O9-BUB-358

Estonia, Latvia, and Lithuania
country studies

Federal Research Division
Library of Congress
Edited by
Walter R. Iwaskiw
Research Completed
January 1995

On the cover: Toompea Castle, Tallinn (upper left); tower of the Dome Cathedral, Riga (right); and wayside wooden sculpture near Druskininkai, Lithuania

First Edition, First Printing, 1996.

Library of Congress Cataloging-in-Publication Data

Estonia, Latvia, and Lithuania : country studies / Federal
    Research Division, Library of Congress ; edited by Walter
    R. Iwaskiw — 1st ed.
        p. cm. — (Area handbook series, ISSN 1057–5294)
(DA pam ; 550–113)
    "Research completed January 1995."
    Includes bibliographical references (pp. 267–279) and
index.
    ISBN 0–8444–0851–4 (hard cover : alk. paper)
    ———— Copy 3 Z663.275 .E86 1996
    1. Baltic States. I. Iwaskiw, Walter R., 1958– . II.
Library of Congress. Federal Research Division. III.
Series. IV. Series: DA pam ; 550–113.
DK502.35.E86 1996   96–4057
947'.4—dc20   CIP

Headquarters, Department of the Army
DA Pam 550–113

For sale by the Superintendent of Documents, U.S. Government Printing Office
Washington, D.C. 20402

Foreword

This volume is one in a continuing series of books prepared by the Federal Research Division of the Library of Congress under the Country Studies/Area Handbook Program sponsored by the Department of the Army. The last two pages of this book list the other published studies.

Most books in the series deal with a particular foreign country, describing and analyzing its political, economic, social, and national security systems and institutions, and examining the interrelationships of those systems and the ways they are shaped by historical and cultural factors. Each study is written by a multidisciplinary team of social scientists. The authors seek to provide a basic understanding of the observed society, striving for a dynamic rather than a static portrayal. Particular attention is devoted to the people who make up the society, their origins, dominant beliefs and values, their common interests and the issues on which they are divided, the nature and extent of their involvement with national institutions, and their attitudes toward each other and toward their social system and political order.

The books represent the analysis of the authors and should not be construed as an expression of an official United States government position, policy, or decision. The authors have sought to adhere to accepted standards of scholarly objectivity. Corrections, additions, and suggestions for changes from readers will be welcomed for use in future editions.

Louis R. Mortimer
Chief
Federal Research Division
Library of Congress
Washington, DC 20540–4840

Acknowledgments

The authors are indebted to the numerous individuals and organizations who contributed to the preparation of this volume. Valuable advice was provided by Stephen R. Burant and Jonathan Bemis of the Department of State. The collection of data was assisted by the contributions of the embassies of Estonia, Latvia, and Lithuania. Sincere thanks go to all individuals who so graciously allowed their photographs to be used in this study, particularly to Priit Vesilind, from whose vast collection many photographs were selected.

The authors gratefully acknowledge Ralph K. Benesch, who oversees the Country Studies/Area Handbook Program for the Department of the Army, and Sandra W. Meditz, the Federal Research Division's coordinator of the handbook series, for her guidance and suggestions. Special thanks also go to Marilyn L. Majeska, who supervised editing; Andrea T. Merrill, who managed production; David P. Cabitto, who provided graphics support and, together with the firm of Maryland Mapping and Graphics, prepared the maps; Thomas D. Hall, who assembled the materials for the maps; Wayne Horne, who prepared the illustrations on the title page of each chapter and on the book cover; Pirkko M. Johnes, who researched and drafted the country profiles; and Helen Fedor, who coordinated the acquisition of photographs. The following individuals are gratefully acknowledged as well: Vincent Ercolano and Janet Willen, who edited the text; Beverly Wolpert, who performed the final prepublication editorial review; Barbara Edgerton and Izella Watson, who did the word processing; Victoria Agee, who compiled the index; and David P. Cabitto, Stephen C. Cranton, Janie L. Gilchrist, and Izella Watson, who prepared the camera-ready copy.

Contents

List of Figures

Preface

Estonia, Latvia, and Lithuania: Country Studies is the latest in a new subseries examining the fifteen newly independent states that emerged from the disintegration of the Soviet Union at the end of 1991. Hitherto, aside from their coverage in the 1991 *Soviet Union: A Country Study*, none had received individual treatment in the Country Studies/Area Handbook series. This volume aims to provide an overview of the history, Soviet legacy, and post-Soviet development of the Baltic states, whose first modern period of independence (1918–40) was a casualty of the 1939 Nazi-Soviet Nonaggression Pact. The authors describe the quest of Estonia, Latvia, and Lithuania for self-determination, their struggle to reestablish independent statehood, and their attempts to cope with the political, economic, and social problems confronting them in the 1990s.

Transliteration of all Slavic names generally follows the system developed by the United States Board on Geographic Names (BGN). Conventional English-language variants, such as Moscow and Yeltsin (rather than Moskva and Yel'tsin), are used when appropriate. Estonian, Latvian, and Lithuanian names appearing in the text of this volume regrettably are missing some diacritics because the typesetting software being used cannot produce all the necessary diacritics (although they do appear on the maps). Measurements are given in the metric system; a conversion table is provided in the Appendix.

The body of the text reflects information available as of January 1995. Certain other portions of the text, however, have been updated. The Introduction discusses significant events and changes that have occurred since the completion of research; the Chronology, Country Profiles, and Glossary include updated information as available; and the Bibliography lists recently published sources thought to be particularly helpful to the reader.

Table A. Chronology of Important Events

Period	Description
CA. 2500–1500 B.C.	Finno-Ugric and proto-Baltic tribes settle on Baltic shores.
FIRST CENTURY–SIXTH CENTURY A.D.	Early Baltic peoples experience rapid cultural progress and expansion of trade with Roman Empire and Germanic tribes.
EIGHTH CENTURY–TWELFTH CENTURY	Scandinavian Vikings and, subsequently, Slavic tribes engage in trade and war with Baltic peoples.
THIRTEENTH CENTURY	Northern Estonia conquered by Danes and rest of Estonia and Latvia by Germans.
1253	Mindaugas crowned king of Lithuania.
FOURTEENTH CENTURY	Grand Duke Gediminas and his descendants expand Lithuania's territories southward to Black Sea.
1343–45	Estonian peasant uprising prompts Danes to relinquish control of northern Estonia to Germans.
SIXTEENTH CENTURY	
1558–83	Army of Russian tsar Ivan IV (the Terrible) invades Livonia; Sweden and Poland help repel invasion.
1569	Lithuania unites with Poland, forming Polish-Lithuanian Commonwealth.
1584	Northern Estonia incorporated into Sweden's Duchy of Estland.
SEVENTEENTH CENTURY	
1629	Swedish-Polish struggle for control of Livonia ends with Poland's being forced to cede entire territory, except southeastern province of Latgale, to Sweden.
1632	Tartu University founded by Swedes.
EIGHTEENTH CENTURY	
1710	Russian tsar Peter I (the Great) succeeds in wresting control of Estland and Livland (southern Estonia and northern Latvia) from Sweden.
1795	Poland partitioned; Lithuania annexed by Russian Empire.
NINETEENTH CENTURY	
1816–19	Serfdom formally abolished in Estland and Livland.
TWENTIETH CENTURY	
1905	Tsarist Russian authorities respond with violence and repression to Baltic demands for radical political change during Revolution of 1905.
1917	Tsar Nicholas II abdicates Russian throne; tsarist regime collapses. Russian provisional government allows Estonia's territorial unification as one province. Bolsheviks take power in Russia and make significant political inroads in Baltic region.
1918 February	Estonia and Lithuania proclaim independence.

Table A. Chronology of Important Events

Period		Description
	November	Latvia proclaims independence.
1918–20		Baltic states engage in war to defend independence; Bolshevik, White Russian, German, Polish, and other forces struggle for control of territories. Lithuania fails to regain Polish-occupied Vilnius region.
1920		Baltic states sign peace treaties with Soviet Russia; Moscow recognizes their independence and renounces all claims to their territories.
1920–22		Land reform carried out in Baltic states. Democratic constitutions introduced.
1921		Estonia, Latvia, and Lithuania admitted to League of Nations.
1923		Lithuania annexes Klaipeda region.
1924		Soviet-backed communist coup attempt in Estonia fails.
1926–29		Military coup in Lithuania; authoritarian regime gradually introduced.
1934		State of emergency declared in Estonia and Latvia amidst growing political instability; parliaments suspended and authoritarian regimes introduced.
1939	August	Nazi-Soviet Nonaggression Pact signed; Estonia, Latvia, and, soon, Lithuania assigned to Soviet sphere of influence.
	October	Baltic states pressured into signing treaties allowing Moscow to station troops on their soil; Vilnius given back to Lithuania.
1940		Red Army occupies Estonia, Latvia, and Lithuania; pro-Soviet governments "elected," and Baltic states annexed to Soviet Union.
1941	June	Soviet authorities arrest and deport tens of thousands of Estonians, Latvians, and Lithuanians to Siberia; deportations interrupted by Nazi Germany's invasion of Soviet Union; Lithuanian resistance movement launches revolt against Soviet rule.
1941–45		Baltic states under German occupation; Nazi regime institutes compulsory draft of Balts into labor or military service; Jews and Gypsies subjected to mass annihilation; nationalist and communist resistance movements active.
1944–45		Soviet forces reoccupy Estonia, Latvia, and Lithuania; hundreds of thousands of refugees flee to West.
1945–52		Anti-Soviet guerrilla war in Baltic republics claims tens of thousands of casualties on both sides.
1947–51		Agriculture collectivized in Baltic republics.
1949	March	Soviet authorities resume campaign of terror in Estonia, Latvia, and Lithuania; more than 100,000 people from Baltic republics deported to Siberia.

Table A. *Chronology of Important Events*

Period		Description
1953		Repression eases after death of Joseph V. Stalin.
1959		Nikita S. Khrushchev purges Eduards Berklavs and other national communists in Latvia.
1968		Repression increases after Soviet invasion of Czechoslovakia; dissident movement grows, particularly in Lithuania.
1970–82		Period of stagnation under Leonid I. Brezhnev; living standards decline; Russification intensifies.
1972		Lithuanian student Romas Kalanta immolates himself in protest against Soviet rule.
1973		Publication of *The Chronicle of the Catholic Church in Lithuania* begins.
1985		Mikhail S. Gorbachev introduces policies of *glasnost* and *perestroika*.
1987–88		Baltic dissidents hold public demonstrations in Tallinn, Riga, and Vilnius.
1988	April	Estonian Popular Front founded.
	June	Estonian communist leader Karl Vaino removed. Sajudis founded in Lithuania.
	October	Popular Front of Latvia holds first congress. Sajudis congress in Lithuania elects Vytautas Landsbergis chairman. Algirdas Brazauskas becomes Lithuanian communist leader.
	November	Estonian Supreme Soviet adopts declaration of sovereignty.
1989	March	Soviet loyalist Intermovement founded in Estonia.
	May	Lithuanian Supreme Soviet proclaims Lithuania's sovereignty.
	July	Latvian Supreme Soviet adopts declaration of sovereignty.
	August	Human chain forms from Tallinn to Vilnius as a protest on fiftieth anniversary of Nazi-Soviet Nonaggression Pact. Intermovement stages strikes in Estonia.
	December	Communist Party of Lithuania splits from Communist Party of the Soviet Union.
1990	February	Elections held for Congress of Estonia, rival parliament to Estonian Supreme Soviet.
	March	Lithuanian Supreme Soviet elects Vytautas Landsbergis chairman of presidium; votes for declaration of independence. Estonian Supreme Soviet votes for transition to independence.
	April	Moscow imposes economic blockade on Lithuania. Baltic Agreement on Economic Cooperation signed by Estonia, Latvia, and Lithuania.
	May	Latvian Supreme Council votes for transition to independence. Baltic countries renew 1934 Baltic Treaty on Unity and Cooperation.

Table A. Chronology of Important Events

Period		Description
	June	Lithuanian Supreme Council agrees to six-month moratorium on independence declaration; Moscow lifts economic blockade.
1991	January	Lithuanian prime minister Kazimiera Prunskiene resigns after dispute with Vytautas Landsbergis. Soviet military intervention in Vilnius and Riga results in massacre of civilians.
	February–March	Referenda in Estonia, Latvia, and Lithuania show overwhelming support for independence.
	August	Estonian Supreme Council and Latvian Supreme Council vote for full independence following coup in Moscow; coup collapses; Baltic states restore diplomatic relations with many countries.
	September	Soviet Union recognizes independence of Baltic states. Estonia, Latvia, and Lithuania admitted to United Nations.
	November	Estonian Supreme Council decides to require naturalization of Soviet-era immigrants.
1992	January	Estonian prime minister Edgar Savisaar resigns; Tiit Vähi forms new government. Latvian Supreme Council reaffirms validity of Latvia's pre-Soviet borders.
	June	New Estonian constitution adopted by referendum.
	July	Lithuanian prime minister Gediminas Vagnorius resigns after vote of no confidence; replaced by Aleksandras Abisala.
	September	Election of new parliament, Riigikogu, in Estonia yields center-right coalition government led by Fatherland Party (Isamaa).
	October	Lithuanian Democratic Labor Party wins absolute majority of seats in Seimas; Algirdas Brazauskas elected chairman; Sajudis fares poorly. Lennart Meri elected president of Estonia; Mart Laar becomes prime minister.
	October–November	Lithuania's new constitution approved by referendum and adopted by Seimas.
	December	Seimas chairman Brazauskas appoints Bronislovas Lubys prime minister of Lithuania.
1993	February	Algirdas Brazauskas elected president of Lithuania.
	March	Lithuanian prime minister Bronislovas Lubys resigns; replaced by Adolfas Slezevicius.
	June	Political crisis in Estonia follows passage of Law on Aliens; measure amended after presidential veto. Latvia's Way finishes first in first post-Soviet national elections to Saeima.
	July	Saeima restores 1922 constitution and elects Guntis Ulmanis president of Latvia; Valdis Birkavs becomes prime minister.
	August	Russian military forces withdrawn from Lithuania.

xvi

Table A. Chronology of Important Events

Period		Description
	October	Isamaa fares poorly in Estonia's first post-Soviet local elections; Tiit Vähi's Coalition Party finishes first.
1994	May	Latvian National Independence Movement finishes first in Latvia's first post-Soviet local elections; ex-communists fare worst.
	July	Ruling coalition in Latvia breaks up; Birkavs government resigns.
	August	Russian military forces withdrawn from Estonia and Latvia. Citizenship bill signed into law in Latvia; controversial restrictive quota on naturalization excluded.
	September	Estonian prime minister Mart Laar loses vote of no confidence; Andres Tarand confirmed as prime minister. Maris Gailis confirmed as prime minister of Latvia.
1995	February	Latvia admitted to Council of Europe, after abandoning restrictive quotas on naturalization.
	March	Coalition Party-Rural Union alliance finishes first in Estonian parliamentary elections; Russophone community gains representation. Lithuanian Democratic Labor Party fares poorly in local elections.
	April	Tiit Vähi confirmed as Estonia's prime minister.
	May	Latvia's Baltija Bank collapses.
	July	Lithuanian economics minister Aleksandras Vasiliauskas resigns after cabinet dispute over economic reform.
	September–October	Democratic Party Saimnieks finishes first in Latvian parliamentary elections; followed closely by far-right For Latvia.
	October	Estonian interior minister Edgar Savisaar implicated in scandal; Vähi government resigns.

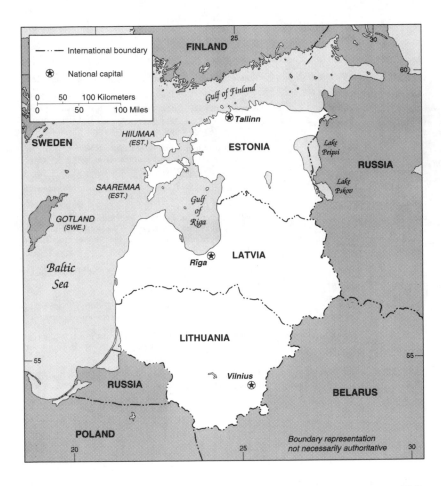

Figure 1. Estonia, Latvia, and Lithuania: Geographic Setting, 1995

Introduction

FORCIBLY ANNEXED TO THE SOVIET UNION fifty-one years earlier, the Baltic states—Estonia, Latvia, and Lithuania—regained independence in 1991 after an abortive coup in Moscow that accelerated the collapse of the Soviet regime. Having been, in the words of former British foreign secretary Douglas Hurd, "stolen or kidnapped from the European family," these nations embarked on a course of political and economic restructuring and reintegration with the West. Their experience with independent statehood and, to a lesser extent, with democracy in the 1920s and 1930s (an advantage not enjoyed by the other former Soviet republics), as well as their ability to maintain a strong sense of national identity under foreign hegemony, has helped them in their efforts to deal with the legacies of Soviet rule. The challenges, nonetheless, remain formidable.

A major demographic shift occurred during the Soviet era in the Baltic region, particularly in Estonia and Latvia, where, according to the 1989 census, the titular nationalities accounted for only 61.5 and 52 percent, respectively, of each country's population. The Russians, by far the largest ethnic minority, made up 30.3 percent of Estonia's population and 34 percent of Latvia's. There were high concentrations of Russians in Tallinn, Riga, and Vilnius—the capital cities of the Baltic republics. Encouraged by the Soviet authorities, a massive influx of immigrants reduced Latvians and Estonians to minority status in a number of their largest cities. After independence, Estonia and Latvia faced the challenge of integrating into their political life these large, mostly insular Russophone communities, whose loyalty to the new states had yet to be demonstrated, without jeopardizing their hard-won independence. Unlike Lithuania, whose higher birth rate and larger indigenous work force permitted the republic to maintain an approximately 80 percent share of ethnic Lithuanians, Latvia and Estonia refused to grant automatic citizenship to the Soviet-era settlers. Lithuania's relatively small ethnic minorities, of which the Russians and the Poles are the most significant, have been easier to accommodate.

The issue of ethnic minority rights in Latvia and Estonia gained prominence primarily in the international arena, especially in 1992 and 1993 when Moscow tried to link it to the departure of Russian (former Soviet) troops from the two countries. Under Western diplomatic pressure, Russian military forces finally were withdrawn in August 1994, yet Moscow continued to view the region as "the near abroad," an area contiguous to Russia and within its sphere of influence. To punish its former colonies—Latvia and Estonia, for allegedly mistreating their Russian minorities, and Lithuania, for refusing to legitimate Russia's right of military transit to and from the exclave of Kaliningrad—Moscow resorted to economic measures. The Russian government levied prohibitive tariffs on imports of Baltic goods and raised prices on Russian fuel and other essential commodities. These actions spurred on efforts by the three countries to mitigate their geopolitical and economic vulnerability through the development of stronger relationships with the West.

In 1994 Estonia, Latvia, and Lithuania signed and ratified free-trade agreements with the European Union (EU—see Glossary), and in 1995 each country signed an Association Agreement with the EU. Estonia and Lithuania became members of the Council of Europe (see Glossary) in 1993; Latvia was admitted in 1995, after its parliament backed down from a controversial quota system that would have restricted the naturalization of permanent residents. All have joined the North Atlantic Cooperation Council, the Organization for Security and Cooperation in Europe, and the Partnership for Peace program of the North Atlantic Treaty Organization (NATO), and all have participated in NATO exercises. They have reaffirmed their desire to join NATO, in spite of Russia's hostile reaction. That reaction included a warning in September 1995 from Russian deputy foreign minister Sergey Krylov that his country reserves the right to employ military, economic, and political measures to prevent the Baltic states from becoming members of the NATO alliance. Shortly afterward, the Moscow newspaper *Komsomol'skaya pravda* quoted high-level Russian military sources discussing a draft military doctrine that would authorize the invasion of Estonia, Latvia, and Lithuania if they were to join NATO.

On the domestic front, although the political exclusion of many Soviet-era immigrants in Estonia and Latvia could impede the process of building stable democratic systems, there has been no political violence against the Russophone population and less ethnic tension than in many other newly independent states. In Latvia 62 percent of the Russian speakers interviewed in a public opinion survey in the fall of 1993 described relations between their group and the ethnic Latvian population as good; only 22 percent said relations were not good. In Estonia 87 percent of the local Russians polled in late 1994 indicated that they had experienced few or no problems with the indigenous population, and 92 percent wanted to stay in the country. According to Aleksandr Kinsburskiy, a Moscow sociologist who studies Russian minorities in the former Soviet republics, "The overwhelming majority of ethnic Russians in Estonia have accepted the Estonian government's tough policy toward them and decided to adapt to it." They do not wish to relocate to Russia, if for no other reason than that they enjoy a higher standard of living in Estonia.

The Baltic countries generally have made greater progress in rebuilding their economies than Russia and the other former Soviet republics. Estonia, at the forefront of economic reform, was the first to introduce its own currency, which is fully convertible today. The country also has had considerable success in attracting foreign aid and investment and reorienting foreign trade to the West. Like Latvia and Lithuania, it has experienced painful economic downturns since reestablishing independence but in the mid-1990s was showing signs of a sustained economic recovery. The Economist Intelligence Unit estimated that Estonia's gross domestic product (GDP—see Glossary) grew by 4.7 percent in 1994 and predicted a growth rate of 5 percent in 1995, citing a continuing fall in unemployment and increases in capital equipment purchases, port and other transit volumes, and foreign trade. Detracting from an otherwise strong economic performance is a large trade deficit, which was estimated to be US$389 million in 1994 and was expected to reach US$600 million in 1995, although the government is taking steps to assist Estonian exporters.

More troublesome is the situation in neighboring Latvia following the collapse in May 1995 of Baltija Bank, the country's largest commercial bank. Baltija's collapse exposed serious weaknesses in what had been considered to be a healthy banking sector, shaking the confidence of foreign investors and dampening economic growth. Latvia's rate of GDP growth, which was earlier expected to increase from an estimated 2 percent in 1994 to 3 percent in 1995 and 4.5 percent in 1996, was scaled down to 1 percent in 1995 and 3 percent in 1996. Latvia also has had to cope with a high unemployment rate (6.7 percent in June 1995) and a worsening budget deficit.

Controlling unemployment and balancing the budget are concerns shared by Lithuania as well, although declining foreign investment is a greater problem there. In part because, unlike Estonia and Latvia, it does not allow foreigners to own land and buildings, Lithuania has had greater difficulty in attracting foreign capital. Direct foreign investment in Lithuania totaled US$170 million at the end of 1994, compared with US$474 million in Estonia and US$327 million in Latvia. Russian companies account for the largest number of joint ventures in Lithuania. Fluctuating industrial output and sales in 1995 made it difficult to determine to what extent the country's economy was recovering. Lithuania's GDP grew by an estimated 0.6 percent in 1994; a growth rate of 3 percent in 1995 was predicted.

Controversy in the Lithuanian Democratic Labor Party (LDLP) government over the pace of Lithuania's economic reform, which is the slowest overall in the Baltic region, resulted in the resignation of the economics minister, Aleksandras Vasiliauskas, in July 1995. Several other members of the cabinet disagreed with Prime Minister Adolfas Slezevicius, who advocated accelerating the pace of reform. Lithuania's banking sector, although more stable than that of Latvia, is arousing public concern and could divide the government further. In July some 1,000 people assembled for a rally in Vilnius to call for improved legislation to protect bank deposits and to demand the resignation of Prime Minister Slezevicius and President Algirdas Brazauskas for their failure to remedy the weakness of the banking and financial system. Another call for the resignation of the government came in September from the Fatherland Union, the main opposition grouping and successor to the Sajudis movement. The Fatherland Union accused the ruling LDLP, successor to the Communist Party of Lithuania, of condoning corruption, intentionally driving businesses to bankruptcy, and impoverishing the population. The opposition has also accused the government of taking a weak negotiating stance toward Russia, particularly over the issue of Russian military transit through Lithuanian territory.

Popular disenchantment with the ruling leftist government and with politics in general was evident in Lithuania's March 1995 local elections, which generated a low voter turnout and gave right-of-center parties more than half the total number of seats. In April, however, the LDLP succeeded in winning a parliamentary by-election in the Kaisiadorys district. The March elections also showed an increase in political fragmentation: seventeen parties were registered in the elections; sixteen of the seventeen secured seats on local councils.

Even greater was the degree of fragmentation on Latvia's political scene in early 1995: more than forty parties prepared to contest the general elections in the fall. Many of these parties merged subsequently in an attempt to pass the threshold for parliamentary representation. After its defeat by the right-wing Latvian National Independence Movement in local elections one year earlier, the Latvia's Way government had just regained some ground in public opinion polls. The collapse of Baltija Bank and the ensuing financial crisis, however, seriously undermined its credibility. Moreover, many Latvians' patience with low wages and meager pension benefits had begun to wear thin. Foreign investment had increased and economic ties to the West had grown stronger, but corruption was widespread, and, according to official estimates, 20 percent of the population lived in poverty. (Unofficial estimates were much higher.)

With 14.6 percent of the vote, Latvia's Way finished third in the September 30–October 1, 1995, parliamentary elections. The center-left Democratic Party Saimnieks was in first place with 15.3 percent of the vote, followed closely by the far-right For Latvia with 15 percent. The latter party is headed by Joachim Siegerist, a failed German politician facing a prison sentence in Germany for inciting racial hatred. His political success in Latvia has stunned many people both in Latvia and abroad. Much of Siegerist's support has come from the country's most vulnerable citizens—young people and the elderly—who have been impressed by his efforts to distribute food, medicine, and clothing to the needy and his promises to crack down on corruption, stabilize the currency, and bring Latvia out of its "deep misery."

Dissatisfaction among elderly and rural voters, who had yet to experience the benefits of Estonia's economic revival, was an important factor in that country's general election in March 1995. Political infighting and bitter disputes among members of former Prime Minister Mart Laar's government, as well as charges of corruption, were other reasons that many voters rejected the center-right grouping of the Fatherland Party (Isamaa) and the Estonian National Independence Party, which received less than 8 percent of the vote. With nearly one-third

(32.2 percent) of the vote, the victorious center-left Coalition Party-Rural Union alliance, led by former Prime Minister Tiit Vähi, took forty-one of the parliament's 101 seats. Next came the staunchly pro-market Estonian Reform Party with 16.2 percent of the vote and the moderate Estonian Center Party with 14.2 percent. Six percent of the vote was garnered by Our Home is Estonia!, an alliance of two ethnic Russian parties. Thus, Estonia's Russophone community secured parliamentary representation.

After negotiating a coalition agreement with Edgar Savisaar, leader of the Estonian Center Party, Vähi was confirmed as prime minister in April and Savisaar became minister of interior. Although somewhat more mindful of the agrarian sector's concerns, the new government pursued policies essentially similar to those of its predecessor. In October, however, Savisaar was implicated in the bugging of conversations of several Estonian political leaders. Consequently, President Lennart Meri relieved Savisaar of his ministerial duties, and the government resigned. President Meri characterized the scandal as a crisis for democracy. Overcoming such crises posed yet another challenge for the nascent democratic institutions of the Baltic states.

October 14, 1995

*   *   *

Following preparation of this manuscript, several significant events occurred in the Baltic states. In Estonia, shortly after the resignation of the government in October 1995, President Meri decided against holding early elections and asked outgoing Prime Minister Vähi to form a new government. Upon negotiating a coalition agreement with Siim Kallas, chairman of the Estonian Reform Party, Vähi was confirmed as prime minister, and Kallas became the foreign minister. Vähi pledged to continue the previous policies of economic reform and integration into European structures. He also stressed the need to reach an agreement with Moscow regarding the Estonian-Russian border, which had been shifted by Soviet leader Joseph V. Stalin at the end of World War II, in violation of the 1920 Tartu Peace Treaty (see fig. 2). The issue of the validity of the 1920 treaty remained unresolved, however, despite several rounds of border talks in late 1995 and early 1996.

Estonian-Russian relations were complicated further in February 1996, when the Estonian Orthodox Church left the jurisdiction of the Moscow Patriarchate and renewed canonical ties with the Ecumenical Patriarchate of Constantinople, the historical center of Orthodox Christianity. In protest against Ecumenical Patriarch Bartholomew's decision to resume his patriarchate's canonical jurisdiction over the Estonian Orthodox Church, Patriarch Aleksiy of Moscow suspended relations between the Russian Orthodox Church and Constantinople. Moreover, Aleksiy accused the Estonian government, which had recognized the newly independent church as the legal successor to the pre-World War II Estonian Orthodox Church, of "stripping the Russian Orthodox Church of its property rights." At Aleksiy's behest, Russian president Boris N. Yeltsin and Russia's Ministry of Foreign Affairs protested to the Estonian government as well.

Also in Estonia, the commander of the armed forces, General Aleksander Einseln, resigned in December 1995. Einseln, a retired United States Army colonel, resigned at President Meri's demand, following a political row with Defense Minister Andrus Oovel. In January 1996, the Estonian parliament approved Meri's nomination of Colonel Johannes Kert, previously commander of the country's paramilitary Defense League (Kaitseliit), as the new commander of the armed forces. In a February address to the Estonian community in Stockholm, Einseln attacked Oovel as a communist who had regained power.

In Lithuania the refusal of Prime Minister Slezevicius to resign after he was implicated in a banking scandal impelled President Brazauskas to ask the Lithuanian parliament, the Seimas, to vote in February 1996 on the dismissal of Slezevicius from office. The banking scandal had erupted in December 1995, when Lithuania's two largest commercial banks, LAIB and Litimpex, were declared insolvent and their accounts frozen. Slezevicius prematurely terminated a fixed-term, high-interest account with LAIB two days before the bank's operations were suspended, prompting media reports that he had used inside information to withdraw his savings and angering thousands of depositors. In January 1996, President Brazauskas asked Slezevicius to resign as prime minister, but, with the backing of the leadership of the ruling LDLP, Slezevicius

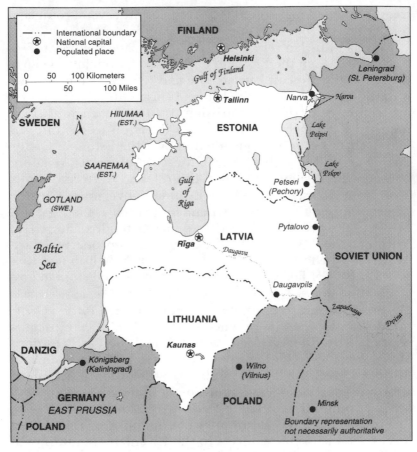

Source: Based on information from Anatol Lieven, *The Baltic Revolution*, New Haven,
1993, 63; and Toivo V. Raun, *Estonia and the Estonians*, Stanford, California,
1987, 138, 221.

Figure 2. Estonia, Latvia, and Lithuania, 1938

refused. In February the Seimas voted by a wide margin to
approve a presidential decree dismissing Slezevicius. One
month later, under pressure from many LDLP members,
Slezevicius was also ousted as party chairman.

After Prime Minister Slezevicius's dismissal, Brazauskas nominated Mindaugas Stankevicius for the post. Stankevicius, hitherto the minister for government reform and local rule, was
confirmed promptly. He retained twelve of the nineteen ministers who had served in the previous government, and he
pledged to continue the policies of economic reform and integration into the EU and other European bodies. His govern-

ment's objectives included admission to NATO, the gradual demilitarization of the neighboring Russian exclave of Kaliningrad, the reduction of Lithuania's dependence on fuel imports from Russia, and the bringing of Lithuania's economic legislation into line with EU standards. Stankevicius also stated that he would give priority to stabilizing and strengthening Lithuania's banking system, stabilizing the national currency, reducing inflation, and improving the social security system.

The strengthening of relations with Poland has become a highlight of Lithuania's foreign policy. In March 1996, President Brazauskas and his Polish counterpart, Aleksander Kwasniewski, met in Vilnius to discuss a broad range of political and security issues. They agreed to coordinate their countries' efforts to gain membership in the EU and NATO, to establish joint airspace control, to allow mutual military overflights under an "open sky policy," to form a joint battalion, and to hold joint military exercises. The two sides also agreed to cooperate in building the Via Baltica highway and a new railroad between Lithuania and Poland, and they reaffirmed their opposition to a Russian-Belarusian proposal to build a highway across either Lithuanian or Polish territory to the heavily militarized Russian exclave of Kaliningrad.

Lithuania and the neighboring Baltic country of Latvia, however, had yet to agree on the demarcation of their common maritime border. The subject of their dispute is a continental shelf area considered rich in oil deposits, where Latvia has unilaterally awarded drilling rights to a United States-Swedish joint venture. Latvian-Lithuanian border talks had been expected to begin in late 1995 but were canceled because of protracted government crises in the two countries. Talks on demarcating the Latvian-Estonian border in the Gulf of Riga were held in February 1996 in Stockholm but did not produce an agreement.

The failure of rival political blocs in Latvia's parliament, the Saeima, to reach an agreement repeatedly obstructed the formation of a new government after the country's September–October 1995 general election. The impasse finally ended in December when President Guntis Ulmanis nominated Andris Skele as prime minister. Skele, a professional agronomist and successful entrepreneur, had widespread appeal as a respected nonpolitical figure and was confirmed shortly afterward.

In December 1995, Latvian government representatives joined their counterparts from Estonia and Lithuania in Madrid to lobby EU leaders assembled there for equal consideration for admission to the EU. Some EU officials and member governments had favored giving priority to the Czech Republic, Poland, and Hungary, but the efforts of the Baltic governments resulted in a decision to treat the Central European and Baltic countries equally. Discussions with individual countries are to begin after mid-1997.

Also in December 1995, the governments of the Baltic countries made final plans for the participation of their armed forces in the Bosnia peacekeeping operation under the command of NATO. Each country will assign one platoon, which will become integrated with NATO forces. Before being airlifted to Bosnia, the Baltic platoons will train with Danish forces in Denmark, a NATO country with which the Baltic countries have established close military cooperation. The Baltic contingent's close integration with the troops of NATO countries is seen by the Baltic countries as an important step toward meeting NATO military standards and toward eventually joining the alliance.

The first joint military force of the three Baltic countries, the Baltic Battalion, held its first combat exercise in Latvia in January and February 1996. It was the largest military exercise held in the Baltic states since they regained their independence in 1991 and the first joint exercise of troops from the three countries. Britain, Norway, Denmark, and Sweden provide military assistance to the integrated battalion. Other forms of military cooperation among the Baltic states are to include linking the three countries' airspace surveillance systems, engaging in joint mine-laying and mine-sweeping operations in the Baltic Sea, and harmonizing equipment and logistics. Moreover, in March 1996 senior naval officials of Estonia, Latvia, and Lithuania met in Tallinn to discuss plans for the formation of a joint naval squadron and joint naval training groups.

Safeguarding their security continues to be the foremost concern of the Baltic states. At a briefing after the first exercise of the Baltic Battalion, the defense ministers of Estonia, Latvia, and Lithuania reaffirmed their countries' common goal of joining NATO. Recent developments in Russia, most notably the Russian Duma's nonbinding resolution of March 15, 1996, declaring the dissolution of the Soviet Union illegal, have reinforced the fear of Russian revanchism. Estonian foreign minister Kallas characterized the action by the communist-dominated lower house of the Russian parliament as "an intention to recreate the Soviet Union, which would pose a threat to the entire world. The world should be concerned, not just us."

March 20, 1996   Walter R. Iwaskiw

Chapter 1. Estonia

Toompea Castle, Tallinn

Country Profile

Country

Formal Name: Republic of Estonia (Eesti Vabariik).

Short Form: Estonia (Eesti).

Term for Citizen(s): Estonian(s).

Capital: Tallinn.

Date of Independence: During abortive Soviet coup, declared immediate full independence August 20, 1991; Soviet Union granted recognition September 6, 1991. February 24, Independence Day, national holiday; on this day in 1918, independent Republic of Estonia proclaimed.

Geography

Size: 45,226 square kilometers (land area 43,200 square kilometers), slightly larger than Vermont and New Hampshire combined; includes 1,520 islands in Baltic Sea.

Topography: Mostly low-lying land with many lakes, rivers, and forests. Forest 1.8 million hectares, arable land 926,000 hectares, meadows 252,000 hectares, and pastureland 181,000 hectares. Highest elevation 318 meters.

Climate: Temperate, influenced by Eurasian land mass to east, Baltic Sea to west, and North Atlantic Ocean farther west. Cool summers and mild winters. Rainfall moderate, averaging about 568 millimeters per year.

Society

Population: 1,506,927 (1994 estimate). Population declined in early 1990s because of negative natural growth rates and net out-migration. In 1993 birth rate 10.0 per 1,000 population; death rate 14.0 per 1,000 population. Total fertility rate 2.0

children per woman in 1994. Population density 33.7 persons per square kilometer. Life expectancy 70.0 years in 1994 (65.0 years for males and 75.2 years for females).

Ethnic Groups: According to 1989 census, Estonians 61.5 percent, Russians 30.3 percent, Ukrainians 3.1 percent, Belorussians 1.7 percent, Finns 1.1 percent, and others (including Jews, Tatars, Germans, Latvians, and Poles) 2.3 percent. In 1994 estimates of Estonian and Russian groups 63.9 percent and 29.0 percent, respectively.

Languages: Official language Estonian; Russian, Ukrainian, Belarusian, Finnish, and other languages also used.

Religion: Predominantly Evangelical Lutheran. Other denominations include Orthodox Christian, Old Believer, Methodist, Baptist, Seventh-Day Adventist, Jewish, and Roman Catholic.

Education: Estonian-language schools have twelve years of education (nine in elementary schools and three in secondary schools). Russian-language education lasts eleven years. Education compulsory to ninth grade. In 1993 some 215,000 elementary and secondary school students in 724 schools. About 142,000 students enrolled in Estonian-language schools and 70,000 in Russian-language schools. Individual schools offered instruction in other languages as well. Seventy-seven vocational schools, in which about 26,000 students enrolled. Literacy nearly universal. According to 1989 census results, 99.7 percent of adult population literate.

Health and Welfare: In 1992 thirty-two doctors and ninety-two hospital beds per 10,000 inhabitants, but shortage of auxiliary staff. Retirement pensions very low (about EKR260 per month); other welfare benefits include financial support for invalids, low-income families, and families having three or more children.

Labor Force: 785,500 (August 1994); industry 33 percent, agriculture 12 percent, education and culture 10 percent, construction 10 percent. Services sector, accounting for 44.7 percent of employment, was the most developed in former Soviet Union and is expected to expand.

Economy

Gross National Product (GNP): Estimated at US$4.7 billion in 1993; per capita income US$3,040. Gross domestic product (GDP) declined from 8,681 million Russian rubles (as expressed in 1990 Russian rubles) in 1989 to 5,320 million Russian rubles in 1993. Annual rate of inflation, which had averaged 3.3 percent in 1980s, jumped to 1,000 percent in 1992. By 1993 government's radical budgetary and monetary reform program had reduced rate of inflation substantially to an average of 2 to 3 percent per month. Rate of inflation averaged 3.5 percent per month in 1994. Annual decline in output, recorded in all sectors in 1991–92, slowed in 1993 and reversed in 1994. Real GDP grew by an estimated 5.0 percent in 1994.

Agriculture: Sector small but largely self-sufficient; in 1991 contributed 15.4 percent of GDP and 12 percent of employment. Fishing and animal husbandry among main activities. About 30 percent of land cultivable; principal crops grains, potatoes, and vegetables. Agricultural production declined by an estimated 19 percent in 1992 and by 22 percent in 1993.

Industry: 42.5 percent of GDP in 1992; main products electricity, oil shale, chemical products, electric motors, textiles, furniture, cellulose and paper products, building materials, ships, and processed foods. Industrial production estimated to have declined by 39 percent from 1991 to 1992, and by 27 percent in 1993. Overall output increased by an estimated 7 percent in 1994.

Energy: Produces roughly 23 million tons of oil shale per year; exports electrical energy but depends heavily on imports of oil and natural gas.

Exports: US$827 million (1993 estimate). Major commodities foodstuffs and animal products, textiles and footwear, base metals and jewelry, minerals, glassware, wood products, furniture, and machinery.

Imports: US$902 million (1993 estimate). Major commodities machinery and transport equipment, mineral products, textiles, food products, and fuel.

Major Trading Partners: Finland, Russia, Germany, Latvia, Lithuania, Netherlands, Denmark, Ukraine, Japan, and United States.

Currency and Exchange Rate: 1 kroon (EKR) = 100 cents; pegged to German deutsche mark (DM) within 3 percent of EKR8 = DM1. In March 1996, EKR11.83 = US$1.

Fiscal Year: Calendar year.

Transportation and Telecommunications

Roads: 30,300 kilometers total; 29,200 kilometers with hard surface, 1,100 kilometers unpaved. Bus routes exist to Poland, Germany, and Denmark. Bus and taxi service within Tallinn and surrounding area good. Rental automobiles available.

Railroads: 1,126 kilometers of railroads, of which 132 kilometers electrified (1993). Chief center Tallinn. Main lines link Tallinn with Narva and St. Petersburg, Tartu with Pskov (Russia), and Pärnu with Riga (Latvia). Train service available to Moscow, St. Petersburg, and Warsaw.

Civil Aviation: Service to many international destinations from Ulemiste International Airport at Tallinn, as well as domestic flights to Estonian islands. National carrier Estonian Air, which had sixteen former Soviet aircraft in 1992 and operated flights to Amsterdam, Copenhagen, Frankfurt, Helsinki, Kiev, Minsk, Moscow, Riga, St. Petersburg, Sochi (Russia), Stockholm, and Vilnius. Service also provided by Aeroflot, Drakk Air Lines, Finnair, Lithuanian Airlines, Lufthansa, and SAS (Scandinavian Airlines).

Shipping: 500 kilometers of inland waterways navigable year round. Inland port Narva; maritime ports Pärnu and Tallinn. Twenty main ports, but Tallinn handles four-fifths of ocean-going transport. Ice-free port of Muuga, near Tallinn, is underused modern facility with good transshipment capability, high-capacity grain elevator, refrigerated/frozen storage, and oil tanker off-loading facilities. Excellent Tallinn-Helsinki and

Tallinn-Stockholm ferry links exist year round.

Telecommunications: One television set per 2.6 persons; one radio per 1.7 persons; one telephone per 3.9 persons. Three radio stations and three television stations.

Government and Politics

Government: Parliamentary democracy. President, elected for term of five years, is head of state and supreme commander of armed forces. Riigikogu (parliament), with 101 members, has broad organizational legislative functions. Members elected in direct elections for term of four years. Candidate for prime minister forms new government (no more than fifteen ministers) after Riigikogu has approved basis for its formation; after selection, president formally appoints government, which has executive power.

Judicial System: Post-Soviet criminal code introduced in 1992, based on civil law system, with no judicial review of legislative acts. Death penalty retained for murder and terrorism. Legal chancellor, appointed by Riigikogu, provides guidance on constitutionality of laws but has no powers of adjudication. Criminal justice administered by local first-level courts as well as second-level appellate courts. Final appeal may be made to National Court, which sits in Tartu. Court system comprises rural and city, as well as administrative, courts (first-level); district courts (second-level); and National Court, highest court in land.

Politics: First post-Soviet elections, held in September 1992, yielded center-right coalition government led by Fatherland Party (Isamaa). Isamaa-led coalition disintegrated in June 1994. Center-left Coalition Party-Rural Union Alliance victorious in March 1995 elections.

Administrative Divisions: Fifteen counties (*maakonnad*), subdivided into 255 local administrative units, of which forty-two are towns and 213 are townships (*vald*).

Foreign Relations: In September 1991, Estonia joined United Nations (UN) and Conference on Security and Cooperation in

Europe (in January 1995, name changed to Organization for Security and Cooperation in Europe) and is a signatory to a number of UN organizations and other international agreements. In February 1994, Estonia joined Partnership for Peace program of North Atlantic Treaty Organization. Member of Council of Europe and Council of the Baltic Sea States. Cooperation with European Union includes significant economic aid as well as talks on a free-trade agreement. Relations with Russia remain cool.

National Security

Armed Forces: Following establishment of Ministry of Defense in April 1992, Estonia began to form independent armed forces. In 1994 total armed forces numbered 3,000, including army (2,500) and navy (500). Also reserve militia of about 6,000. Paramilitary border guard of 2,000 under command of Ministry of Interior. Military service lasts twelve months. By end of 1993, fewer than 3,500 Russian troops remained in Estonia; last Russian troops withdrawn in August 1994.

Military Budget: About EKR250 million allocated for defense in 1994.

Figure 3. Estonia, 1995

10

ESTONIA'S FOUR-YEAR STRUGGLE for sovereignty and independence from the Soviet Union culminated in victory in August 1991. A failed coup d'état in Moscow was followed by a final declaration of freedom in the Estonian capital, Tallinn, and by worldwide recognition of the country's renewed statehood a few days later. The determination of the Estonians to regain their independence, lost since 1940, had been proclaimed by artist and future politician Heinz Valk in 1988: "One day we will win in the end!" ("Ükskord me võidame niikuinii!"). Indeed, when victory came, it was at a surprisingly low cost. Unlike Latvia and Lithuania, Estonia suffered no casualties in its independence struggle. Unlike Lithuania, Estonia was spared any direct economic blockade by Moscow. Unlike most secessionist campaigns, that of Estonia, like those of the other Baltic states, enjoyed the tacit support and acknowledgment of Western governments, which had not recognized the incorporation of the Baltic states into the Soviet Union a half-century earlier and which supported their right to seek redress. The events of 1988–91 were in many ways a process of advancing step by step, keeping the pressure on a wavering Soviet Union and laying the groundwork for a leap to statehood.

In campaigning for independence, most Estonians were intent on escaping and reversing their Soviet past: years of stifling social and political rule, growing economic inefficiency and languor, cultural deprivation under a policy of Russification, and increasing environmental waste and destruction. This was the sentiment that came forth in the "singing revolution" of 1988, when Estonians gathered in large, peaceful rallies to sing their national songs and give voice to their pent-up frustrations. At the same time, the Estonians were equally intent on a future as an independent nation enjoying economic prosperity in a post-Cold War Europe.

In the mid-1990s, several years after independence, Estonia's past as a Soviet republic was proving itself a legacy that could not easily be put aside. The challenges Estonians faced included integrating a 500,000-strong Russophone population that was largely the product of Soviet-era immigration policy, as well as restructuring an economy that had been developed along impractical guidelines dictated by an overbearing center. The future, meanwhile, was not unfolding entirely as had been

11

expected. The process of regaining prosperity by means of economic shock therapy was beginning to tear at the fabric of Estonian society, which, despite Soviet rule, had achieved a certain equilibrium since the 1960s. Widening gaps between the newly rich and the newly poor were putting a strain on the Estonians' erstwhile social cohesion. On the diplomatic front, a new Europe and genuine Estonian sovereignty also were proving slow to materialize. Estonia's proximity to vast Russia was still a given, despite a desire to be rid of Russian influence once and for all. Post-Cold War Europe calculated its policies with an eye to the superpower to the east just as much as it had in the days when the Soviet Union was still intact. Still, as Estonia marked four years of independence in 1995, domestic peace and a measured pace of progress—the hallmarks of the independence struggle—had been maintained; these two factors offered the best guarantee of the country's continued advancement.

Historical Setting

Early History

Estonia's struggles for independence during the twentieth century were in large part a reaction to nearly 700 years of foreign rule. Before 1200 the Estonians lived largely as free peasants loosely organized into parishes (*kihelkonnad*), which in turn were grouped into counties (*maakonnad*). In the early 1200s, the Estonians and the Latvians came under assault from German crusaders seeking to impose Christianity on them. Although the Estonians' resistance to the Teutonic Knights lasted some twenty years, the lack of a centralized political organization as well as inferior weaponry eventually brought down the Estonians in 1227. The Germans, moving from the south, were abetted by Danish forces that invaded from the north and captured Tallinn. Together with present-day Latvia, the region became known as Livonia; the Germans and Danes settled down as nobility, and the Estonians were progressively subordinated as serfs. During 1343–45 an Estonian peasant uprising against the German and Danish nobility prompted the Danes to relinquish their control of northern Estonia to the Germans. After this resistance was crushed, the area remained generally peaceful for two centuries.

Commerce developed rapidly because Estonia's larger urban centers at the time—Tallinn, Tartu, Pärnu, and Narva—were

*Anti-Soviet demonstration on the fiftieth anniversary of the Nazi-
Soviet Nonaggression Pact, Tallinn, 1989
St. George's Eve commemoration of 1343–45 rebellion by Estonian
peasants against their German and Danish overlords, Tallinn, 1991
Courtesy Priit Vesilind*

all members of the Hanseatic League, an organization established by merchants of various, mostly German, cities to protect
their mutual trading interests. Still, foreign rivalries over the
strategic Livonian region began to reemerge in the mid-six-
teenth century as the fighting capacity of the Germans diminished and that of neighboring Muscovy began to increase. The
ensuing twenty-five-year struggle for control of Livonia was pre-
cipitated by an invasion by Ivan IV (the Terrible) (r. 1533–84)
in 1558. The advancing Russians wiped out the disintegrating
forces of the Teutonic Knights and nearly succeeded in con-
quering the whole area. However, Swedish and Polish intervention reversed the Russian gains and forced Ivan eastward, back
behind Lake Peipsi. Peace between Sweden and Poland in
Livonia was also slow in coming, with Sweden eventually winning most of the territory by 1629. By this time, decades of war
had caused huge population losses (in some areas, over 50 percent), affecting urban and rural areas alike.

Under Swedish rule, northern Estonia was incorporated into
the Duchy of Estland. The southern part, together with northern Latvia, became known as Livland. This division of Estonian
lands would last until 1917. The German-based nobility in both
areas retained and even strengthened its position under Swedish suzerainty. Meanwhile, the Estonian peasants saw their lot
worsen as more and more of their land and output were appropriated by seigniorial estates. Still, during the Swedish era,
Estonian education got its start with the founding of Tartu University in 1632 and the establishment of the first Estonian par-
ish schools in the 1680s. Although the population also began to
grow during this period of peace, war and suffering once again
were not far away. Swedish hegemony during the late seventeenth century had become overextended, making the Swedes'
holdings a prime target for a newly expansionist Russia.

In his first attempt to conquer Estland and Livland, during
the Great Northern War (1700–09), Peter I (the Great) (r.
1682–1725) met with defeat at Narva at the hands of Sweden's
Charles XII (r. 1697–1718). A second campaign in 1708 saw
Peter introduce a scorched-earth policy across many parts of
the area. The outcome was victory for Russia in 1710 and acquisition of a "window to the West." In taking control of Estland
and Livland for what would be the next 200 years, tsarist Russia
recognized the rights and privileges of the local German nobility, whose members amounted to only a small fraction of the
population. Although the extent of the nobles' autonomy in

the two areas was always contested, especially under Catherine II (the Great) (r. 1762–96), the Baltic Germans did develop a strong loyalty to the Russian tsars as guarantors of their landed privileges. German control over the Estonian peasantry reached its high point during the eighteenth century. Labor overtook taxes-in-kind as the predominant means of controlling the serfs. The first real reforms of serfdom, which gave peasants some rights, took place in 1804. In 1816 and 1819, the serfs were formally emancipated in Estland and Livland, respectively.

By the mid-nineteenth century, the Estonians were fast developing into an independent society and nation. The number of urbanized Estonians had grown considerably, overtaking what had been German majorities in the cities. Industrialization was also breaking down the old order. An Estonian cultural awakening began in the 1850s and 1860s (see Religion; Language and Culture, this ch.). Tsarist reaction and a fierce Russification campaign in the 1880s could not extinguish the new Estonian spirit, although for the most part Estonian demands continued to focus on culture. Political demands for Estonian autonomy found strong expression during the Revolution of 1905, and an All-Estonian Congress was organized in Tartu that same year. Although radical Estonian politicians such as Jaan Teemant and moderate leaders such as Jaan Tõnisson were deeply divided on tactics, there were widespread calls from the Estland and Livland provinces for a unification of Estonian lands and an official end to Russification. Repression of the 1905 movement was severe in Estland, although Tõnisson's moderate Estonian Progressive People's Party survived and went on to participate in Russia's new assembly, the Duma. Amid the turmoil, Baltic Germans also grew apprehensive; they would be upset even more with the outbreak of World War I, which would pit Russia against their conationals.

The fall of the tsarist regime in February 1917 forced the issue of Estonia's political future. Vigorous lobbying in Petrograd by Tõnisson and the large Estonian population living there forced the provisional government to accept Estonia's territorial unification as one province and the election of a provincial assembly, the Maapäev, later that year. The election results showed significant support for leftist parties, including the Bolsheviks, Social Democrats, and Social Revolutionaries. Voting was complicated, however, by the presence of numerous military personnel from outside Estonia.

15

The Bolshevik takeover in Petrograd in November 1917 extended to Estonia as well, until Germany occupied Estonia in February 1918. Most of Estonia's other political parties realized they were caught between the two forces and agreed to begin an active search for outside support. Representatives were sent to the major European capitals to secure Western recognition of an Estonian declaration of independence. As the Bolsheviks retreated from Tallinn and the German occupation army entered the city, the Committee of Elders (or standing body) of the Maapäev declared the country independent on February 24, 1918.

Interwar Independence, 1918–40

In contrast to its later peaceful return to independence in 1991, Estonia's first modern era of sovereignty began with a fifteen-month war (1918–20) against both Russian Bolshevik and Baltic German forces. In the end, the War of Independence took the lives of about 3,600 Estonians and left about 14,000 wounded. In the Tartu Peace Treaty, which was concluded with Russia in February 1920, Moscow relinquished all claims to Estonia in perpetuity. A year later, Estonia gained international recognition from the Western powers and became a member of the League of Nations. In June 1920, Estonia's first constitution was promulgated, establishing a parliamentary system.

With a political system in place, the new Estonian government immediately began the job of rebuilding. As one of its first major acts, the government carried out an extensive land reform, giving tracts to small farmers and veterans of the War of Independence. The large estates of the Baltic German nobility were expropriated, breaking its centuries-old power as a class.

Agriculture dominated the country's economy. Thanks to land reform, the number of small farms doubled to more than 125,000. Although many homesteads were small, the expansion of landownership helped stimulate new production after the war. Land reform, however, did not solve all of Estonia's early problems. Estonian agriculture and industry (mostly textiles and machine manufacturing) had depended heavily on the Russian market. Independence and Soviet communism closed that outlet by 1924, and the economy had to reorient itself quickly toward the West, to which the country also owed significant war debts. The economy began to grow again by the late 1920s but suffered another setback during the Great Depression, which hit Estonia during 1931–34. By the late 1930s, however, the industrial sector was expanding anew, at an average annual rate of 14 percent. Industry employed some 38,000 workers by 1938.

Independent Estonia's early political system was characterized by instability and frequent government turnovers. The political parties were fragmented and were about evenly divided between the left and right wings. The first Estonian constitution required parliamentary approval of all major acts taken by the prime minister and his government. The Riigikogu (State Assembly) could dismiss the government at any time, without incurring sanctions. Consequently, from 1918 to 1933 a total of twenty-three governments held office.

The country's first big political challenge came in 1924 during an attempted communist takeover. In the depths of a nationwide economic crisis, leaders of the Estonian Communist Party (Eestimaa Kommunistlik Partei—EKP), in close contact with Communist International (Comintern—see Glossary) leaders from Moscow, believed the time was ripe for a workers' revolution to mirror that of the Soviet Union. On the morning of December 1, some 300 party activists moved to take over key government outposts in Tallinn, while expecting workers in the capital to rise up behind them. The effort soon failed, however, and the government quickly regained control. In the aftermath, Estonian political unity got a strong boost, while the communists lost all credibility. Relations with the Soviet Union, which had helped to instigate the coup, deteriorated sharply.

By the early 1930s, Estonia's political system, still governed by the imbalanced constitution, again began to show signs of instability. As in many other European countries at the time, pressure was mounting for a stronger system of government. Several constitutional changes were proposed, the most radical being put forth by the protofascist League of Independence War Veterans. In a 1933 referendum, the league spearheaded replacement of the parliamentary system with a presidential form of government and laid the groundwork for an April 1934 presidential election, which it expected to win. Alarmed by the prospect of a league victory and possible fascist rule, the caretaker prime minister, Konstantin Päts, organized a preemptive coup d'état on March 12, 1934. In concert with the army, Päts began a rule by decree that endured virtually without interruption until 1940. He suspended the parliament and all political parties, and he disbanded the League of Independence War Veterans, arresting several hundred of its leaders. The subsequent "Era of Silence" initially was supported by most of Estonian political society. After the threat from the league was neutralized, however, calls for a return to parliamentary democracy resurfaced. In 1936 Päts initiated a tentative liberalization with the election of a constituent assembly and the adoption of a new constitution. During elections for a new parliament, however, political parties remained suspended, except for Päts's own National Front, and civil liberties were only slowly restored. Päts was elected president by the new parliament in 1938.

The Soviet Era, 1940–85

Although the period of authoritarian rule that lasted from 1934 to 1940 was a low point in Estonian democracy, in perspective its severity clearly would be tempered by the long Soviet era soon to follow. The clouds over Estonia and its independence began to gather in August 1939, when Nazi Germany and the Soviet Union signed the Nazi-Soviet Nonaggression Pact (also known as the Molotov-Ribbentrop Pact), dividing Eastern Europe into spheres of influence. Moving to capitalize on its side of the deal, the Soviet Union soon began to pressure Estonia, Latvia, and Lithuania into signing the Pact of Defense and Mutual Assistance, which would allow Moscow to station 25,000 troops in Estonia. President Päts, in weakening health and with little outside support, acceded to every Soviet demand. In June 1940, Soviet forces completely occupied the country, alleging that Estonia had "violated" the terms of the mutual assistance treaty. With rapid political maneuvering, the regime of Soviet leader Joseph V. Stalin then forced the installation of a pro-Soviet government and called for new parliamentary elections in July. The Estonian Communist Party, which had only recently reemerged from underground with fewer than 150 members, organized the sole list of candidates permitted to run. Päts and other Estonian political leaders meanwhile were quietly deported to the Soviet Union or killed. With the country occupied and under total control, the communists' "official" electoral victory on June 17–18 with 92.8 percent of the vote was merely window dressing. On July 21, the new parliament declared Estonia a Soviet republic and "requested" admission into the Soviet Union. In Moscow, the Supreme Soviet granted the request on August 6, 1940.

For all the ups and downs Estonia's independent government experienced during the interwar period, its termination by Stalin in 1940 was clearly not among the range of solutions favored by most Estonians. Yet, chances of holding off the Soviet onslaught with an army numbering about 15,000 men were slim at best. Thus, Estonia's only real hope for the future lay in continued Western recognition of its de jure statehood, which other European countries and the United States declared in 1940. Over the next fifty years, this Western policy of token recognition nearly fell into desuetude. Yet, the policy's survival into the late 1980s would allow it to become a rallying point for Estonia's new drive for independence. Thanks to this continuing Western recognition, Estonia's calls for sovereignty from Moscow by early 1990 could not be considered merely secessionism. Rather, they represented demands for the restoration of a state still existent under international law. This appeal to international legality dating to 1940 would frustrate the attempts of Soviet leader Mikhail S. Gorbachev to control Estonia and the other Baltic states in the late 1980s.

Estonia's absorption into the Soviet Union as the Estonian Soviet Socialist Republic was interrupted in June 1941 by the German invasion. Still, that one year of Soviet rule left a deep mark on the Estonians. In addition to the takeover of their country and the rapid nationalization of their capitalist economy, on June 13–14, 1941, before the German invasion, Estonians also saw the mass deportation of some 10,000 of their countrymen to Siberia. Of those seized during the one-night operation, over 80 percent were women, children, or elderly people. The purpose of this action seemed to be to create terror rather than to neutralize any actual threat to the regime. The 1941–44 German occupation witnessed more repression, especially of Estonia's Jewish population, which numbered about 2,000. In September 1944, as the Red Army again neared Estonia, the memories of Soviet rule resurfaced vividly enough to prompt some 70,000 Estonians to flee the country into exile. These émigrés later formed ethnic communities in Sweden, the United States, Canada, Britain, Australia, and elsewhere, continuing to lobby for Estonia's rights during the next fifty years. Altogether, from 1939 to 1945 Estonia lost over 20 percent of its population to the turmoil of Soviet and German expansionism.

After the war, the Sovietization of Estonia resumed. The republic's war-ravaged industry was rebuilt as a component of the centrally planned economy. Agricultural collectivization was enforced, climaxing in March 1949 with another, more brutal wave of deportations involving some 25,000 people. The Estonian Communist Party was purged in 1950 of many of its original native leaders; they were replaced by several prominent Russified Estonians who had grown up in Russia. After Stalin's death in 1953, Nikita S. Khrushchev's liberalization also touched Estonia. Efforts at economic reform were undertaken, and repression was eased. By the late 1960s, consumerism had taken root, and intellectual life was relatively vibrant. Following the Soviet Union's suppression of Czechoslovakia's "Prague Spring" reform movement in 1968, the trend toward openness suffered a reversal, but Estonia continued to maintain a standard of living well above the Soviet average. In 1980, during the period of stagnation under Soviet leader Leonid I. Brezhnev, some 2,000 schoolchildren demonstrated in the streets of Tallinn against a major Russification campaign launched from Moscow. Several dozen Estonian intellectuals later came together to write their own protest letter, but to no avail. Karl Vaino, the Russified Estonian leader of the Estonian Communist Party at the time, was particularly hostile toward dissent of any kind.

The Pursuit of Independence, 1985–91

The dawning of *glasnost* (see Glossary) and *perestroika* (see Glossary) in the Soviet Union initiated a period of liberalization from which the dying superpower would never recover. Estonia seized on this opportunity in 1987, beginning with public protests against a phosphorus-mining project proposed by the central government that would have seriously damaged the country's environment. Pressure for economic reform became acute later in the year when a group of four Estonian liberals put forth a plan for economic autonomy for the republic. In 1988 Estonia's "singing revolution" took off, energized by the removal of Karl Vaino as Estonian Communist Party chief in June and his replacement by a native son, Vaino Väljas. In April the Estonian Popular Front was founded as the capstone to a summer of political activity unparalleled since 1940. This mobilization proved effective in November when Estonia opposed attempts by Gorbachev to strengthen central authority through changes in the Soviet Union's constitution. In an act of defiance, the Estonian parliament, then known as the Supreme Soviet, declared the republic's right to sovereignty on November 16. It also called for a new union treaty to be drawn up to govern the Soviet state.

By the spring of 1989, Estonia had thrown down the gauntlets of political sovereignty and economic autonomy. A two-year effort to force their acceptance by Moscow followed. On the political front, Estonia's strongest strategy was to invoke history. At the Soviet Union's first Congress of People's Deputies (see Glossary) in Moscow, in 1989, Estonian and other Baltic deputies battled with Gorbachev to have the Soviet Union reveal the true story of the Nazi-Soviet Nonaggression Pact in time for the fiftieth anniversary of the pact in August. Just days before the anniversary, a commission charged with studying the pact concluded that secret protocols dividing up Poland and the Baltic states had indeed existed. Armed with this finding, Estonia literally linked up with its Baltic neighbors on August 23 to form a 600-kilometer human chain from Tallinn to the Lithuanian capital, Vilnius, to draw worldwide attention to the anniversary of the pact and to their cause. An estimated 2 million Baltic residents participated in the show of unity, but the action also elicited a harsh rebuke from Moscow several days later. Tensions quickly mounted in Estonia, and the Estonian Popular Front decided to cancel a major song festival and rally planned for early September. In early August, Estonian nationalists had already been shaken by their first confrontation with Soviet loyalists. Members of the International Movement of Workers in the Estonian Soviet Socialist Republic (Intermovement), primarily made up of ethnic Russians, had staged strikes in Tallinn and northeastern Estonia protesting a set of new electoral rules and a new language law requiring all service workers to speak both Estonian and Russian. Many Russians in Estonia, fearful of growing Estonian national feeling and of losing their privileges, looked to Moscow for help. But direct intervention would not come.

Throughout the fall, independence sentiment continued to mount. In October the Estonian Popular Front issued a campaign platform for upcoming municipal elections in which it publicly endorsed full independence. Meanwhile, more radical groups had begun organizing their own campaign to restore independence, completely bypassing the Soviet system. These groups, known as Estonian Citizens Committees, maintained that because their country had been illegally occupied and annexed by the Soviet Union and because the prewar republic still retained international recognition, it could not legitimate

Soviet authority by negotiating "secession." Rather, Estonia had to insist on the continuing legal authority of the prewar republic as the only sure way to ward off Soviet attempts to keep it in the union. By invoking international law, Estonia could also enlist Western support and protection at a time when the Soviet Union needed good relations with the West to facilitate its own reforms. By the fall of 1989, it was clear that this argument and strategy would become essential to the independence movement and, indeed, to politics thereafter.

To raise popular awareness of the independence issue, the Estonian Citizens Committees mounted a year-long campaign to register all citizens of the prewar republic and their descendants. Of an estimated 1 million such citizens, the grassroots movement succeeded in registering about 700,000. It was this electorate that, according to the radical committees, possessed the sole right to decide the future of Soviet-occupied Estonia—not the Soviet-era Supreme Soviet, its government, or even the half-million Soviet-era immigrants to Estonia and their descendants, whom the committees claimed had taken up residence under the terms of the Soviet occupation and who would later be denied automatic citizenship. Rather, the committees asserted the need to elect a new representative body to lead the independence struggle and the restoration of the prewar republic. In February 1990, they organized nationwide elections for a Congress of Estonia, which held its first session the following month.

Although their campaign enabled the citizens committees and the Congress to gain a fair amount of popular support, most Estonians were not totally willing to forsake the Supreme Soviet because it, too, was up for election in March 1990. The more moderate Estonian Popular Front favored the Supreme Soviet as a more realistic path to independence. The Estonian Popular Front campaigned heavily in March and won about forty of the 101 seats. The Supreme Soviet elections also allowed all residents of Estonia to vote, including Soviet-era immigrants and their descendants. These were mostly Russians who, still led primarily by Estonian Communist Party functionaries, finally elected a total of twenty-seven pro-Soviet deputies. Although the two-thirds Estonian majority consequently was slim, it was enough for the Supreme Soviet to declare at its first full session, on March 30, the country's official intention to reestablish its independence.

Unlike Lithuania's declaration of independence, Estonia's declaration was not an outright break with the Soviet Union. Rather, it was an attempt to find a compromise between the radical Congress of Estonia and moderate Estonian Popular Front positions. Still, the message of asserting independence from Moscow was the same. The Kremlin's reaction was subdued; no economic sanctions were imposed on Estonia. Neither, however, was any recognition accorded Estonia's declaration, nor were any serious attempts made to begin talks with the new government in Tallinn. In the meantime, therefore, Estonia attempted to shore up its stance by finding new allies and initiating independent economic policies. In May 1990, the leaders of Estonia, Latvia, and Lithuania met formally in Tallinn to coordinate their strategy. In July representatives of the three countries met for the first time with Boris N. Yeltsin, who had just been elected chairman of the Russian Supreme Soviet. Estonian politicians and government officials traveled in Western Europe and the United States to renew Western contacts.

Domestically, in the fall of 1990 the Estonian government, led by Estonian Popular Front leader Edgar Savisaar, began a series of moves to assert the republic's economic independence and begin market reforms. Financial contributions to the all-union budget were stopped, and wide-ranging price reform was initiated. Plans for a separate currency, begun in 1989, continued to be worked on. In October the government dispatched militia forces to patrol the republic's border with Russia and to control the movement of goods; control over western gateways remained under Soviet control.

Moscow's bloody military assault on civilians in Vilnius and Riga in January 1991 sent shock waves through Estonia as well. Although there were no violent incidents in Estonia, Soviet loyalists staged a noisy demonstration in Tallinn, and the government installed huge boulders in front of the parliament building for protection. On January 12, Tallinn was the site of a hastily organized summit meeting between the Baltic leaders and Yeltsin, who supported the sovereignty of the three republics against Gorbachev. Yeltsin and Estonian parliament chairman Arnold Rüütel signed a bilateral treaty recognizing the sovereignty of each other's republic. When, later in the month, Gorbachev announced a nationwide referendum on the issue of preserving the Soviet Union, Estonia decided to preempt the ballot with a referendum of its own on independence. The

March 3 Estonian poll showed 78 percent in favor of independence and indicated significant support for independence among Russian residents—as much as 30 percent. Most Estonians boycotted the Soviet referendum held two weeks later. With public opinion clearly favoring independence, Gorbachev agreed to official talks with Estonia beginning on March 28. The talks continued through August and the Moscow coup, but no progress was made. Estonia refused to join negotiations for a new union treaty, while the Kremlin avoided any specifics on independence. The talks were further upset by several hit-and-run attacks on Estonia's border outposts during the summer of 1991. These were generally attributed to units of the Soviet Ministry of Internal Affairs Special Forces Detachment (Otryad militsii osobogo naznacheniya—OMON), commonly known as the Black Berets, over which Gorbachev apparently had lost control.

Independence Reclaimed, August 1991–October 1992

On the night of August 19, 1991, Estonia was caught up in the uncertainty generated by the attempted coup in Moscow. A column of Soviet light tanks and troop carriers had already started to move on Tallinn as the commander of Soviet forces in the Baltics announced his support of the coup. Fearing a total crackdown by the Soviet army, the Estonian parliament met in emergency session on August 20. At 11:00 P.M., the Supreme Council, as the legislature was now known, passed a final resolution declaring full independence and requesting de facto international recognition. Volunteers were mustered to defend key government buildings and communications centers; there was no bloodshed, however. As Heinz Valk, an artist and a member of parliament, later declared, "The coup in Moscow [gave] us a chance comparable to that in 1918."

Once the coup finally collapsed, Estonia resumed its efforts to gain international recognition and otherwise reestablish itself as an independent state. Iceland was the first to acknowledge Estonian independence, on August 22; Yeltsin's Russia was quick to follow, on August 24. The United States hesitated until September 2. The Soviet Union recognized Estonia on September 6. The process of state building also began soon after the coup. In contrast to Latvia and Lithuania, Estonia, in its August 20 independence declaration, took the additional step of convening a constitutional assembly immediately to draft a new basic law for the country. The assembly drew thirty members each from the Supreme Council and the Congress of Estonia, thus defusing rivalries between the two organizations. In mid-October the assembly settled on a working draft focused on a generally parliamentary form of government. Deliberations then slowed as the country got caught up in debates over citizenship.

In Estonia's fight to regain independence, the overall strategy of asserting the country's legal continuity as a state clearly had paid off. Yet, in terms of offering a path for the future, this strategy had many complications. One of these was the question of what to do with the 500,000 mostly Russian, Soviet-era immigrants living in Estonia. In 1990 the Congress of Estonia had been the first representative body to lay down the principle that because these people had settled in Estonia under Soviet rule, they were not automatically citizens of the legally restored Estonian state. Rather, under independence they would have to be "naturalized" on the basis of specific language and residency criteria. This position was also argued as a means of better integrating the mostly Russian noncitizen population, the majority of whom did not speak Estonian. In mid-1991, as the independence struggle seemed to languish, the Estonian government, led by Prime Minister Edgar Savisaar, showed signs of readiness to compromise on the citizenship issue in order to gain more local Russian support. However, after the failed August coup and the immediate onset of full independence, the Congress and other radical groups were emboldened to insist on the principle of restricted citizenship. Thus, the Supreme Council decided on November 11, 1991, to require the naturalization of all Soviet-era immigrants to Estonia while automatically renewing the citizenship of all prewar citizens and their descendants. In February 1992, the parliament set naturalization terms, which included a two-year residency requirement, the ability to speak conversational Estonian, and a one-year waiting period after applying.

Although these terms were relatively mild, the implications in Estonia's particular situation remained less than clear. Most Soviet-era immigrants had already fulfilled the residency requirement, but at best only 20 percent were prepared to meet the language requirement. Most Russians living in Estonia had not bothered to learn the rudiments of the national language, forcing Estonians to speak Russian to them instead. It would take time for many to begin learning. In any case, the naturalization procedures would delay nationalization for at

25

least the one-year waiting period. This outcome had serious implications because the resident Russians would then be ineligible to vote in the September 1992 elections for a new parliament. As the only consolation to noncitizens, the Constitutional Assembly later accorded them the right to vote in local elections under the terms of the new constitution.

The citizenship issue generally heightened tensions between Estonians and Russians. The more nationalistic Estonian deputies in parliament began to accuse the moderate government of Savisaar of foot-dragging. In January 1992, in the midst of a severe economic crisis and problems securing heating oil, Savisaar asked parliament for emergency powers. When the vote on emergency powers was taken on January 16, Savisaar won, thanks only to the votes of several Russian deputies. This narrow margin revealed the extent of Savisaar's unpopularity among the Estonian deputies, and a week later he resigned. Savisaar's transportation minister, Tiit Vähi, was charged with forming a new government, which was billed as one of technocrats and caretakers in advance of parliamentary elections in the fall.

As Vähi formed his regime, several major issues remained outstanding. The new prime minister's first task was to oversee the passage of the naturalization requirements for citizenship, which occurred in late February. Then, the language and residency requirements were put into effect. Thereafter, the draft constitution drawn up by the Constitutional Assembly neared completion and required approval by popular referendum. This referendum was set for June 28, 1992, with only citizens allowed to participate. Alongside the proposed constitution, a second question asked the people whether to allow the earliest applicants for citizenship to vote on an exceptional basis in the upcoming nationwide elections. Because these applicants numbered just over 5,000, the gesture would be largely symbolic. However, a strong campaign by nationalist Estonian parties led to the defeat of the measure, 53 percent to 46 percent. The constitution was passed by a 91 percent majority.

On June 20, one week before the referendum, the Vähi government completed its third remaining task: currency reform. On that day, Estonian residents proudly cashed in their old, worn Russian rubles for crisp, new Estonian kroons (for value of the kroon—see Glossary). The kroon, pegged to the stable deutsche mark, would soon bring inflation tumbling down and serve as the basis for a new economy (see Economy, this ch.).

Typical rural landscape near Viljandi
Industrial pollution on the northern coast
Courtesy Priit Vesilind

27

With the constitution approved and a new state structure in place, the campaign began for Estonia's first post-Soviet elections. The election of a new legislature, the Riigikogu, on September 20 would mark the full restoration of the legal Republic of Estonia. On October 5, 1992, in its first session, the Riigikogu, which replaced the transitional Supreme Council, issued a declaration establishing its legal continuity with the prewar republic and declaring an official end to the transition to independence announced two-and-one-half years earlier.

Physical Environment

Geographic Features

Estonia is a low, flat country covering 45,226 square kilometers. It is about the size of Vermont and New Hampshire combined. Estonia has a long, shallow coastline (1,393 kilometers) along the Baltic Sea, with 1,520 islands dotting the shore. The two largest islands are Saaremaa (literally, island land), at 2,673 square kilometers, and Hiiumaa, at 989 square kilometers. The two islands are favorite Estonian vacation spots. The country's highest point, Suur Munamägi (Egg Mountain), is in the hilly southeast and reaches 318 meters above sea level. Estonia is covered by about 1.8 million hectares of forest. Arable land amounts to about 926,000 hectares. Meadows cover about 252,000 hectares, and pastureland covers about 181,000 hectares. There are more than 1,400 natural and artificial lakes in Estonia. The largest of them, Lake Peipsi (3,555 square kilometers), forms much of the border between Estonia and Russia. Located in central Estonia, Võrtsjärv is the second-largest lake (270 square kilometers). The Narva and Emajõgi are among the most important of the country's many rivers.

Estonia has a temperate climate, with four seasons of near-equal length. Average temperatures range from 16.3°C on the Baltic islands to 17.1°C inland in July, the warmest month, and from –3.5°C on the Baltic islands to –7.6°C inland in February, the coldest month. Precipitation averages 568 millimeters per year and is heaviest in late summer.

Estonia's land border with Latvia runs 267 kilometers; the Russian border runs 290 kilometers. From 1920 to 1945, Estonia's border with Russia, set by the 1920 Tartu Peace Treaty, extended beyond the Narva River in the northeast and beyond the town of Pechory (Petseri) in the southeast (see fig. 2). This territory, amounting to some 2,300 square kilometers, was incorporated into Russia by Stalin at the end of World War II. Estonia is now disputing that territorial loss (see Relations with Russia, this ch.).

Environmental Issues

One of the most burdensome legacies of the Soviet era is widespread environmental pollution. The worst offender in this regard was the Soviet army. Across military installations covering more than 80,000 hectares of Estonian territory, the army dumped hundreds of thousands of tons of jet fuel into the ground, improperly disposed of toxic chemicals, and discarded outdated explosives and weapons in coastal and inland waters. In the 1990s, during the army's withdrawal from Estonia, extensive damage was done to discarded buildings and equipment. In October 1993, the Estonian Ministry of Environment issued a preliminary report summing up part of the degradation it had surveyed thus far. The report described the worst damage as having been done to Estonia's topsoil and underground water supply by the systematic dumping of jet fuel at six Soviet army air bases. At the air base near Tapa, site of the worst damage, officials estimated that six square kilometers of land were covered by a layer of fuel; eleven square kilometers of underground water were said to be contaminated. The water in the surrounding area was undrinkable. With Danish help, Estonian crews began cleaning up the site, although they estimated the likely cost to be as much as EKR4 million. The Ministry of Environment assigned a monetary cost of more than EKR10 billion to the damage to the country's topsoil and water supply. However, the ministry was able to allocate only EKR5 million in 1993 for cleanup operations.

In a 1992 government report to the United Nations Conference on the Environment and Development, Estonia detailed other major environmental concerns. For instance, for several consecutive years Estonia had led the world in the production of sulfur dioxide per capita. Nearly 75 percent of Estonia's air pollution was reported to come from two oil shale-based thermal power stations operating near Narva. The mining of oil shale in northeastern Estonia also left gigantic mounds of limestone dotting the region. Near the town of Sillamäe, site of a former uranium enrichment plant, about 1,200 tons of uranium and about 750 tons of thorium had been dumped into the Gulf of Finland. This was said to have caused severe health problems among area residents. In the coastal town of Paldiski, the removal of waste left by Soviet army nuclear reactors was also a major concern. The combined cost of environmental cleanup at both towns was put at more than EKR3.5 billion.

Society

Population

According to 1989 census figures, Estonia had a population of 1,565,662 (see table 2, Appendix). By 1994 this number had dropped to an estimated 1,506,927 as a result of negative natural growth rates and net out-migration beginning in 1990. Females outnumbered males by some 100,000 in 1991 (see fig. 4). Seventy percent of the population was urban. The birth rate in 1993 was 10.0 per 1,000 population, and the death rate was 14.0 per 1,000.

Tallinn, the capital, is the largest city, with about 479,000 inhabitants in 1989. Tartu, the second most populous city, had about 113,000 residents in the same year, and Narva, on the Russian border, had 81,000 (see table 3, Appendix). Since the late 1980s, many place-names have had their pre-Soviet names restored. These include the Saaremaa town of Kuressaare (formerly Kingissepa) and some 250 streets throughtout the country.

In 1934 Estonia had a population of 1,126,413. War losses and Soviet deportations brought that figure down to an estimated 850,000 by 1945. During the Soviet era, the population grew steadily, fueled largely by in-migration from other areas of the Soviet Union (see table 4, Appendix). During the 1950s and 1960s, net in-migration accounted for more than 60 percent of the total population growth. In recent years, net migration has reversed, with some 84,000 people, mostly Russians, having left between 1989 and 1993. In the mid-1990s, these trends were continuing, though more slowly. Since 1992 Estonia has been offering financial assistance to people wishing to resettle in Russia; in October 1993, it signed a treaty with Russia regulating repatriation and resettlement. According to public opinion polls conducted in 1993 and 1994, however, the vast majority of local Russians were not inclined to leave Estonia.

The reverse flow of migration is thought to have contributed in the early 1990s to a slight rise in the Estonian proportion of the population. In 1989 Estonians constituted only 61.5 percent of the population, while Russians made up 30.3 percent, Ukrainians 3.1 percent, Belorussians 1.7 percent, and Finns 1.1

percent; Jews, Tatars, Germans, Latvians, and Poles constituted the remaining 2.3 percent. This was in sharp contrast to 1934, when Estonians represented 88.2 percent of the population and Russians only 8.2 percent. This demographic shift was a major concern for Estonians, who feared losing control of their own country. Another worrisome statistic for Estonians was their disproportionately small share of the yearly natural population growth (births minus deaths) until 1990 and their large share of the population's decrease in 1991 (see table 5, Appendix). Although Estonians dominate in the countryside, the Russian population in Estonia is nearly 90 percent urban, living mainly in Tallinn and in the northeastern industrial towns of Kohtla-Järve, Sillamäe, and Narva. Tallinn is about 47 percent Estonian. Kohtla-Järve is only about 21 percent Estonian, Sillamäe 5 to 6 percent, and Narva 4 percent.

Health

In the mid-1980s, the average life expectancy in Estonia peaked at about sixty-six years for males and seventy-five years for females. Thereafter, these figures declined somewhat, especially for males, most likely because of deteriorating living standards. In 1994 overall life expectancy was estimated to be 70.0 years (65.0 years for males and 75.2 years for females). Infant mortality was about 19.1 deaths per 1,000 live births, according to a 1994 estimate. Fertility rates dropped from an estimated 2.3 children born per woman in 1988 to about 2.0 in 1994. Abortion remained the main form of birth control, more so among Russians than Estonians. There were 24,981 abortions in 1992 (1,389 per 1,000 live births), although that figure was down from about 36,000 a decade earlier. Most women who have abortions are married. Nearly half of all marriages end in divorce. In recent years, a greater number of people have begun living together instead of marrying. Such couples account for 17 percent of all births in the country.

The primary cause of death is cardiovascular diseases, accounting for about 64 percent of all deaths in the mid-1990s. Cancer and accidents account for a large share as well. Estonia's suicide rate over the years has reflected the country's sociopolitical condition. In the mid-1970s, during the politically stagnant Brezhnev years, there were about 530 suicides per year. In 1990, after Estonia's political reawakening, suicides dropped to 425. In 1992, as economic conditions worsened, suicides climbed again, to 498. In November 1993, twenty-nine

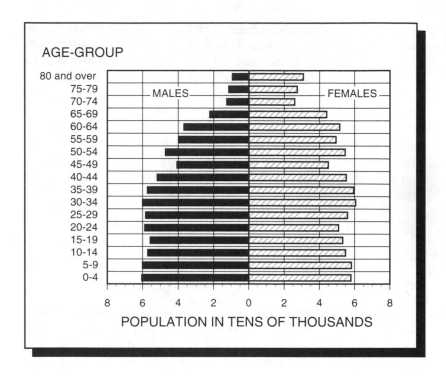

Source: Based on information from Marje Jõeste, Ülo Kaevats, and Harry Õiglane, eds., *Eesti A & Õ*, Tallinn, 1993, 104.

Figure 4. Population of Estonia by Age and Gender, 1991

cases of acquired immune deficiency syndrome (AIDS) were reported in Estonia, with two deaths having resulted from AIDS-related illnesses.

The state-run health care system inherited from the Soviet regime was being decentralized in the early 1990s and had yet to meet Western standards. In 1992 the number of physicians, equivalent to thirty-two per 10,000 inhabitants, was relatively high, but there was a shortage of nurses and other auxiliary medical staff. Hospital beds numbered ninety-two per 10,000 inhabitants, down from 121 in 1990. Although the cost of medicines increased, new imports from the West eased some of the chronic shortages of the Soviet era. But overall, shortages of basic medical supplies, including disposable needles, anesthetics, and antibiotics, remained a serious problem.

Welfare

In 1990 and 1991, Estonia began taking over more of the administration of its social welfare system from the central Soviet authorities. The government instituted its own system of payments, for example, to compensate the population for the removal of state subsidies and an increase in food prices. In April 1991, the republic passed its own pension law, the implementation of which was upset by inflation, although later the situation improved with the introduction of a new currency. Still, with some 307,000 pensioners and a rapidly aging population, pensions accounted for a large share of the country's social fund (see Recent Economic Developments, this ch.). In response, the government began gradually raising the retirement age from fifty-five for women and sixty for men to sixty for women and sixty-five for men. In January 1993, more than 1,000 angry retirees staged a protest in front of Toompea Castle to demand higher pensions. At EKR260 a month, pensions were so low that many people complained that they could barely pay their rent and utility bills.

Other welfare benefits provided by the state included financial support for invalids, low-income families, and families having three or more children. The state also provided institutional care for elderly people and orphans.

Education System

With a half-century of Soviet rule behind it, independent Estonia began a process of thorough educational reform. In addition to a restructuring of curricula, the government began a reorganization of the secondary school system with the goal of increasing specialization among the country's high schools. In 1993 there were some 215,000 elementary and secondary school students in 724 schools across Estonia. About 142,000 students were enrolled in Estonian-language schools and about 70,000 in Russian-language schools, mainly in Tallinn and northeastern Estonia. In addition, there were individual schools teaching in other minority languages, including Hebrew, Swedish, and Ukrainian. Estonian-language schools offer twelve years of education—nine elementary and three secondary. Education in Russian-language schools lasts eleven years. Under a 1993 law, education was made compulsory up to the ninth grade. Estonia's vocational education network is also extensive, with seventy-seven schools across the country and about 26,000 students in 1993. Literacy is nearly universal.

Estonia's system of higher education centers on six universities. Tartu University, founded in 1632, is the country's largest, with about 7,600 students in 1993. The Tallinn Technical University had about 6,800 full-time students in 1993, and the Tallinn Pedagogical University had about 3,150. The Estonian Agricultural University in Tartu had about 2,800 students, and the Tallinn Art University and the Estonian Academy of Music each enrolled about 500.

Higher education was restructured in the early 1990s into a four-year system after the five-year Soviet system was dropped. A new degree structure comparable to the Western one of baccalaureate, master's, and doctoral degrees was established. Soviet ideological subjects such as "scientific communism" were abandoned soon after the independence movement began in 1988. With the help of exchange programs and guest lecturers from the West, new programs were begun in economics, business, foreign languages, religion, political science, and sociology.

Religion

The dominant religion in Estonia is Evangelical Lutheranism. Estonians were Christianized by the Teutonic Knights in the thirteenth century. During the Reformation, Lutheranism spread, and the church was officially established in Estonia in 1686. Still, Estonians generally tend not to be very religious, because religion through the nineteenth century was associated with German feudal rule. In 1992 there were 153 Lutheran congregations in Estonia with an estimated 200,000 members. Active members totaled about 70,000.

Orthodox Christianity is the second largest faith, with eighty congregations and about 15,000 members in 1992. Forty-three Orthodox congregations are Estonian, twenty-five are Russian, and twelve are mixed. There are eleven congregations of Old Believers (see Glossary) and a convent in Kuremäe, in northeastern Estonia. After independence, ethnic divisions among Orthodox Christians resurfaced over the question of their allegiance to Moscow. Many Estonian Orthodox Church leaders favored greater autonomy from Moscow or total allegiance to the Ecumenical Patriarchate of Constantinople, the situation that existed during Estonia's first period of independence. In 1992 the Estonian Orthodox Church, despite local Russian

Old city gate with modern hotel in background, Tallinn
Courtesy David Walker
"Kali," a nonalcoholic beverage made from rye bread, dispensed
in the southern town of Pärnu
Courtesy Priit Vesilind

objections, requested autonomy from Moscow. The issue was a delicate one for Russian Orthodox patriarch Aleksiy II, who had been born in Estonia and had served there as a metropolitan. However, in April 1993 he agreed to grant the Estonian Orthodox Church autonomy.

Among other religions in Estonia in the early 1990s there were eighty-three Baptist congregations with about 6,000 adult members, as well as about fifteen Methodist and several Seventh-Day Adventist congregations. Estonia's small Roman Catholic community was visited by Pope John Paul II during a tour of the Baltic states in September 1993, and the Dalai Lama came to Estonia soon after independence, in October 1991. The Jewish community has a synagogue in Tallinn.

Language and Culture

The Estonian language belongs to the Finno-Ugric family of languages, closely related to Finnish and more distantly related to Hungarian. It is among the most difficult languages in Europe, with fourteen cases for the declension of nouns and complicated rules for their use. There are no articles, however, nor any grammatical gender in Estonian. Indeed, the same word is used for both "he" and "she": *tema.* Over the years, the language has been standardized, but many dialects and accents remain, especially on the islands. Most of the foreign words used by Estonians come from German. Russian, Finnish, and English also have influenced Estonian, especially in the formation of slang.

Estonian culture developed in earnest during the nineteenth-century period of national awakening. Elements of Estonian peasant culture, such as songs and folktales, were brought together by the country's first cultural elite after 1850. Between 1857 and 1861, Friedrich Reinhold Kreutzwald compiled and published the Estonian national epic, *Kalevipoeg* (Son of Kalev), which was based on various folklore themes. Written in verse, the epic tells the story of Kalevipoeg, the mythical ancient ruler of Estonia. Another achievement of this period was the establishment of Estonia's first regularly published Estonian-language newspaper, *Perno Postimees,* originally published in Pärnu by Johann Voldemar Jannsen in 1857. In 1878 Carl Robert Jakobson established the newspaper *Sakala,* which would soon become a major promoter of the cultural renaissance. Jakob Hurt, a schoolteacher and Lutheran minister, organized a collection of folk songs in the 1880s and gave several speeches extolling the value of Estonian culture.

The national literature had an earlier beginning, in the 1810s, with the patriotic poetry of Kristjan Jaak Peterson. In the second half of the nineteenth century, romanticism and love of country found equal expression in the poetry of Lydia Koidula, Estonia's first woman poet and a key figure of the cultural awakening. The first Estonian song festival was organized in 1869 in Tartu, attracting some 800 participants and about 4,000 spectators. This event would become a major tradition in Estonian cultural life and was held roughly every five years. At the end of the nineteenth century, Estonian theater also got its beginnings in Tartu with the formation of the Vanemuine theater group.

During the first independence period, Estonian culture thrived. During 1926–33 writer Anton Hansen Tammsaare published his five-volume epic novel, *Tõde ja Õigus* (Truth and Justice), which covered the period 1870–1930. Lyrical poetry grew with the works of Marie Under, Henrik Visnapuu, and Betti Alver. In 1919 the Pallas art school was founded in Tartu, giving rise and expression to several new artistic currents. Architecture became a new mode of expression for Estonians as the first architects were educated in Tallinn. Their works came to include the parliament building on Toompea Hill and several functionalist buildings in the resort town of Pärnu. The Estonian Drama Theater was established in 1926, complementing the already existing Estonia Theater, which featured operettas and ballet. By 1940 Estonia had eleven professional or semiprofessional theaters.

The return of the Red Army in 1944 after the German occupation caused much of Estonia's cultural elite to flee the country. Many writers and poets settled in Sweden, where they continued to issue works through their own publishing cooperative. Under Stalin, Estonian culture was subordinated to the propagandistic needs of the regime. In 1950, as the Estonian Communist Party was being purged, so too was Estonian culture. Many writers and artists were accused of "formalism" (adherence to bourgeois standards) or nationalism and were dismissed or deported. It was only in the 1960s, during the thaw under Khrushchev, that Estonian culture regained vibrancy, the result of increased foreign contacts and the arrival on the scene of a new generation of writers, artists, composers, and poets. The last category included Paul-Eerik

Rummo (appointed minister of culture in 1992), Jaan Kaplinski (elected a member of parliament in 1992), and Hando Runnel. Novelist Jaan Kross made his debut during this period as a writer of historical works; his 1978 book, *The Czar's Madman*, was published in English in 1993 to critical acclaim. Graphic art became popular in Estonia during the 1960s, as did abstractionism among painters. The Estonian music scene saw the coming of age of Arvo Pärt, who would emigrate in 1980 to West Germany; Veljo Tormis, a composer drawing on themes from Finno-Ugric folk music; and Neeme Järvi, who emigrated in 1980 and later became director of the Detroit Symphony Orchestra. Song festivals still were held continuously, often providing a popular outlet for national feeling. In the place of the banned national anthem, the song *My Fatherland Is My Love*, based on a poem by Lydia Koidula and music by composer and conductor Gustav Ernesaks, became Estonians' de facto anthem.

During the late 1970s and early 1980s, Estonian culture again felt some of the cold drafts of official control, but by 1986 the influence of *glasnost* began to stir cultural activity anew, this time far into the realm of politics. One of the first groups to mobilize in 1987 was the Estonian Heritage Society, which led volunteer projects to restore many of Estonia's cultural landmarks. At a 1986 writers' conference, the first complaints were publicly aired about censorship and Russification. In the main literary publications—*Sirp ja Vasar, Vikerkaar,* and *Looming*—an unprecedented number of articles began to appear dealing with hitherto banned topics. In April 1988, during a two-day public forum, nearly fifty of Estonia's most prominent cultural figures met to voice their concerns about the state of Estonia's culture, language, and people. Open criticism was leveled against the old-guard party leadership of Karl Vaino, and demands were made for real political reform. The forum was an awe-inspiring event for the hundreds of thousands of Estonians who listened on radio; yet it was only a prelude to the "singing revolution" that would follow that summer.

During the next several years, many of Estonia's artists, poets, and writers would become involved in politics. Thirteen cultural figures were elected to the Supreme Soviet in 1990, nearly twenty to the Riigikogu, the new legislature, in 1992. Culture suffered, however, because of economic decline. Paper shortages in 1990 and 1991 limited the number of books and literary journals that could be published. Art supplies, in high demand, often were available only in exchange for hard currency. Still, foreign contacts opened up completely with opportunities to view new creative works and to spread Estonian culture abroad. With independence again in hand, Estonia could look forward to another era of free cultural development in a common European home.

Economy

Estonia's transition to a free-market economy in the early 1990s reflected the difficulties of building an independent economy from the ruins of one that hitherto had been developed for a single market, that of the Soviet Union. The creation of new economic institutions such as a separate monetary system, new regulatory agencies, and new development strategies had to keep pace with the decline of the old economy and its institutions. Real gross domestic product (GDP—see Glossary) dropped continuously in the early 1990s (see table 6, Appendix). Yet, among the former Soviet republics, in roughly four years of far-reaching market reforms Estonia became a model of economic transformation. The right-of-center government of Mart Laar, which took office in 1992, maintained a promarket stance despite criticism from opposition parties and agricultural interests, which were most vulnerable to foreign competition. After the introduction of the kroon in June 1992, inflation fell rapidly to an average of less than 3 percent per month in 1993. Consumer goods were again in abundant supply. Foreign trade grew, although in 1993 the trade balance began to show deficits. Under a program of privatization, 80 percent of the country's state-owned small businesses were sold off, and three rounds of large-scale privatization with foreign participation resulted in the acquisition of thirty major enterprises. By January 1995, after several more rounds of privatization, only twenty large enterprises had yet to be privatized. Official unemployment dropped to 1.4 percent in November 1994, but real unemployment may have been as high as 10 percent. The squeeze on the economy and the state budget intensified as many large, privatized firms were downsized and the transition neared the decisive stage of open competition.

Economic Reform History

Estonia began its reform process in 1987 with the development of a plan for economic autonomy within the Soviet

Union. Drawing on examples from both China and Hungary, the radical proposal called for an end to central economic control over Estonia, a separate tax system, and the adoption of a convertible ruble. Until then, it had been said that as much as 90 percent of the Estonian economy was controlled from Moscow; very little was left for the Estonians to decide for themselves. The decline in living standards beginning in the early 1980s and the "years of stagnation" were viewed as direct consequences of this overcentralization. With Gorbachev calling for a "restructuring" (or *perestroika*) of the economy, the Estonian proposal was meant to respond to and test this new call for change. The idea was popular among Estonians, not least of all because of the plan's name, Isemajandav Eesti, whose acronym, IME, also means "miracle" in Estonian.

Despite initial resistance from the old-guard Estonian Communist Party leadership, IME became official policy soon after the appointment of native-born Vaino Väljas as first secretary of the party in June 1988. Teams of economists were put to work mapping out the laws and decrees that would enable the plan to begin by January 1, 1990. Much of this work would improve Estonians' knowledge of reform economics by the time more radical measures proved necessary. In May 1989, the Estonian Supreme Soviet approved the plan by an overwhelming majority, sending it on to the Supreme Soviet in Moscow. Kremlin bureaucrats, however, sought to water down the scheme, injecting contradictory clauses that would make the plan unworkable. While the final law passed by the Soviet parliament accorded economic autonomy to Estonia, along with Latvia and Lithuania, it also stipulated that all reform measures be in accord with central Soviet laws.

In the following months, as the popular mood in Estonia shifted toward full independence, it became clear that the IME plan, too, would get nowhere within the increasingly outdated Soviet system. Still, many of the details and general impetus of IME proved very useful for economic reform down the road. In December 1989, the Estonian Supreme Soviet voted to create a central bank, the Bank of Estonia, for the republic as part of the plan for an eventual Estonian currency. Price-reform policies were in full force by October 1990, and an independent law on foreign trade was adopted. Prime Minister Edgar Savisaar sought to broaden Estonia's economic contacts with other Soviet republics, organizing several economic summits in Tallinn with Central Asian and Caucasian leaders. A new tax system was put in place in Estonia, replacing the state budget's dependence on enterprise turnover taxes and phasing in income and sales taxes. In short, economic reform simply was carried out without regard to the Kremlin.

By August 1991, with Estonia's leap to full independence, the economy was beginning to feel the pain of both market reform and collapsing ties to the Soviet Union. Gasoline shortages had been endemic since 1990, and many enterprises were forced to cut production because of a lack of raw materials previously imported from other Soviet republics. Lax Soviet monetary policy also fueled Estonian inflation, undermining reform efforts as long as the new country remained in the Russian ruble zone. An unprecedented fuel and food shortage in January 1992 prompted Prime Minister Savisaar to ask parliament for emergency powers to deal with the crisis. Deputies in parliament, however, had lost confidence in Savisaar, and in the ensuing political crisis he was forced to resign. Savisaar was replaced by his transportation minister, Tiit Vähi.

A temporary fuel loan from Finland helped stabilize the situation, but the need to hasten the introduction of Estonia's own currency became apparent. Other economic reforms such as privatization and foreign trade were also being held up by the country's dependence on the Russian ruble.

On June 20, 1992, against earlier objections from the International Monetary Fund (IMF—see Glossary), Estonia introduced its new currency, the kroon. With only US$120 million in gold reserves and no internationally backed stabilization fund, Bank of Estonia president Siim Kallas said the country could wait no longer. At 800 exchange points across the country, residents were allowed to exchange up to 1,500 rubles at a rate of ten rubles to one kroon. Excess cash was exchanged at a rate of fifty to one. Bank accounts were converted in full at ten to one. By the end of the three-day transition period, the move was declared a success, with only minor glitches reported. For stability, the kroon was pegged by special agreement to the deutsche mark (DM) at EKR8 = DM1. This would make the kroon worth about 7.7 United States cents, or EKR13 = US$1. The kroon would be the only Baltic currency to be officially pegged to any outside value.

Recent Economic Developments

Monetary and Fiscal Policy

The new Estonian currency became the foundation for rational development of the economy. Money began to have clear value; the currency supply could be controlled from Tallinn, not Moscow; and long-term investment decisions could be made with greater confidence by both the state and private enterprise. The president of the central bank, Siim Kallas, made "hard money" the benchmark of his policy. In return, the bank saw its reserves grow rapidly, to US$184 million by the end of 1992 and US$365 million by December 1993. The central bank was independent of the government but subordinate to the parliament. In addition to its president, the bank was managed by a board of directors, whose chairman was also appointed by parliament.

Although the initial success of the kroon was gratifying, many fiscal challenges remained that threatened to upset monetary policy in the future. Among these was a high enterprise tax debt to the state. In December 1992, this debt, mostly unpaid revenue taxes from large state firms, amounted to about EKR565 million. A year later, this sum had fallen to roughly EKR400 million, but the possibility that the state might need to use its own funds to bail out these ailing firms remained. Another danger to monetary stability was posed by the possible collapse of several private banks in Estonia. In November 1992, the Bank of Estonia ordered the shutdown of three private banks because of insolvency. One of these was the Tartu Commercial Bank, which in 1988 had become the first private bank to be founded in the Soviet Union. Bad loans, increased competition, and poor management were expected to force other bank closures, with which the state would have to deal.

Following the enactment of reform laws during 1989–90, the state budget in Estonia was broken into three parts: the central government budget, local government budgets, and nine extrabudgetary funds. In 1993 (the first year for which figures are provided entirely in kroons), the central state budget ran a surplus of EKR216 million on total revenues of roughly EKR4.2 billion (US$323 million). This surplus, however, was immediately spent in a secondary budget drawn up in October. The central budget included the financing of government operations (ministries, schools, police, cultural subsidies, and so

Farm laborers in northern Estonia
Small Estonian farmstead
Courtesy Priit Vesilind

forth) as well as roughly EKR500 million in aid to cities and towns. About half of the revenue for the central budget came from an 18 percent value-added tax (VAT—see Glossary) on most goods and services. Another 35 percent came from personal income and business taxes. Social welfare taxes on employer payrolls went directly into the state's extrabudgetary social welfare and health insurance funds, which amounted to slightly more than EKR2 billion. In all, general government taxes (including local taxes) in 1991 amounted to about 47.7 percent of GDP. Although successive governments pledged to reduce the overall tax burden, the transition was slow. In 1994 the previous three-tiered progressive tax scale was replaced with an across-the-board income tax rate of 26 percent. Estonia's central budget in 1995 was expected to total EKR8.8 billion, exceeding the 1994 budget and its supplements by EKR2.3 billion, mainly because of additional expenditures on social welfare, the civil service, the police, and the border guard. It was to be a balanced budget, nonetheless, for the second consecutive year. Various forms of taxation, including the income tax, an 18 percent VAT, and a corporate tax were to provide most of the revenue.

Wages and Prices

After the beginning of economic reform in Estonia, real wages dropped precipitously. From the fourth quarter of 1989, when the first price rises began, to the third quarter of 1991, when Estonia became independent, real wages fell by more than half. Food prices rose an estimated sevenfold as state subsidies were eliminated and the population received only partial government compensation for the higher prices. Fuel prices and apartment rents also increased. Inflation soared even more after independence as trade with Russia broke down even though Estonia remained in the ruble zone. In January 1992 alone, the cost-of-living index rose 88 percent, and in February it rose another 74 percent. The average rate for the year was 1,000 percent according to some estimates. Nominal monthly wages skyrocketed to keep pace, rising from 648 rubles in May 1992 to 3,850 rubles by May 1993.

The introduction of the kroon in June 1992 did much to stabilize wages and inflation. In 1993 increases in the consumer price index averaged about 3.0 percent per month; in 1994 they averaged 3.5 percent per month. The average monthly wage settled around EKR500 in August 1992. Thereafter, it began a steady climb, reaching roughly EKR1,200 by the end of 1993. Yet, according to Arvo Kuddo, an official of the Bank of Estonia, real wages in mid-1993 still amounted to only 95 percent of their June 1992 levels and barely 50 percent of their levels from early 1991. In the meantime, wage differentials between the highest- and lowest-paying jobs grew markedly, from 3.4 times to ten times. According to the Estonian State Statistics Board, in mid-1993 the top 10 percent of wage earners received 32.9 percent of all income, while the bottom 10 percent received only 2.1 percent. Residents of Tallinn had the highest average monthly wage, some 20 percent above the national average. Personal savings also declined during this period. In December 1992, 41 percent of survey respondents said they had no significant savings at all. In 1993 some 17 percent said they were behind in paying their utility bills for lack of money.

Employment

The complexion of the Estonian labor market changed rapidly in the early 1990s in the wake of property reform and the growth of private enterprise. In 1990 some 95 percent of the labor force was employed in state-owned enterprises or on collective farms. Only 4.3 percent worked in private cooperatives or on private farms. In 1993 a public opinion survey indicated that less than half of the respondents now received their main income from a state enterprise. As privatization continued and the privately owned share of production increased, the share of state employment was expected to drop even more. Industry (in both the public and the private sectors) employed about 33 percent of workers in 1990; agriculture, 12 percent; education and cultural activities, 10 percent; construction, 10 percent; and trade and catering, 9 percent. The remainder of the labor force engaged in a variety of other activities in the services sector (see table 7, Appendix).

As of December 1, 1993, Estonia's official unemployment rate was still very low, 1.7 percent, or 14,682 people. This figure represented the proportion of working-age people officially registered as unemployed with the government's Employment Board and hence receiving unemployment benefits. During the second half of 1993, unemployment had in fact steadily declined from a high of 22,699 in May. In addition, the number of people on unpaid or partially paid leave declined during the first half of the year. By contrast, however, more people were reported working part-time, most often with their full-time workweek having been reduced to three or four days. These people were not included in the official figure. The highest official unemployment rates in December 1993 were in the towns of the southeast (Võru, 5.3 percent; Põlva, 4.8 percent) and the northeast (Narva, 4.4 percent). Tallinn posted the lowest unemployment rate (0.2 percent), with just 594 registered jobless people. In 1994 official unemployment peaked at 2.3 percent in April, then fell steadily to a rate of 1.4 percent in November, the lowest rate among the Baltic states.

The official unemployment figures, however, did not tell the whole story. The unemployment rate was based on the working-age population (about 880,000 people), not the smaller number of active persons in the population (about 795,000). In addition, the figure did not include unregistered jobless people. In general, the low level of unemployment benefits also discouraged many people from even registering as unemployed. In October 1992, unemployment benefits in Estonia were reduced from 80 percent to 60 percent of the minimum monthly wage. Benefits were paid for 180 days with the possibility of a ninety-day renewal. In 1993 the government allocated EKR90 million for an expected 40,000 unemployed but ended up disbursing only EKR30 million because of the low number of registered jobless people. Still, in the final quarter of 1993, the Economist Intelligence Unit estimated that the real level of unemployment was as high as 10 to 12 percent.

Foreign Trade

An integral part of Estonia's transition to a market economy during the early 1990s involved reorienting foreign trade to the West and attracting foreign investment to upgrade the country's industry and commerce. In 1990 only 5 percent of Estonia's foreign trade was with the developed West, and of this, only 21 percent represented exports. About 87 percent of Estonia's trade was with the Soviet Union, and of that, 61 percent was with Russia. In 1991 trade with Western and other foreign countries fell further as available hard currency for imports dried up and as many producers of Estonian exports had to cut output because of a lack of raw materials. Although trade with Russia struggled on during the first half of 1991, trade relations broke down after independence was attained in August. New agreements were signed in December 1991, but precise licensing procedures and bilateral trade quotas took several more

Women laborers in Viljandi
Ethnic Russians selling produce at Tallinn's central market
Courtesy Priit Vesilind

months to work out. This delayed shipments of fuel and raw materials to Estonia, causing a severe economic crisis.

The introduction of the Estonian kroon in June 1992 proved decisive in stabilizing foreign trade. By the third quarter of 1992, Estonia experienced strong growth in foreign trade, finishing the year with an EKR136 million surplus. The total volume of trade amounted to nearly EKR11 billion, two-thirds of that coming during the second half of 1992. Moreover, by the end of the year, the very structure of Estonia's foreign trade had begun to change. European countries accounted for 56 percent of Estonia's trade in 1992. While 28.4 percent of Estonia's imports continued to be from Russia, 22.6 percent now came from Finland. In 1993 Finland surpassed Russia as a source of Estonia's imports, 27.9 percent to 17.2 percent. The two countries were roughly equal as a destination for Estonian goods, both accounting for just above 20 percent in 1992 and 1993 (see table 8, Appendix). Textiles constituted Estonia's leading trade article in 1992, accounting for 14 percent of exports. Among imports, Estonia primarily continued to receive mineral products (27.2 percent) and machinery and equipment (18.3 percent) (see table 9, Appendix).

In 1993 Estonia ran a trade deficit estimated at US$135 million. The trade balance deteriorated partly because of the strength of the kroon and partly because of a growing need for automobiles, agricultural products, and other essential goods. There was a 131 percent increase in imports from 1992 to 1993, compared with a 91.8 percent increase in exports. This imbalance was offset by a strong increase in services, leaving the country's current account in the black at EKR493 million. The trade deficit, however, continued to swell, reaching an estimated US$389 million in 1994.

Foreign Investment and Loans

Foreign investment in Estonia began during 1987–88 with the creation of several dozen joint ventures under the Soviet Union's early reform strategy. The number of joint ventures in Estonia grew steadily after April 1990, when Estonian authorities began registering joint ventures themselves. By January 1991, 232 joint ventures had been registered in Estonia; by October 1991, there were 313. Finland led in the number of joint ventures (159), but Sweden accounted for the most foreign capital in Estonia (35 percent). In mid-1990 foreign investment also started coming into Estonia via joint-stock com-

Woman serving sour rye bread
at Lahemaa National Park
cabin on the northern shore
Courtesy Priit Vesilind

Boatman in Viljandi
Courtesy Priit Vesilind

panies—a more flexible form of ownership for both foreign investors and local capital. Joint-stock companies soon surpassed joint ventures as the prime attraction for foreign capital, totaling 803 by October 1991. In fact, many joint ventures later were converted into joint-stock companies. In September 1991, Estonia passed a new foreign investment law offering tax breaks (new ventures were granted a two-year tax exemption) and import-export incentives to foreign investors. This legislation stimulated further activity. In 1993 foreign investors were also given the right to buy land, but only through the purchase of privatized state enterprises. Non-Estonians could not own more than 50 percent of the equity in joint ventures without government permission.

From the beginning, foreign capital was heavily concentrated in Tallinn. About 75 percent of the first joint ventures were established in the capital; in March 1993, it was reported that 87 percent of all foreign capital invested in Estonia was

49

located in Tallinn and the surrounding area. Although the government hoped that lower property taxes and lower wages might eventually entice more foreign capital to southern Estonia, most investors continued to be drawn to Tallinn for its higher-quality communications, better-trained personnel, and broader transportation opportunities.

Among individual countries, Sweden continued to lead all others in both overall value of investments and as a percentage of total foreign investment—37.7 percent in 1993 (see table 10, Appendix). Both the Norwegian company Statoil and the Finnish firm Neste also were heavily involved in the national economy, building gasoline stations across Estonia. Tallinn's premier hotel, Hotel Palace, was owned by the Estonian-Finnish consortium Fin-Est. In 1992 Coca-Cola set up a joint venture with the Estonian bottling plant AS Tallinna Karastusjoogid to produce soft drinks for the Estonian and Russian markets. In 1993 a four-story office building, the Tallinn Business Center, was opened by a United States development group.

Estonia's transition to a market economy during 1991–93 was eased considerably by the availability of more than US$285 million in foreign aid, loans, and credits. Receipt of this financial assistance was facilitated by the fact that Estonia, unlike many of the other countries of Eastern Europe, had no prior foreign debt. In addition, by claiming legal status as a formerly occupied country, Estonia, along with the other Baltic states, refused to accept liability for the Soviet Union's foreign debt. Instead, it claimed—and received the rights to—more than US$100 million worth of Estonian gold deposited in Western banks by the prewar republic and frozen after 1940.

During 1992–93 Estonia received a total of about US$125 million in humanitarian aid, including emergency shipments of fuel, grain, and medical supplies. In August 1992, Estonia signed its first memorandum with the IMF to secure a US$32 million loan from the IMF and US$30 million from the World Bank (see Glossary). The memorandum obligated the Estonian government to balance its budget, to limit wage increases, to privatize state enterprises, and to maintain a strict monetary policy. Fourteen months later, the IMF released the first US$16 million of its loan to Estonia, after it was satisfied that the government has maintained its economic reforms. In early 1992, Estonia also had become a member of the European Bank for Reconstruction and Development, from which it would later receive a total of US$46 million in loans for improving its energy industry. Other foreign loans were received from Japan, the United States, Sweden, and the European Union (see Glossary), among others (see table 11, Appendix). In addition, in December 1993 the European Investment Bank gave Estonia a credit worth 5 million European currency units (ECUs—see Glossary) for loans to small businesses. The credit was the first from an ECU200 million fund allocated to Baltic states through the European Union's Poland/Hungary Aid for Restructuring of Economies (PHARE) program.

Property Reform

Privatization, or the selling off of state property, represented the cornerstone of Estonia's efforts at property reform during 1990–93. Although growth in simple private enterprise during this period contributed to the country's shift to capitalism, the allocation to private initiative of state-owned resources ranging from factories to kiosks was considered a more formidable engine for encouraging economic recovery. Much of Estonia's economy had been developed in accordance with central Soviet planning requisites, and it was unclear at first how viable many of Estonia's machine-building and metallurgical factories would be in the context of its small national economy. The fate of these enterprises remained unclear in the mid-1990s. In the meantime, however, Estonia had launched a successful small- and medium-scale privatization program, which showed impressive results after only two years. By August 1993, more than half of all registered Estonian enterprises were privately owned.

As in many other East European countries, property reform in Estonia was intimately linked to issues of property restitution. In Estonia's case, this meant the return of, or compensation for, property nationalized by the Soviet regime in 1940. Estonia's political strategy for independence, with its stress on the illegality of Soviet rule, raised corollary questions and debates during 1989–90 about the legality of the Soviet Union's early nationalization of the economy. The principle of a political restoration of the prewar republic also generated pressures to recognize a kind of economic restoration—recognition of the right of previous property owners to reclaim their property or at least to receive just compensation. This, it was argued, was a simple matter of fairness to society. Thus, the tension between the equally compelling needs for efficient privatization and for judicious restitution was acute. If one accepted the necessity of fostering new economic activity, the imperative to privatize was clear. Yet, in selling off state property, the government was in danger of wrongfully profiting from the sale of property taken from Estonian citizens in 1940. Determining which property could be privatized and which property might have claims on it soon became a legal tangle with long-term consequences.

Despite some individual warnings as to the cost and rationality of such a move, in December 1990 the Estonian Supreme Soviet adopted a resolution voiding the Soviet government's 1940 nationalization of property and recognizing the continuity of all prewar property rights. In addition, it set a deadline of December 27, 1991, for the submission of claims to local government authorities for the return of property or compensation. The authorities thereafter would decide upon the validity of these claims. In June 1991, the parliament passed a second law laying out the basic principles of property reform. Among this law's three explicit objectives was one calling for the "redress of injustice committed by the violation of property rights" under Soviet rule. More than 200,000 property restitution claims were submitted, and much work in municipal archives to verify the claims lay ahead.

Although opposed to restitution, the government of Prime Minister Edgar Savisaar (1990–92) relented, with the stipulation that for any prewar property radically altered during the Soviet era, such as reconstructed factories, only compensation would be offered. In addition, persons currently in houses and apartments subject to restitution claims got assurance that they would not be summarily evicted by the previous owners. With these ground rules, in June 1990 the Supreme Soviet passed the Law on Property, legalizing various forms of property, including individually owned property. The government moved to create the State Property Board (Riigivaraamet) in August to supervise the privatization of at least small businesses and services, which would help to stimulate the economy. These enterprises mostly had been created during the Soviet era and thus were free from potential restitution claims. In early 1991, the board began selling off an estimated 3,000 such enterprises, among them small booths and shops, service outlets, and catering facilities. Initially, preference was given to employee buyouts, but public auctions later became the method of choice in order to speed up the process. By Septem-

View of historic Tallinn
Street in small town near Viljandi
Courtesy Priit Vesilind

53

ber 1992, out of a total of 855 enterprises approved for sale, 558 had been sold. Service enterprises proved easiest to sell, although retail establishments were not far behind.

Experimentation with large-scale privatization began in mid-1991. Two machine-building factories, as well as the Tallinn taxi depot, were chosen as the first properties to be sold. Preference again was given to employee buyouts, which in the case of large-scale enterprises, however, proved to be unwieldy because several competing groups emerged. The experimental enterprises soon became mired in controversy, and the policy of relying solely on local capital was abandoned. After the adoption of the new currency in mid-1992, privatization was reinvigorated.

In a change of procedure, the government set up the Estonian Privatization Enterprise (Eesti Erastamisettevõte—EERE) to begin dealing with the direct sale of large-scale enterprises to foreign and domestic investors. The EERE was modeled after the successful German agency Treuhandanstalt, with which the EERE signed a cooperation agreement. In November 1992, the EERE offered its first thirty-eight enterprises for sale through widespread advertising in local and Western newspapers. Yet, scarcely ten days later, the newly elected prime minister, Mart Laar, halted the process. He claimed that several restitution claims were outstanding vis-à-vis the advertised properties and charged that the EERE had too much power. Although the controversy took some time to resolve, the EERE's program was back on track by 1993. In May it offered another fifty-four enterprises for sale; in November forty enterprises were put on the block. In each case, sealed bids were accepted by the EERE from foreign and local investors until a certain date. Thereafter, the EERE attempted to negotiate a sale with the highest bidder based on development plans for the new enterprise as well as promises to retain a certain number of employees. The early sale offers by the EERE attracted widespread interest. In April 1993, the Estonian parliament sweetened the incentive to bid by allowing foreign investors to buy the land underneath any privatized property, rather than rent. About half of the enterprises put up in the first two rounds found buyers. Often, however, enterprises were broken up, with only parts being sold off. Many initial sales secured guarantees of employment for up to 60 percent of the acquired enterprise's employees.

In the summer of 1993, Estonia merged its two privatization firms, the State Property Board and the EERE, to create the Estonian Privatization Agency (Eesti Erastamisagentuur—EEA). The privatization of small enterprises was coming to a close, and the process needed to be consolidated. During 1991–92 the government sold 676 properties for a total of EKR64.3 million. By October 1993, another 236 small enterprises had been sold for a total of EKR169 million. Roughly 40 percent of these were in Tallinn. A total of EKR117.8 million had been garnered from the sale of the first thirty large-scale enterprises. According to an EEA official, these deals had secured some EKR52 million in investment and provided guarantees for 4,900 jobs.

By 1993 three property reform tasks remained. First, a wide variety of mostly unprofitable state enterprises had yet to be sold off. Second, the issue of how to provide compensation for prewar property claimants remained unresolved. Third, the process of housing privatization, in which the average resident was most interested, had yet to begin. These three tasks were all addressed in a Law on Privatization passed by the Riigikogu in June 1993. Throughout 1993 all adult residents had begun registering themselves and their work histories to qualify for a specific amount of national capital vouchers (*rahvakapitali obligatsioonid*—RKOs) based on their years of active employment and service to the economy. According to the new Law on Privatization, residents could use their RKOs toward the purchase of their apartments based on apartment values set by the government. If a resident lived in a house or did not wish to buy an apartment, he or she could buy into investment funds, which were to be the main players in the sale of remaining state property. In addition, individuals could invest in pension funds backed by the government. Finally, prewar property claimants who were due compensation for their losses were issued compensation securities, which they could use in any of the new investment modes. According to Liia Hänni, a former government minister, in 1992 the state still held about EKR36 billion worth of property, of which EKR7 billion worth was housing stock. An estimated EKR15 to EKR25 billion worth of RKOs would be issued, along with EKR12 to EKR15 billion in property compensation.

Economic Sectors

Industry

The Estonian industrial sector suffered more than other sectors during the country's transition to a market economy. Most of Estonia's heavy industry had been developed and managed by central planners in Moscow with imported labor from Russia. In 1990 only sixty-one of 265 industrial enterprises were under direct Estonian control. Forty enterprises, which accounted for 12 percent of Estonia's industrial production, were controlled directly from Moscow. Because many of these were defense related, even Estonian authorities had limited access to them. After independence was regained in 1991, Estonia acquired all of the industrial enterprises on its territory and faced the challenge of finding them a place in a market economy.

In 1990 industry accounted for about 40 percent of GDP (42.5 percent in 1992) and 33 percent of employment. Within the sector, food processing was the largest subsector, accounting for 30.4 percent of production in 1992 (up from 24.5 percent in 1990). It was followed by light industry at 17.9 percent (down from 26.3 percent in 1990) (see table 12, Appendix).

Industrial production began to fall drastically as supplies of raw materials from the Soviet Union dwindled. The World Bank reported that in the first nine months of 1991, industrial activity decreased by 10 percent over the previous year's corresponding period. According to the Estonian State Statistics Board, during 1992 total production fell another 39 percent from 1991. In 1993, as enterprises began slowly buying raw materials on the world market, production in some areas began to increase. Although overall output was still down in 1993, it increased by an estimated 7 percent in 1994. Estonia's best hope lay with its lighter industries: food processing, textiles, furniture, paper, and glass. Many of these relied on domestic raw materials and hence were able to continue producing during the transition. Estonia's metallurgical and chemical industries showed the greatest decline, and their future was in doubt without new technology and markets.

Agriculture

Like the rest of the economy, Estonian agriculture has been in great flux since the degeneration of the collective and state farm systems. In 1991 roughly 12 percent of the labor force was

*Strip mining of oil shale in
northeastern Estonia
Courtesy Priit Vesilind*

employed in agriculture, producing 15.4 percent of Estonia's GDP. Estonia has some 1.3 million hectares of agricultural land, nearly 1 million hectares of which are arable. During the Soviet era, arable land decreased by nearly 405,000 hectares, much becoming forest. Collectivization in the late 1940s and 1950s brought great hardship to Estonian agriculture, which during the first independence period had been the mainstay of Estonian society. Still, Estonian agriculture remained more productive than the Soviet average. In 1990 there were 221 collective and 117 state farms with an average of 350 to 400 workers each. The average livestock herd per farm included 1,900 cattle and 2,500 pigs. Estonia was a net exporter of meat and milk to the other republics. Agriculture also served as the basis for the republic's strong food-processing industry (see table 13, Appendix). For its meat production, however, Estonia relied heavily on feed grain from Russia. When the republic sought to cut back on meat exports in the late 1980s, Russia retaliated by slowing the provision of feed grain, which cut Estonian production even further. Increases in fuel prices and a general fuel crisis in early 1992 also hit agricultural production very hard. Although the total area of field crops grew in the early 1990s, total production and average yields fell markedly (see table 14, Appendix).

Reform of Estonia's agricultural system began in December 1989 with adoption of the Law on Private Farming. The law allowed individuals to take up to fifty hectares of land for private planting and for growing crops. The land was heritable but could not be bought or sold. The goal of the reform was to stimulate production and return the spirit of private farming to a countryside worn down by decades of central planning. Six months after implementation, nearly 2,000 farms were set up, with several thousand waiting for approval. A year later, more than 3,500 private farms were operating. Starting in October 1991, farmers were allowed to own their land. This boosted the number of farms to 7,200 by early 1992. As of the first half of 1993, a total of 8,781 farms had been created, covering approximately 225,000 hectares, or a quarter of Estonia's arable land.

In May 1993, the Estonian parliament passed a law on property taxes, which had been a major concern for many farmers before getting into business. The law mandated a 0.5 percent tax on property values to be paid to the state and a 0.3 to 0.7 percent share to be paid to local governments. More than property taxes, the costs of commodities such as fuel and new

Kunda cement factory
Dock facilities at harbor of Tallinn
Courtesy Priit Vesilind

equipment were considered most likely to prove burdensome to many new farmers.

With the introduction of private agriculture, many collective farms began to disintegrate. Corruption and "spontaneous privatization" of farm equipment by farm directors grew. A number of Estonia's more successful farms were reorganized into cooperatives. Over the long term, the government predicted that 40,000 to 60,000 private farms averaging fifty hectares would be optimal. At the same time, Estonians were likely to maintain a very high rate of consumption of home-grown fruits and vegetables. A 1993 survey by the Estonian State Statistics Board indicated that nearly 80 percent of all potatoes consumed by Estonians either were privately grown or were received from friends or relatives. Thirty percent of eggs were received outside the market as well as 71.5 percent of all juice. Overall, Estonians reported getting over 20 percent of their food from private production or from friends or relatives.

Estonia has 1.8 million hectares of forest with approximately 274 million cubic meters of timber. Accounting for about 9 percent of industrial production in 1992, forest-related industries seem likely to grow further in the 1990s, thanks to expanding furniture and timber exports.

The fishing industry, once entirely under Soviet control, also has the potential to contribute to the country's economy. With 230 ships, including ninety oceangoing vessels, this profitable industry operated widely in international waters. A large share of Estonia's food-industry exports consists of fish and fish products. In 1992 about 131,000 tons of live fish were caught.

Energy and Natural Resources

Estonia is an exporter of electrical energy, but it is wholly dependent on the outside market for oil fuels and natural gas. Oil shale deposits estimated at 5 billion tons in the country's northeast help to fuel two large thermal power plants near the town of Narva (see fig. 5). Roughly 23 million tons of oil shale were mined per year up to the early 1990s. In 1990 Estonia produced about 17.2 billion kilowatt-hours of electricity, of which about 8.5 billion were exported to Russia and Latvia. By 1992, however, export production of electricity had dropped by more than one-half because of falling demand in Russia. These cutbacks in turn forced a slowdown in oil-shale mining, although no exact figures were available. In many mines, miners were employed only three or four days per week. The decline in tonnage also increased relative production costs. In order to start bringing Estonian oil shale closer to world prices and to cover costs, mining officials called in 1993 for an increase in the state price per ton from EKR36 to EKR50. The government resisted at first, fearing a corresponding rise in electricity prices and a new wave of inflation throughout the economy but eventually allowed oil shale producers to raise the price of their products to EKR45 per ton.

After independence, Estonia endeavored to sign barter agreements with Russia to exchange Estonian electricity and food for Russian oil and gas. Transportation problems in Russia caused this arrangement to break down in early 1992. The ensuing fuel shortages forced Estonia to venture onto the open market for the first time. In the interim, Russian oil prices began to approach the world price, meaning Estonia would find it just as competitive to begin buying fuel from other countries. In March 1993, two new oil terminals were opened near Tallinn, which will facilitate imports in the future. Foreign companies, such as Finland's Neste and Norway's Statoil, also began entering the Estonian gasoline market, building several modern filling stations in Tallinn and the surrounding areas. Meanwhile, the Estonian state oil company, Eesti Kütus, was forced to sell off many of its holdings and drastically scale back its operations in mid-1993 in order to pay an estimated EKR250 million in debts and back taxes. The company's market share was expected to drop from 70 percent to 30 percent.

Dependence on Russia for natural gas continued, with Estonia consuming about 1.3 billion cubic meters of Russian natural gas in 1990. Energy was in fact often used as a political weapon during the early 1990s. Estonia's two thermal power plants, for example, were staffed mostly by Russian workers who, to protest Estonian government policies, repeatedly threatened to shut down the plants. Although any disruption in production would also affect neighboring Russia, the possibility of problems persisted. Russia in turn threatened Estonia with a cutoff of gas supplies in June 1993 during the crisis surrounding Estonia's Law on Aliens (see Government and Politics, this ch.). The Russian gas company Lentransgas once shut down its pipelines to Estonia for a single day, ostensibly because of Estonia's US$10 million in unpaid bills. Also, Russian leaders often threatened economic sanctions for what they called discrimination against Estonia's Russian minority.

Figure 5. Economic Activity in Estonia, 1995

Transportation and Telecommunications

Estonia had a total of 30,300 kilometers of public roads (29,200 kilometers hard-surfaced and 1,100 kilometers unpaved) in the early 1990s. These was little traffic congestion, thanks to the relatively low number of automobiles per person—140 per 1,000 inhabitants. Estonia's major roads include Highway M11 to St. Petersburg and Highway M12 to Riga. In 1990 the roads carried 214 million tons of freight, or 85 percent of the total freight for that year. Estonian officials, for their part, were seeking to increase international truck transport through the country by encouraging the development of an international highway project, Via Baltica, from Tallinn to Warsaw (see fig. 6).

Bus transportation was widely developed during the Soviet period, totaling 4.5 billion passenger-kilometers in 1990. By 1993 the removal of state subsidies had forced an increase in ticket prices, a decline in ridership, and a contraction of service. New international routes, however, were opened to Germany and Denmark.

With a total of 1,126 kilometers of track, railroads in Estonia carried 30 million tons of freight and 16 million passengers in 1993. Estonia's main rail lines link Tallinn with Narva and St. Petersburg, Tartu with the Russian city of Pskov, and Pärnu with Riga. More than 130 kilometers of rail line are electrified.

The country's main airport, located in Tallinn, can serve medium-sized jets and accommodate up to 2 million passengers per year. Airports are also located in Tartu and Pärnu at former Russian air force bases. Domestic air service is provided only to Estonia's islands. In September 1991, the country inherited a fleet of about fifteen airplanes from the Soviet airline Aeroflot. It had a fleet of sixteen aircraft in 1992. A state airline, Estonian Air, was launched in December. In 1992 it served twelve international destinations—Amsterdam, Copenhagen, Frankfurt, Helsinki, Kiev, Minsk, Moscow, Riga, St. Petersburg, Sochi (Russia), Stockholm, and Vilnius—and carried nearly 175,000 passengers. Service is also provided by other airlines, including Aeroflot, Drakk Air Lines, Finnair, Lithuanian Airlines, SAS (Scandinavian Airlines), and Lufthansa.

International shipping was a major source of foreign currency for Estonia under the Soviet regime. In the early 1990s, the state-owned Estonian Shipping Company operated a fleet of eighty-two vessels with a carrying capacity of 500,000 tons. Narva is the main inland port. Five hundred kilometers of inland waterways are navigable year round. Estonia's three main commercial ports are all located around Tallinn; together they handled about 10 million tons of cargo in 1991. The Tallinn port continued to be a transit point for trade shipments to Russia, particularly grain. Ferry traffic out of Tallinn grew exponentially in the early 1990s. In 1992 an estimated 1.3 million people crossed between Tallinn and Helsinki, while traffic was said to be still growing at 50 to 60 percent a year. In 1990

Figure 6. Transportation System of Estonia, 1995

overnight ferry service was started to Stockholm; freight service to Germany followed later. Disaster struck on September 28, 1994, however, when a ferry owned by Estline, a Swedish-Estonian joint venture, sank in the Baltic Sea, killing more than 900 passengers.

Telecommunications required much modernization in Estonia after independence. Poor-quality telephone connections and outmoded equipment were among the major problems. The number of international lines was increased during the early 1990s, and beginning in 1993 new digital switchboards were being installed to replace old mechanical ones. The country's first mobile telephone networks were set up in 1990. Esttelecom, the state telecommunications company, had approximately 341,000 subscribers in 1992. However, unmet demand because of a shortage of lines indicated the existence of another 150,000 potential customers. Only two-thirds of telephone customers had long-distance access within Estonia and to the former Soviet Union. To improve service, Esttelecom was negotiating with Swedtel of Sweden for outside investment and the creation of a joint telecommunications venture. In 1993 there were approximately 600,000 television receivers in use, or one television per 2.6 persons. There was one radio per 1.7 persons and one telephone per 3.9 persons.

Tourism

Tourism was a major area of growth for Estonia in the late 1980s and even more so after independence. With the expansion of ferry and air links, Estonia began to receive a growing number of visitors from Western countries as the number of tourists from the former Soviet Union dropped off. In 1990 the number of tourists was estimated at 500,000; by the mid-1990s, that figure was expected to top 1 million. New accommodations were being built, and several of Tallinn's major hotels were being privatized. Estonia established visa requirements for visitors after independence but soon rescinded them for many European countries, the United States, and Canada. The Baltic states also signed agreements allowing foreigners to travel with one country's visa in all three states. Tallinn's medieval old town, although in need of repairs, is Estonia's main tourist attraction. Many visitors also tour Tartu and the island of Saaremaa. The greatest number of visitors come from Finland and Sweden. Net tourism receipts totaled about EKR26 million in 1992.

Government and Politics

Estonia's new era of democratic politics began slowly in the 1990s with the adoption of a new constitution and the formation of stable political groupings. Several mechanisms in the constitution were beginning to function to ensure a balance of power and steady government. Citizenship issues, however, caused tensions among the country's 500,000-strong Russophone population, most of whom had been denied automatic citizenship rights in 1991. Their naturalization and integration into Estonian society remained a significant challenge.

Current Politics

The election in September 1992 of a new parliament, the Riigikogu, and the formal restoration of the Republic of Estonia marked the opening of a new political era. Not only was a new set of deputies elected, but Estonia took a further step in defining its political forces and developing a new political culture. As expected, right-wing parties did best in the electoral poll, promising "to clean house" and offer a fresh beginning after the Soviet era. The contest for the 101-seat Riigikogu yielded a three-party center-right coalition government holding fifty-two seats. The Fatherland Party (Isamaa) led the coalition with thirty seats, the Estonian National Independence Party (Eesti Rahvusliku Sõltumatuse Partei) had ten seats, and the Moderates (Mõõdukad—made up of the Social Democratic Party and the Rural Center Party) had twelve seats. In opposition were the Coalition Party (Koonderakond), the Rural Union (Maaliit), the Estonian Center Party (Eesti Keskerakond), the Royalist Party (Rojalistlik Partei), and the Estonian Citizens Union (Eesti Kodanike Liit). Because noncitizens were not allowed to vote in the election, most of Estonia's Russian population was excluded from the poll. Consequently, the new Riigikogu was 100 percent ethnic Estonian.

The 1992 elections also saw a special contest for the largely ceremonial post of president. Although the new constitution stipulates that the president shall be elected by the parliament, the Constitutional Assembly in early 1992 succumbed to popular pressure and agreed to have the country's first president elected by the people. In the resulting poll, the incumbent chairman of the parliament, Arnold Rüütel, topped the list. But with only 41.8 percent of the vote, he did not muster the majority needed for direct election under the special rules. Although a former communist, Rüütel had been widely admired for his steady, balanced leadership during the independence struggle. Yet, his electoral shortfall was enough to throw the final decision into the Riigikogu, where the runner-up, with 29.5 percent, Isamaa candidate and former foreign minister Lennart Meri, had the advantage. At the parliament's opening session on October 5, Meri defeated Rüütel by a vote of fifty-nine to thirty-one.

In mid-October Mart Laar, the thirty-two-year-old chairman of Isamaa, was appointed prime minister by President Meri. The youngest person ever to hold that post, Laar promised immediately to expand Estonia's free-market reforms and defend Estonian national interests. During his first fourteen months in office, Laar cut tax rates and maintained control over expenditures (see Economy, this ch.). He also posted some foreign policy successes, such as Estonia's admission to the Council of Europe (see Glossary) in May 1993. His cabinet, however, was plagued by inexperience. Four months into office, Laar's choice for economy minister resigned after accusations that he was not up to the job. In January 1993, the defense minister, an émigré Estonian, Hain Rebas, caused a scandal when he allowed some 250 Russian soldiers to enter Estonia just as the country was negotiating their withdrawal with President Yeltsin. In August a mutiny by a handful of Estonian soldiers in western Estonia prompted Rebas to resign altogether. In December 1993, President Meri was obliged to dismiss Minister of Interior Lagle Parek, a longtime dissident during Soviet rule, for several scandals involving her management of ministerial affairs (see National Security, this ch.).

In June 1993, Laar's government suffered its greatest turmoil when a major political crisis erupted over passage of a law meant to regulate the status of noncitizens (mostly Russians) in the country. Russian groups criticized the 1993 Law on Aliens as discriminatory, and for the first time some of Estonia's key Western allies, including the United States, the Scandinavian states, and the European Union, raised objections. The Law on Aliens as originally adopted would have required all noncitizens to reapply for residency permits within two years without any guarantee of acceptance. In July, after President Meri vetoed the law and requested a review of it from the Council of Europe and the Conference on Security and Cooperation in Europe (CSCE—see Glossary), the Riigikogu agreed to amend the measure and guarantee most noncitizens new permits. The domestic crisis prompted President Meri to establish the Nationalities Roundtable for future discussion of minority affairs. The United States and Sweden immediately supported the roundtable with financial contributions to cover its operating costs. In the ensuing months, the roundtable met several times, but no major decisions were reached.

The results of Estonia's first post-Soviet local elections, held in October 1993, reflected public reaction to the government's series of setbacks and the continuing hardships caused by economic reform. In all the major cities, Isamaa did poorly. Former prime minister Tiit Vähi's Coalition Party was the big winner, especially in Tallinn, where it won eighteen of sixty-four seats. Russian parties also reemerged on the political scene, supported mostly by noncitizen voters, who, under a special constitutional provision, were allowed to vote. In Tallinn the moderate Russian Democratic Movement won eighteen seats. Despite this midterm upset and a continuing decline in public opinion polls, the Laar government later easily survived a vote of no confidence in parliament. In December it succeeded in passing a tax cut as well as a budget for 1994. To shore up the Isamaa-led coalition, in January 1994 four key portfolios in the Council of Ministers (defense, economy, finance, and foreign affairs) were reshuffled. However, the coalition disintegrated in June 1994 after a series of embarrassments, most notably the allegation that the prime minister had been involved in the secret transfer of a large sum of Russian rubles to the breakaway Russian republic of Chechnya in 1992. In September 1994, Laar lost a vote of no confidence in the Riigikogu. After President Meri's nomination of Bank of Estonia president Siim Kallas to succeed Laar was rejected, the Riigikogu confirmed Andres Tarand, the outgoing minister of environment, as prime minister in October. Tarand was to serve as a caretaker until the general elections in March 1995.

Constitutional Foundations

Under the constitution adopted on June 28, 1992, Estonia has a parliamentary system of government, with a prime minister as chief executive. Parliament also elects a president, whose duties are largely ceremonial, although the first holder of this office, Lennart Meri, sought to assert his independence. The constitution also governs the work of a legal chancellor, an auditor general, and the National Court.

The constitution opens with a set of general provisions and a forty-eight-article section establishing the fundamental rights, liberties, and duties of citizens. Freedom of expression and assembly, freedom of information, the right to petition the courts, and the right to health care are all guaranteed. Censorship and discrimination on the basis of nationality, gender, religion, or political belief are forbidden. The official language of Estonia is Estonian. However, in deference to heavily Russian areas of northeastern Estonia, the constitution allows for the use of other languages in local government where the majority of the population is non-Estonian. Article 9 of the constitution guarantees equal constitutional rights to both citizens and noncitizens living in Estonia. Noncitizen permanent residents are also allowed to vote in local elections. Noncitizens may not, however, join political parties or hold elected office.

Parliament building, Toompea Hill, Tallinn
Courtesy Stanley Bach

The Riigikogu (State Assembly), which replaced the transitional Supreme Council in 1992, has 101 members, who are chosen every four years by popular election. Members must be at least twenty-one years old. Each member may belong to only one committee. The president of the republic is elected to a five-year term by a two-thirds majority of the Riigikogu. The president nominates the prime minister, who must receive a vote of confidence from the Riigikogu. The Riigikogu passes legislation as well as votes of no confidence in the government. The president can dissolve parliament if there is a prolonged delay in the nomination of a prime minister or in the adoption of a state budget, or after a vote of no confidence in the government.

The president promulgates all laws after their adoption by the Riigikogu. However, he or she may also refuse to promulgate (i.e., veto) a law and send it back to the Riigikogu for reconsideration. If the Riigikogu passes the same law again by a simple majority, the president's veto is overridden. In 1993 President Meri vetoed seven laws, most of which were later modified by the Riigikogu. An early string of vetoes in the spring of 1993 especially angered members of the government coalition in parliament who had helped to elect him. Meri declared it his obligation, however, to protect the balance of power in government. His involvement was particularly critical during the domestic and international crisis surrounding Estonia's Law on Aliens.

The legal chancellor is appointed by the Riigikogu to a seven-year term and provides guidance concerning the constitutionality of laws. This official has no powers of adjudication but can issue opinions and propose amendments. Both the legal chancellor and the president may appeal to a special committee of the National Court for a binding decision on any law, national or local, that they consider unconstitutional. The court system comprises rural and city, as well as administrative, courts (first-level); district courts (second-level); and the National Court, the highest court in the land. Criminal justice is administered by local first-level courts as well as by second-level appellate courts. Final appeal may be made to the National Court, which sits in Tartu.

Central government policy at the regional level is carried out by the administrations of Estonia's fifteen counties (*maakonnad*). These counties are further subdivided into 255 local administrative units, of which forty-two are towns and 213 are townships (*vald*). Local councils are elected for a three-year term by permanent residents of the towns and townships.

Mass Media

The mass media in Estonia played a catalytic role in the democratic upsurge of the late 1980s that led to independence. Responding during 1985–86 to Mikhail S. Gorbachev's call for *glasnost* (openness), the Estonian media, especially newspapers, began to focus on the many social and economic problems afflicting the country at the time. Yet, the blame for these social and economic ailments soon began to fall on the political system, an outcome that Gorbachev had not intended. For instance, the fight against an extensive and environmentally dangerous plan to mine phosphorus in northeastern Estonia was energized in 1987 by several articles in the monthly *Eesti Loodus*. The Tartu daily *Edasi* (later renamed *Postimees*) would become a lively forum for the discussion of economic reforms such as Estonia's economic autonomy plan, the IME plan. The daily newspaper of Estonia's Komsomol, *Noorte Hääl*, took the lead in exposing the abuse many young Estonian men were suffering in the Soviet army. Many Estonian cultural publications, such as the weekly newspaper *Sirp ja Vasar* and the monthly journals *Looming* and *Vikerkaar*, carried historical overviews of Estonia's annexation in 1940 and of the deportations that followed. Finally, on television and radio, several roundtable debate programs were aired, where more ideas were articulated. As political mobilization grew, the mass media became interactive players, reporting on the new events while giving further voice to varied opinions.

The Estonian-language media operated in sharp contrast to Estonia's two main Russian-language dailies, *Sovetskaya Estoniya* (later renamed *Estoniya*) and *Molodezh' Estonii*, whose editors took a defensive stance toward rising Estonian nationalist feeling. The Russian community in Estonia was more heavily influenced by local communist party leaders, who remained loyal to Soviet rule. The Russian-language newspapers also echoed some of the views of the Intermovement and other Soviet loyalist groups. In the aftermath of independence, both newspapers were left searching for a new identity, as was most of the Russian community now living as a minority cut off from Russia.

In the early 1990s, the Estonian media diversified greatly as competition among newspapers grew. The flashy weekly *Eesti Ekspress*, run by a Finnish-Estonian joint venture, captured much of the early market, but it was soon joined by other rivals. Business-oriented publications emerged, such as *Äripäev*, a joint venture with Sweden's *Dagens Industri*. In 1992 a new daily, *Hommikuleht*, was launched by a group of private investors. Estonia was also the base for the Baltics' largest circulating English-language newspaper, *Baltic Independent*. Still, the growth in the number of newspapers could not compensate for a rise in subscription rates and a decline in overall readership. Print runs fell from nearly 200,000 in 1990, when newsstand copies cost the equivalent of US$0.05, to an average of 40,000 in 1993. Still, in 1993 there were approximately 750 serial publications in Estonia, three times the number in 1987.

Television and radio changed as well. During 1992–93 three commercial radio stations went on the air. Each offered a mix of rock music, news, and features. State-owned Estonian Radio spun off one of its two stations to compete with the new formats. Several regional radio stations also began broadcasting. Estonian state television received competition in the fall of 1993 when the government gave rights to three companies to start broadcasting on two channels previously used by Russian television. Earlier, the government had decided to stop paying for the rebroadcast of the Moscow and St. Petersburg channels in Estonia.

Foreign Relations

Both before and after independence, Estonia's foreign policy had a strong Western orientation. Western recognition of Estonia's legal independence was a key source of strength for the republic in its struggle with the Soviet Union. After 1991 Estonia worked to maintain that relationship and integrate with European political institutions as a further safeguard against potential threats from Russia. The last Russian troops stationed in Estonia after 1991 finally were withdrawn in August 1994, but relations with Yeltsin's Kremlin remained cool. Growing instability in Russia and Western attempts to placate Russian nationalism left Estonia anxious for greater European security guarantees but wary of being squeezed again in great-power politics.

Relations with the West

During 1990–91 Estonia undertook a vigorous lobbying campaign on behalf of international support for its bid for independence from the Soviet Union. The Estonian foreign minister at the time, Lennart Meri, was one of several Estonian officials who traveled widely to sustain the Western commitment to the republic's independence. Although the West generally remained in favor of renewed statehood for Estonia and the other Baltic states, Western leaders believed that the real key to that independence lay in Moscow. In August 1991, release of that key came in the form of the attempted coup d'état by conservative elements of the Soviet government.

In the wake of independence, Estonia moved quickly to join the international community. In September it was admitted to both the United Nations (UN) and the CSCE. In the UN, Estonia would later find common ground with the East European countries as well as participate in the organization's various committees and auxiliary bodies, such as the United Nations Educational, Scientific, and Cultural Organization (UNESCO), the United Nations Conference on Trade and Development (UNCTAD), the International Atomic Energy Agency (IAEA), and the United Nations Development Programme (UNDP). In March 1992, Estonia took part in the creation of the Council of Baltic Sea States, an association of all the countries bordering the Baltic Sea and dedicated to furthering regional economic and political cooperation. A year later, the Estonian representative was elected to a one-year term as president of the organization. In the realm of security, Estonia joined the North Atlantic Cooperation Council (NACC) in late 1991 and actively sought support for its efforts to become a member of the North Atlantic Treaty Organization (NATO). Cooperation with the European Union included significant economic aid as well as talks on a free-trade agreement.

Estonia's greatest foreign policy success came in May 1993 with its admission to the Council of Europe. After applying in September 1991, Estonia had to hold its first free parliamentary elections in 1992 before being seriously considered for membership. Although Estonia's citizenship policy came under close scrutiny by council delegations, in the end they accepted Estonia's legal arguments for denying automatic citizenship to Soviet-era immigrants, taking encouragement from the noncitizens' right to participate in local elections. Estonia considered admission the equivalent of a clean bill of health for its young democracy, which Russia had sought to tarnish with accusations of human rights violations.

In the mid-1990s, Estonia's staunchest foreign allies were the Scandinavian countries, particularly Denmark and Sweden. In 1990 the three Baltic states established regular contacts with the Nordic Council, the main political organization uniting the five Scandinavian states. Denmark's prime minister, Poul Schlüter, became in 1991 the first Western head of government to visit Estonia. The Swedish prime minister, Carl Bildt, became an outspoken defender of Estonia after Russian threats to impose economic sanctions on Tallinn heightened tensions in 1993.

In some respects, the development of Scandinavian ties appeared to be a higher priority for Estonia than the fostering of greater Baltic cooperation, begun during the three republics' common struggle for independence. Baltic leaders held regular summit meetings beginning in 1990 and issued numerous joint declarations concerning their relations with Russia. An interparliamentary Baltic Council was established in 1990 to promote further cooperation at semiannual meetings. In mid-1993 Baltic military commanders even met to discuss plans for a joint infantry battalion that would be offered for peacekeeping missions around the world. Yet, progress on a free-trade agreement among the three countries was slow, and this situation was not helped in 1992 when Estonia elected a center-right government while Lithuania voted back in Algirdas Brazauskas and the former communists. Ultimately, a free-trade agreement was signed in April 1994.

Estonia's relations with the United States were strong, although the George H.W. Bush administration's initial delay in establishing diplomatic ties with the republic disappointed many in Tallinn. The United States held off recognition for several days in deference to Mikhail S. Gorbachev. However, Secretary of State James A. Baker visited all three Baltic states in September 1991 and five months later was followed by Vice President J. Danforth Quayle. Relations with the William J. Clinton administration appeared solid, although some Estonian officials expressed concern about what they perceived as its unqualified support for Russian president Boris N. Yeltsin.

Relations with Russia

Estonia's ties with Boris N. Yeltsin had weakened since the Russian leader's show of solidarity with the Baltic states in January 1991. Issues surrounding Russian troop withdrawals from the Baltic republics and Estonia's denial of automatic citizenship to noncitizens ranked high on the list of points of contention. Immediately after independence, Estonia began pressing the Soviet Union, and later Russia, for a speedy withdrawal of Soviet troops from its territory. Estonia insisted that the process be completed by the end of the year. The Soviet government, citing a lack of available housing for its troops, said not before 1994. In January 1992, some 25,000 troops were reported left in Estonia, the smallest contingent in the Baltic states. Still, more than 80,000 hectares of land, including an inland artillery range, remained in the Russian military's hands. More than 150 battle tanks, 300 armored vehicles, and 163 battle aircraft also remained. The last troops did not leave until August 1994.

In the fall of 1991, as Estonia laid down its new citizenship policy, the Soviet Union called the move a violation of human rights. Under the citizenship policy, most of the country's large ethnic Russian minority were declared noncitizens. The Soviet government linked the further withdrawal of troops from Estonia to a satisfactory change in Estonia's citizenship stance. In response, Estonia denied the human rights charges and invited more than a dozen international fact-finding groups to visit the country for verification. As the propaganda war and negotiations dragged on, Estonia and the other two Baltic countries gained international support for their position on troop withdrawal at a July 1992 summit of the CSCE in Helsinki. The final communiqué called on Russia to act "without delay . . . for the early, orderly and complete withdrawal" of foreign troops from the Baltic states. Resolutions also were passed in the United States Senate in 1992 and 1993 linking the issue of troop withdrawals to continued United States aid to Russia.

Yet, Estonian and Russian negotiators remained deadlocked throughout 1993. At several points, President Yeltsin and other Russian officials called an official halt to the pullout, but the unofficial withdrawal of forces continued. By the end of 1992, about 16,000 troops remained. A year later, that number was down to fewer than 3,500, and more than half of the army outposts had been turned over to Estonian defense officials. The Estonian and Russian sides continued to disagree, primarily over the pace of Russia's withdrawal from the town of Paldiski, on the northern coast some thirty-five kilometers west of Tallinn. The Soviet navy had built a submarine base there that included two nuclear submarine training reactors. Russian officials maintained that dismantling the reactor facility would take time; Estonia demanded faster action along with international supervision of the process. The last Russian warship, carrying ten T–72 tanks, departed in August 1994. However, Russia was to retain control of the reactor facility in Paldiski until September 1995.

Territorial issues also clouded Estonian-Russian relations. Estonia continued to stick by its demand for the return of more than 2,000 square kilometers of territory annexed to Russia by Stalin in 1945. The annexed land was within the borders Estonia and Russia had originally agreed to as part of the 1920 Tartu Peace Treaty. However, the Yeltsin government disavowed any responsibility for acts committed by the Soviet regime.

National Security

Although the ultimate goal of ensuring protection against an outside attack appeared remote, Estonia was hard at work building up a defense force in the mid-1990s, with plenty of outside help. The most dramatic step the country took was the appointment in May 1993 of Aleksander Einseln, a retired United States Army colonel and émigré Estonian, to command Estonia's fledgling armed forces. The decision drew strong objections from the United States Department of State, which feared upsetting Russia by allowing former United States military personnel to serve in high posts in the former Soviet Union. The United States threatened to revoke Einseln's military pension and even his citizenship. Support for the new Estonian general from several United States senators, however, helped ease the controversy.

Armed Forces

The armed forces in 1994 numbered about 3,000, including a 2,500-member army and a 500-member navy. There were also a 6,000-member reserve militia, known as the Defense League (Kaitseliit); a 2,000-member paramilitary border guard under the command of the Ministry of Interior; and a maritime border guard, which also functioned as a coast guard. The army's equipment included eight Mi–8 transport helicopters. The navy possessed two former Soviet and four former Swedish patrol craft, as well as two small transport vessels. The government allocated some EKR250 million for defense in 1994.

The armed forces of which Einseln took command offered no shortage of work. Serious divisions existed between several commanding officers, including the army chief of staff, who had received their training in the Soviet military and younger officers and recruits who distrusted leaders who had served in the "Soviet occupation army." The appointment of an outsider as commander was meant to close this rift, but the antipathies remained strong.

Especially independent minded was the Defense League, a patriotic volunteer group from the interwar years that was revived in early 1990. The league staged several attention-grabbing maneuvers in 1990 (including an attempt to place border posts along Estonia's prewar frontier, now in Russia), which often drew criticism as being provocative. After independence the Defense League refused to merge with Estonia's budding army, preferring to remain a separate auxiliary force.

In July 1993, Estonia saw the dissension within the army erupt into a minor mutiny among a group of several dozen recruits serving in Pullapää in western Estonia. The unit was upset over poor treatment during a mission in which it had been ordered to take control of parts of the former Russian military town of Paldiski. In protest, members of the group declared their intention to leave the Estonian army and devote their efforts to fighting organized crime. The Estonian government ordered the dissolution of the unit but eventually backed down. Hain Rebas resigned as defense minister over the government's inaction while also claiming an inability to work with some of the army's Soviet-trained commanders. The leaders of the infantry unit went free until their capture in November following a shoot-out with police.

More outside help in improving Estonia's armed forces came with the purchase in January 1993 of more than US$60 million in Israeli light arms. The contract, signed by the government in private talks with TAAS-Israel Industries, later caused a political storm when many deputies in parliament questioned whether Estonia had gotten a fair deal. The government nevertheless convinced the Riigikogu in December to ratify the agreement. While increasing the army's firepower, part of the weaponry was also to go to Estonia's border guard.

Estonia's Nordic neighbors also were active in building up the country's defenses. Finland, Sweden, and Germany all donated patrol boats, uniforms, and small transport aircraft to equip the new soldiers. No arms sales, however, were considered.

In 1990 Estonia had been the first Soviet republic to defy the Soviet army by offering alternative service to Estonian residents scheduled to be drafted. Most Estonians, however, simply began avoiding the draft. After independence, Estonia instituted its own compulsory military service, with a minimum term of one year beginning at age eighteen. About 12,000 males reach the age of eighteen every year. Young Estonian men continue to spurn the call, however; only one-third of eligible draftees turned out for the spring 1993 conscription. In addition, the Estonian military faces a limited pool from which to choose because only citizens can be drafted and because restrictions have been placed on the induction of university students.

Estonia's security strategy was dubbed by one observer in 1993 as the "CNN defense." Ideally, Estonia would attempt to delay a presumed Russian invasion until it could draw international attention and at least diplomatic intervention. As in the case of Poland and the Czech Republic, talks with NATO about extending Western security guarantees to the Baltic area did not meet with ready success. Still, the Nordic countries seem intent on improving Baltic defense arrangements, in part to bolster their own regional security. Another gambit is Estonia's strengthening of relations with Ukraine.

Crime and Law Enforcement

The number of reported crimes in Estonia rose to 41,254 in 1992, an increase of 250 percent over 1987. The overwhelming majority represented cases of theft (33,128). In Tallinn, where many residents had begun traveling to the West and acquiring Western goods, apartment break-ins accounted for 31 percent of all thefts. Street crime also mounted, especially in the capital. In 1992 the number of murders or attempted murders climbed 75 percent, to 239. In 1993 that total was equaled in only nine months. Meanwhile, only 21 percent of all crimes were being solved as of mid-1993.

Organized crime is a major worry for law enforcement officials. Various groups originating in Russia are believed to be operating in Estonia, conducting illicit trade and exacting protection money from new shops and restaurants. A major black market in copper and other nonferrous metals developed in 1992, when lax export controls and high trading prices encouraged the theft of copper communications wire, monument plaques, and even graveyard crosses. Losses in 1992 were estimated at nearly EKR10 million. The spread of prostitution beyond hotel lobbies into fully operating brothels prompted some officials in 1993 to call for its legalization to gain at least some control over the situation.

Popular frustration at the growth in crime focused in 1993 on the interior minister, Lagle Parek. A prominent dissident during the Soviet era, she had become head of the Estonian National Independence Party, one of the three parties in the governing coalition. She was unable, however, to shake up the ministry that had once kept tabs on her protest activities, and she was forced to resign.

The penal code introduced in 1992 retained the death penalty for terrorism and murder. In 1993 two persons were sentenced to death for aggravated murder. In August 1993, about 4,500 persons were in custody in the country's eleven prisons.

Outlook

As Estonia entered its fourth year of independence, it had already built a strong record of achievements. In the midst of the August 1991 coup, Estonia's politicians had had the foresight to convene a constitutional assembly and seize the moment for political restructuring. The process of constitution making was completed in a relatively orderly manner, and the new basic law was successfully implemented. Lasting political parties had yet to develop, however. Half a decade after open parliamentary politics began with the Supreme Soviet elections of 1990, the factions in parliament continued to fragment and regroup. Part of Estonia's problem may have been its small size. Because the circle of politicians was not very large in a country of only about 1.5 million people, there was relatively little turn-over, and old rivals and allies were constantly pitted against each other. The first era of independence had witnessed the same problem. Yet, Estonia's decision to stick to a parliamentary system of government in 1992 appeared to be a good one, even though it was the same system that had been the undoing of the country's first democracy in 1934. More safeguards had been built into the 1992 constitution against parliamentary domination of politics. Lennart Meri's tenure as Estonia's first postwar president appeared to mold the new office into a source of balance, despite grumblings from his Isamaa backers. A new court system was also put into place, with effective use being made of provisions for testing the constitutionality of laws.

Yet, politics did not reach the lives of all of Estonia's residents. Having been left out of the parliamentary elections in 1992 because of citizenship requirements, Estonia's large Russophone population was virtually absent from national politics. Russians dominated in the city councils of the heavily Russian towns of Narva and Sillamäe, in the northeastern part of the country, but their political presence rarely extended beyond the city limits. Even a last-ditch local referendum on territorial autonomy for the northeastern region, declared in July 1993 in response to the Law on Aliens crisis, largely failed because of numerous reports of voting irregularities. Most of these Russian leaders—who had long histories as communist party functionaries, who had tacitly supported the August 1991 coup, and who had held on to their political turf since then—finally were ousted in the local elections of October 1993. A new core of Russian leaders began to emerge in Tallinn, where two Russian-based parties did well at the polls and were poised to play an important role in the capital's city council. From that point, a responsive mainstream political society could begin to serve a Russian population that seems determined to remain in Estonia and willing to contribute to its future.

The progress of Estonia's economic reforms in the early 1990s, if only in comparison with Russia, was clearly a source of confidence among both Estonians and Russians in the future of the country. Estonia was the first of the Baltic states to jump out of the ruble zone and create its own currency, a move that was soon rewarded by low inflation, rising wages, and an apparent bottoming out of the country's economic decline. Nevertheless, a large section of the population continued to fear unemployment. Retraining for new skills needed on the open market (such as learning the Estonian language for many Russians) also was a pressing need. The growing gap between the newly rich and the newly poor could be seen in the comparison between new Western luxury automobiles racing around Tallinn's streets and pensioners counting their kroons at a store to buy a half-kilogram of meat. For better or worse, the transition to capitalism was reordering society.

Estonia was not alone on its long road to recovery nor in its return to the European community of nations. Yet, even among so many countries with a kindred past and a common desire for a better future, the hoped-for dawning of a new geopolitical age did not appear to have taken place by the mid-1990s. Estonia and the other Baltic states remained of strategic interest to the Kremlin, and the West appeared to have little intention of crossing Russia on its very doorstep. European, and especially Scandinavian, support for Estonia's defense forces was noticeable. But it would take a long time before a credible Estonian force could be assembled. Although the Russian troops had finally departed, full security for Estonia seemed to remain distant.

*   *   *

The two most comprehensive works on Estonia are Rein Taagepera's *Estonia: Return to Independence* and Toivo V. Raun's *Estonia and the Estonians.* Both contain complete overviews of Estonian history, including the most recent struggle for independence. Tõnu Parming's small book on the interwar years, *The Collapse of Liberal Democracy and the Rise of Authoritarianism in Estonia,* provides an extended analysis of that period. *Ot dogovora o bazakh do anneksii: Dokumenty i materialy,* a collection of documents edited by Jüri Ant et al. that pertain to the Nazi-Soviet Nonaggression Pact and to Estonia's annexation by the Soviet Union, dramatizes the fateful end of Estonia's first era of independence.

The World Bank's extensive survey of the Estonian economy is an excellent source of economic and social statistics up to 1991–92. For later statistics reflecting the introduction of the kroon, as well as social trends under the market economy, the Estonian State Statistics Board has issued a statistical yearbook regularly since 1991.

Other useful sources on Estonia can be found in several general works on the Baltic states. Anatol Lieven's *The Baltic Revolution* is an incisive look at the politics of independence from an outsider's point of view. Lieven includes discussion of Estonia's Russian minority and its future. Graham Smith's *The Baltic States: The National Self-Determination of Estonia, Latvia, and Lithuania* also treats Estonia extensively. (For further information and complete citations, see Bibliography.)

Chapter 2. Latvia

Tower of the Dome Cathedral, Riga

Country Profile

Country

Formal Name: Republic of Latvia (Latvijas Republika).

Short Form: Latvia (Latvija).

Term for Citizen(s): Latvian(s).

Capital: Riga.

Date of Independence: During abortive Soviet coup, declared immediate full independence August 21, 1991; Soviet Union recognized it September 6, 1991. November 18, Independence Day, national holiday; on this day in 1918, independent Republic of Latvia proclaimed.

Geography

Size: 64,589 square kilometers, slightly larger than West Virginia.

Topography: Undulating plains cover 75 percent of country. Forest 42 percent; cultivable land 27 percent; meadows and pastureland 13 percent; peat bog, swamp, and marsh 10 percent; and other 8 percent. Highest elevation 300 meters.

Climate: Temperate, with mild winters and cool summers. Average January temperatures range from –2.8°C in Liepaja to –6.6°C in Daugavpils; average July temperatures range from 16.7°C in Liepaja to 17.6°C in Daugavpils. Frequent precipitation, averaging 180 days per year in Riga. Annual precipitation 500 to 700 millimeters.

Society

Population: 2,565,854 (1994 estimate). Population declined in early 1990s because of negative natural growth rates and net out-migration. Birth rate 9.5 births per 1,000 population; death rate 16.3 deaths per 1,000 population (1994). Total fertility rate 2.0 children per woman (1993). Population density 39.7 persons per square kilometer. Average life expectancy estimated in 1994 at 69.4 years (64.4 years for males and 74.8 years for females).

Ethnic Groups: According to the 1989 census, Latvians 52.0 percent, Russians 34.0 percent, Belorussians 4.5 percent, Ukrainians 3.4 percent, Poles 2.3 percent, Lithuanians 1.3 percent, and others (including Jews, Germans, Estonians, Tatars, and Gypsies) 2.5 percent. In 1994 estimates of Latvian and Russian groups 54.2 percent and 33.1 percent, respectively.

Languages: Official language Latvian; Russian, Belarusian, Ukrainian, Polish, Lithuanian, and other languages also used.

Religion: Mostly Evangelical Lutheran; Roman Catholics, Orthodox Christians, Old Believers, Baptists, Pentecostals, Seventh-Day Adventists, Jews, and Methodists also represented.

Education: Latvian adopted as official state language in 1989, making its study compulsory for all students. Nine years of primary education compulsory; may be followed by three years of secondary education or one to six years in technical, vocational, or art schools. In 1993–94 school year, total of 76,619 students enrolled in primary schools, 242,677 in secondary schools, 27,881 in vocational schools, 19,476 in special secondary institutions, and 7,211 in special schools for physically and mentally handicapped. Literacy rate close to 100 percent.

Health and Welfare: In 1992 some 176 hospitals and 130 beds per 10,000 inhabitants. Most hospitals lacked modern facilities and were concentrated in urban areas. Forty-one physicians per 10,000 inhabitants, but too few nurses and other auxiliary staff. Retirement pensions LVL15 to LVL23.5 per month; many pensions awarded also to survivors and disabled persons.

Labor Force: 1,407,000 (August 1994); industry 30 percent; agriculture 16 percent; trade 9 percent; transportation and communications 9 percent; construction 10 percent; and financial services and other 27 percent. Distribution of economic sectors began to shift away from industry and toward services in early 1990s.

Economy

Gross National Product (GNP): Estimated at US$5.1 billion in 1992; per capita income US$4,810 (1993 estimate). Gross domestic product (GDP) increased from LVL1.6 billion in 1993 to an estimated LVL2.2 billion in 1994. Real GDP fell 33.8 percent in 1992 and 11.7 percent in 1993, but grew an estimated 2.0 percent in 1994. Inflation rate averaged less than 3 percent per month in 1993 and less than 2.4 percent per month in 1994; annual inflation rate decreased from more than 958 percent in 1992 to 35 percent in 1993 and 28 percent in 1994.

Agriculture: Supplanted by industry as foremost economic sector in postwar era. Aggressive capital formation and forced labor movements under Soviet rule reduced agriculture's share of labor force from 66 percent in 1930 to about 16 percent in 1990. Accounted for 20 percent of GDP in 1990 and 15 percent of GDP in 1994. Livestock main subsector. Nearly 1.7 million hectares of arable land, used mainly for growing fodder crops and grain. Number of private farms increased from nearly 4,000 in 1989 to more than 57,500 in 1993.

Industry and Mining: Foremost economic sector during Soviet period; employed more than 30 percent of labor force in 1990. Supplanted by services subsequently; share of GDP declined from about 43 percent in 1990 to 22 percent in 1994. Production declined sharply in 1992 and 1993. Highly dependent on energy and raw material imports. Main industries engineering (including machine building and electronics), textiles, food, wood and paper, chemicals, and building materials.

Energy: Relies heavily on imports of fuels and electric power. Energy generated domestically by three hydroelectric power plants on Daugava River and two thermal power plants near Riga.

Exports: LVL701.6 million (1993 estimate). Major commodities oil products, wood and timber, food products, metals, and buses.

Imports: LVL647.4 million (1993 estimate). Major commodities oil, natural gas, machinery, electric power, and automobiles.

Major Trading Partners: Russia, Germany, Ukraine, Sweden, Belarus, Netherlands, Estonia, Finland, Lithuania, and Britain.

Currency and Exchange Rate: 1 lats (LVL) = 100 santims. Lats reintroduced in March 1993, replacing Latvian ruble in October 1993 at rate of 1 lats = 200 Latvian rubles. In March 1996, LVL0.55 = US$1.

Fiscal Year: Calendar year.

Transportation and Telecommunications

Roads: 64,693 kilometers total, of which 7,036 kilometers highways and 13,502 kilometers secondary roads (1994). Bus service between Riga and Warsaw. Urban centers also served by minibuses and taxis. Rental automobiles available.

Railroads: 2,406 kilometers of railroads, of which 270 kilometers electrified (1992). Train service available to Moscow, St. Petersburg, and Warsaw.

Civil Aviation: Main airport in Riga. Regular flights to many international destinations, including Amsterdam, Berlin, Copenhagen, Frankfurt, Kiev, Helsinki, London, Moscow, Oslo, St. Petersburg, and Stockholm. National carrier Latvian Airlines. Service also provided by Baltic International Airlines, Riga Airlines Express, Finnair, Lufthansa, SAS (Scandinavian Airlines), Estonian Air, and LOT (Polish Airlines).

Shipping: Main coastal ports Riga, Ventspils, and Liepaja, a former Soviet naval port. Main inland port Daugavpils. Most Russian petroleum exports pass through Ventspils (16.3 million tons in 1993). Total freight transported through Latvian ports in 1993 about 27.2 million tons. Shipping service exists between Riga and Western Europe.

Telecommunications: In 1992 about 700,000 telephone subscribers (more than 50 percent in Riga); nearly 1.4 million radio receivers and more than 1.1 million television receivers in use. In 1995 more than twenty-five radio stations and thirty television broadcasting companies.

Government and Politics

Government: Parliamentary democracy. Electoral system based on that existing before Soviet annexation; 1922 constitution restored in 1993. Saeima, supreme legislative body, composed of 100 members elected on basis of proportional representation. Saeima elects president (head of state), who appoints prime minister. Cabinet of Ministers, headed by prime minister, has executive power.

Judicial System: Inherited from Soviet regime; undergoing reorganization. Regional, district, and administrative courts, as well as Supreme Court. Final appeals in criminal and civil cases made to Supreme Court.

Politics: Parties include Latvia's Way (Latvijas Cels), centrist in orientation; Democratic Party Saimnieks, center-left; Latvian National Independence Movement; Popular Front of Latvia; For Latvia, far-right; Latvian Farmers Union; Christian Democratic Union; National Union of Economists; and Ravnopraviye (Equal Rights Movement), a Russophone group.

Administrative Divisions: Four provinces: Vidzeme, Latgale, Kurzeme, and Zemgale; subdivided into twenty-six districts, seven municipalities, fifty-six towns, and thirty-seven urban settlements.

Foreign Relations: Latvia joined United Nations (UN) in September 1991 and is a signatory to a number of UN organizations and other international agreements. Member of Organization for Security and Cooperation in Europe (until January 1995 known as Conference on Security and Cooperation in Europe), North Atlantic Cooperation Council, and Council of the Baltic Sea States. In February 1994, Latvia joined Partnership for Peace program of North Atlantic Treaty Organization. Some improvement in relations with Russia after

Russian troop withdrawal in August 1994.

National Security

Armed Forces: Based on Swedish-Finnish rapid response force model. In 1994 armed forces totaled 6,600, including 1,650 in army, 630 in navy, 180 in air force, and 4,140 in border guard. Plans call for 9,000 active members in armed forces. Additional forces include security service of Ministry of Interior and reserve Home Guard (Zemessardze), latter organization having an estimated 17,000 members. Mandatory one-year period of active duty for men at age nineteen. Alternative service available for conscientious objectors.

Military Budget: About US$48 million allocated to defense in 1993.

Figure 7. Latvia, 1995

AMONG THE BALTIC STATES, Latvia lies "in the middle," not merely geographically but also in a cultural sense. It has been suggested that average Estonians are cool, rational, and somewhat aloof, whereas Lithuanians are warm, emotional, and gregarious. Latvians incorporate a mixture of these traits. Although they have much in common with Estonians and Lithuanians, on most questions—whether in economics, politics, or social policies—the Latvian people have chosen a slightly different path of development.

There is a widespread perception that Latvia is a "tiny" country. Its actual size, however, surprises most first-time travelers. It is only slightly smaller than Ireland and is larger than many other European countries, such as the Netherlands, Switzerland, Belgium, and Denmark. Its significant contribution to history, especially in the dissolution of the tsarist and Soviet empires, belies its comparatively limited geographical dimensions beside its giant and unpredictable neighbor to the east.

Latvia was occupied by the Soviet Union for half a century. This occupation has left serious demographic, economic, and psychological legacies, whose burdens will be borne by the inhabitants of Latvia for the foreseeable future. In spite of these burdens, however, Latvia and the other two Baltic republics have made greater progress toward Westernization than any of the other former Soviet republics.

Historical Setting

Early History

Latvians have resided in their present geographical area for more than 2,000 years. Their closest ethnic relatives are the ancient Prussians, the Galinds, the Jatvings, and the Lithuanians. Only the Lithuanians have avoided extinction. All the other peoples were conquered or assimilated by their neighbors, demonstrating one of the realities of history—the ebb and flow of the creation and disappearance of nations. This aspect of history has been taken to heart by Latvians, who regularly use their experience of extinction as a tocsin of potential danger to the survival of their own group. Ironically, Latvians themselves have been in the position of having assimilated another group. The first settlers in the territory of Latvia were

Livonians, or "Libiesi." Whereas the Latvians originated from the Indo-European family, the Livonians were akin to the Estonians and the Finns and formed a part of the Finno-Ugric complex of nations. The Livonians were once heavily concentrated in the northern part of Latvia's present-day provinces of Kurzeme and Vidzeme, but today only about 100 individuals retain their ancient language. Livonians have also contributed to the development of a prominent Latvian dialect.

Until about 1300, the Latvian people lived within half a dozen or so independent and culturally distinct kingdoms. This lack of unity hastened their conquest by German-led crusaders, who brought with them more efficient weaponry, war experience, and technology, including stone and mortar fortifications. During the next 600 years, various parts of the territory of Latvia were taken over by a succession of foreign regimes, including those of Denmark, Prussia, the Polish-Lithuanian Commonwealth, Sweden, and Russia. In this maelstrom of changing rulers, the descendants of the German conquerors were able to maintain their autonomy and their title to feudal estates by adapting to new circumstances and by offering loyalty to whoever was the dominant power. These Baltic barons formed the bulk of the upper classes and set the tone of the Baltic establishment. Although their dominance over the Latvian serfs has often been justifiably criticized, their profound impact on Latvian cultural and social development can be observed even to this day.

Besides the Baltic barons and other Germans, the greatest impact on the formation of the Latvian nation came from Russia, the giant neighbor that began the conquest of Latvia in 1710 under Peter I (the Great) (r. 1682–1725) and completed the process eighty-five years later. For more than 200 years, Latvians had a unique mixture of elites. The German nobility was dominant in economic, cultural, social, and local political life, and the Russian bureaucracy was in charge of higher politics and administration. Some Latvians aspiring to higher status tried to emulate the Germans, but other Latvians thought that salvation was to be found with the Russians. Indeed, a large part of the Latvian intelligentsia was inspired by alumni of the higher educational institutes of St. Petersburg. Several prominent intellectual leaders agitated for the migration of Latvians to the interior of Russia, where free land was available. Some Latvians adopted the Orthodox faith, Russia's predominant religion.

During the second half of the nineteenth century, Latvians experienced a resurgence of national consciousness. There was an intense development of Latvian culture and a new stress on the need for protecting this culture against the inroads of both Germanization and Russification. A new Latvian-oriented elite appeared and began to press for a larger input by Latvians in the determination of their own local affairs. This period is known as the first Latvian awakening.

The favorable geographical position of Latvia alongside the Baltic Sea and on the outer frontier of a vast, mostly landlocked Russian Empire provided the impetus for an extremely rapid economic development of the region. The most rapid growth occurred between 1880 and World War I. Riga became the third largest port in the Russian Empire; in 1913 its port had a larger trade turnover than St. Petersburg's. Many huge factories were constructed, attracting great masses of new workers from the Latvian countryside and from the interior of Russia.

Working-class discontent and the spread of Marxism created a volatile situation in Latvia. This radicalism was exacerbated by the shooting of seventy peaceful demonstrators in Riga in January 1905. Massive strikes by workers and the uprising of peasants with the attendant burning of feudal manor houses resulted in a very vindictive reaction by authorities, who shot some 3,000 people and sent many into exile in Siberia. Others managed to flee abroad. In 1905 almost all segments of Latvian society were united in their anger against the Russian authorities and the German barons.

This legacy of 1905, together with the disruption of World War I, when half the Latvian population was forced to evacuate ahead of the invading Germans, created propitious conditions for the growth of Marxism and especially its radical variant, Bolshevism. Of the votes for the All-Russian Constitutional Assembly from Latvians in the Russian-controlled northeastern part of Latvia, the Bolsheviks received a majority (71.9 percent). By contrast, in the entire empire less than a quarter voted for the Bolsheviks.

This infatuation with Bolshevism suffered a severe jolt, and support plummeted dramatically, during the half-year of Bolshevik rule of Latvia, which ended in May 1919. Nevertheless, a significant contingent of Latvian Red Riflemen fled to Russia, where they formed an important part of the leadership and infrastructure of the Red Army. Many Latvians also became prominent in the top hierarchy of the first Soviet political police, known as the Cheka (see Glossary), and the Russian Communist Party (Bolshevik). Their days of glory were cut short by the mass executions initiated by Joseph V. Stalin in the 1930s.

Independence, 1918–40

Latvian independence was proclaimed on November 18, 1918, but its real advent came only in 1920 after the cessation of hostilities between pro- and anti-Bolshevik forces and the withdrawal of all foreign armies from Latvian territory. The peace treaty signed with Soviet Russia on August 11, 1920, was a critical step. As stated in Article 2 of this treaty, "Russia unreservedly recognizes the independence and sovereignty of the Latvian State and voluntarily and forever renounces all sovereign rights over the Latvian people and territory." Latvia became a member of the League of Nations in 1921.

Latvia's ensuing period of independence lasted for twenty years and has become embedded in the Latvian consciousness as a golden era of progress and achievement, now referred to as the second awakening. The period of independence was characterized by both economic viability and political instability. The Latvian currency, the lats, became relatively stable. Farming and exports flourished. Inflation was low. Welfare provisions were generous. Foreign debt was minimal. One of the more important indexes of economic achievement was the volume of gold—10.6 tons—that the Latvian government placed for safekeeping in the United States, Britain, France, and Switzerland.This period is also important in understanding a significant thread of present-day Latvian political culture. The state intervened as a direct economic actor in many areas, including heavy industry, building materials, electricity, tobacco, brewing, confectionery, textiles, insurance, and food processing. The government also made a conscious attempt to provide stability and, even more important, to help expand Latvian control of the economy.

Until 1934 Latvia had a system of democracy similar to that in Weimar Germany (1919–33). The use of proportional elections and the absence of any dominant party encouraged participation by more than forty different political parties. The 1931 parliament (Saeima) had representatives from twenty-seven parties. It is not surprising, then, that Latvia had eighteen different parliamentary governments with new combinations of coalition partners in fewer than fourteen years. The evident political instability and the threat of a coup d'état from both the left and the right encouraged Karlis Ulmanis, a centrist, to take the reins of power into his own hands in May 1934. Ulmanis had been one of the founders of independent Latvia and had also been prime minister several times. His acknowledged experience and the public's general disgust with politicking assured little protest against the "setting aside" of Latvia's constitution.

Ulmanis was a populist ruler who did not countenance opposition. He banned all parties and many press organs. It is important to note, however, that not a single person was executed during this period, although several hundred activists from the left and right were incarcerated for brief periods of time. Ulmanis tried to maintain a neutral stance between the Soviet Union and Nazi Germany, but his best efforts failed when these two totalitarian systems connived to carve out spheres of dominance in the heart of Europe.

Ulmanis was deported by the Soviet authorities and died in captivity in Russia in 1942, but his legacy remains alive in Latvia. Today, Ulmanis is a powerful symbol of selfless dedication to Latvia, and his memory is honored even by organizations with high concentrations of former communists. These groups realize that the once-vilified dictator has tremendous appeal among Latvians, especially in rural areas, and that their association with Ulmanis can provide long-term political dividends. At the same time, the historical experience of such a dictatorship, even if beneficial in some respects, has been used in debates as a warning against a repetition of dictatorial rule.

The fate of Latvia and the other Baltic republics was sealed on August 23, 1939, when the foreign ministers of the Soviet Union and Nazi Germany, Vyacheslav Molotov and Joachim von Ribbentrop, respectively, signed a secret protocol giving Estonia and Latvia to the Soviet Union and Lithuania to Germany. Within five weeks, however, Lithuania was added to the Soviet roster of potential possessions in exchange for other territories and sizable sums of gold.

The Nazi-Soviet Nonaggression Pact (also known as the Molotov-Ribbentrop Pact) was not acknowledged by the Soviet Union until it was forced to do so, fifty years later, by the Baltic delegation to the Congress of People's Deputies (see Glossary) in Moscow in 1989. The pact was seen by Latvian and other Baltic independence supporters as the Achilles' heel of the carefully constructed myth by Moscow propagandists of how the

Baltic countries had joyfully embraced the Soviet Union and had voted to become new Soviet republics. Indeed, the Latvian dissident group known as Helsinki '86 had organized demonstrations on August 23, 1987, to underscore the secret pact's existence. These demonstrations had reverberated throughout the world and had put Soviet leader Mikhail S. Gorbachev's regime on the defensive.

For the Baltic countries, the half-century following the 1939 pact was a particularly tragic time. During that period, hundreds of thousands of people perished, and much effort was expended to obliterate the memory of independence.

On October 5, 1939, soon after the Nazi-Soviet Nonagression Pact was signed, the Soviet Union coerced Latvia into signing the Pact of Defense and Mutual Assistance. It then forced Latvia to accept occupation by 30,000 Soviet troops. Similar treaties were imposed on Estonia and Lithuania, whose forces also were vastly outnumbered by Soviet forces. (The Baltic states' northern neighbor, Finland, refused to accept such a demand, however, and, after it was attacked on November 30, 1939, valiantly fought the Red Army in what became known as the Winter War. The Soviet Union was expelled from the League of Nations for this unprovoked attack on Finland.)

Stalin made his next move in the Baltics when world attention was riveted on the imminent surrender of France to the Nazis in June 1940. An ultimatum was sent to each one of the Baltic countries demanding replacement of their existing governments by those capable of ensuring the proper fulfillment of the previously signed pacts of mutual assistance. Moscow also demanded the free entry of unlimited troops to secure strategic centers. With no hope of external support, all three countries capitulated to these demands.

The Soviet Period

The new Soviet troops moved into Latvia, together with a special emissary, Andrey Vyshinskiy, who was entrusted with the details of mobilizing enthusiastic mass support for the Sovietization of Latvia. Vyshinskiy had learned political choreography well when he staged the infamous Moscow show trials against the theoretician Nikolay I. Bukharin and other enemies of Stalin.

A so-called "people's government" was assembled, and elections were held to help legitimate the changes in the eyes of the world. Only the communist slate of candidates was allowed

Flowers laid at base of Liberty
Monument in Riga
Courtesy Linda Sudmalis

Candles line roads connecting
the three Baltic capital cities
on the anniversary of the
Nazi-Soviet Nonaggression
Pact (1939), Riga, 1991.
Courtesy Linda Sudmalis

on the ballot, and the improbable result of 97.6 percent in favor—with a more than 90 percent turnout—was never found to be credible by any of the Western governments. For the purposes of Soviet strategy and mythmaking, however, they sufficed. On July 21, 1940, the newly elected delegates proclaimed the Latvian Soviet Socialist Republic and voted to petition the Soviet Union to allow Latvia to join as a constituent republic. Not surprisingly, their wishes were granted. The process of Sovietizing Latvia was interrupted, however, when Stalin's ally and co-conspirator attacked the Soviet Union on June 22, 1941. One week before the Nazi attack, the Soviet regime had arrested and deported to Siberia, in sealed cattle cars, about 15,000 of the former Latvian elite, as well as suspected anticommunists, including 5,154 women and 3,225 children. In all, during the first year of occupation, Latvia lost 35,000 people to deportations or executions. Most deportees died in Siberia.

The equally brutal Nazi occupation lasted until May 8, 1945. Latvia's Jews and Gypsies were particularly subjected to mass annihilation, and only a small number of each group survived this holocaust. The Nazis had no intention of liberating Latvia or providing renewed independence. Even the bulk of nationalized property was not returned. They did, however, draft young men into the armed forces—an illegal move in occupied territories, according to international law. These young people fought against the Red Army in two divisions, suffering high casualties.

With the advance of the Red Army into Latvia, about 200,000 Latvian refugees fled in panic to the West. Many lost their lives in the Baltic Sea, and others were bombed, together with their horse-drawn wagons. A sizable group was captured and turned back to await punishment for their "disloyalty." About 150,000 refugees from Latvia settled in the West, where many of them continued a half-century-long struggle against the occupation of their homeland.

The reestablishment of Soviet control in the mid-1940s was not welcomed. Many Latvians joined the guerrilla movement, which fought the occupying power for close to a decade. To break this resistance and also to force peasants into collective farms, new deportations to Siberia, involving more than 40,000 people (10,590 of them children under sixteen years of age), were completed on March 25, 1949. This date was to become a focal point of demonstrations in 1988.

The leading positions in postwar Latvia's political, economic, and cultural life were filled by Russians or Russified Latvians, known as *latovichi*, who had spent much or all of their lives in the Soviet Union. Political power was concentrated in the Communist Party of Latvia (CPL), which numbered no more than 5,000 in 1945. The rapid growth of industry attracted migrant workers, primarily from Russia, further facilitating the processes of Russification and Sovietization. Net immigration from 1951 to 1989 has been estimated at more than 400,000.

After Stalin's death in 1953, conditions for greater local autonomy improved. In Latvia, beginning in 1957, a group of national communists under the leadership of Eduards Berklavs, deputy premier of the Latvian Council of Ministers, began a serious program of Latvianization. He and his supporters passed regulations restricting immigration, requested that party and government functionaries know the Latvian language, and planned to limit the growth of industry requiring large inputs of labor. Increased funding was planned for local requirements, such as agricultural machines, urban and rural housing, schools, hospitals, and social centers, rather than for Moscow-planned "truly grandiose projects."

These programs were not well received in Moscow, and a purge of about 2,000 national communists was initiated in July 1959. Many of the most gifted individuals in Latvia lost their positions and had to endure continuous harassment.

Berklavs himself was exiled from Latvia and expelled from the CPL. Later, upon returning to Latvia, he was one of the leaders of the Latvian underground opposition and coauthored a 1974 letter with seventeen Latvian communists, detailing the pace of Russification in Latvia. In 1988 Berklavs became one of the key founders of the Latvian National Independence Movement (Latvijas Nacionala neatkaribas kustiba—LNNK), and as an elected deputy in the Latvian parliament he vigorously defended Latvian interests.

After the purge of the national communists, Latvia experienced a particularly vindictive and staunchly pro-Moscow leadership. Under the iron fist of hard-liner Arvids Pelse (CPL first secretary, 1959–66), who later became a member of the Political Bureau (Politburo) of the Central Committee of the Communist Party of the Soviet Union (CPSU), Latvia suffered many restrictions and petty harassments in all fields of national culture and social development. Sovietization and Russification programs were of an intensity and dimension not found in either Estonia or Lithuania. Pelse was replaced by Augusts Voss (CPL first secretary, 1966–84), who was equally insensitive to Latvian demands. With the advent of a new period of *glasnost* (see Glossary) and national awakening, Voss was transferred to Moscow to preside over the Supreme Soviet's Council of Nationalities and was replaced by Boris Pugo, a former chief of Latvia's Committee for State Security (Komitet gosudarstvennoy bezopasnosti—KGB). Pugo, who served as CPL first secretary until 1988, subsequently gained prominence as a participant in the abortive Soviet coup of August 1991.

The Pursuit of Independence, 1987–91

The national awakening came about in large measure as a result of Gorbachev's loosening of the reins of repression and his public stress on truth and freedom of expression. When open demonstrations started in 1987, Latvians were no longer lacking in social cohesion. The purpose of these "calendar" demonstrations was to publicly commemorate the events of June 13–14, 1941 (the mass deportations of Latvians to the Soviet Union); August 23, 1939 (the signing of the Nazi-Soviet Nonaggression Pact); and November 18, 1918 (the proclamation of Latvian independence). During the several years leading up to the first demonstrations by Helsinki '86 on June 14, 1987, several groups had labored with missionary zeal to inspire Latvians to work for a number of social and political causes.

One group that organized in 1976 committed itself to the revival of folk culture and, in spite of harassment, succeeded in rekindling interest in Latvian traditions and in awakening pride in being Latvian. Parallel to the folk culture group, another movement focused on the repair of old churches and monuments and the protection of the environment. The founder of this movement, the Environmental Protection Club (EPC), acknowledged that its primary goal was to raise the consciousness of the general public. Indeed, the EPC became the organization within which many individuals opposed to various aspects of Sovietization and Russification could unite. Under the seemingly nonpolitical umbrella of the EPC, they could organize far more radical bodies, such as the Latvian National Independence Movement.

A dynamic group of young theologians within Latvia's moribund Evangelical Lutheran Church also began a campaign to reactivate their congregations and the structure of the church itself. The Rebirth and Renewal (Atdzimsana un Atjaunosana) group did not have many members, but its activism and confrontation with communist party officials and policies energized people within the growing religious communities as well as in the wider society. Indeed, several individuals from this group served as catalysts for the creation of the Popular Front of Latvia (Latvijas Tautas Fronte—LTF).

The mobilization of a larger constituency of Latvians occurred as a result of the successful campaign to stop the construction of a hydroelectric dam on the Daugava River in 1987. The initiator of this campaign, journalist Dainis Ivans, was later elected the first president of the LTF.

The "calendar" demonstrations, led by Helsinki '86 during 1987, electrified the Latvian population. Most people expected the authorities to mete out swift and ruthless retribution. When they did not, even more people joined in. In 1988 this grassroots protest was joined by the Latvian intelligentsia, whose demands for decentralization and democratization were forcefully articulated at the June 1–2 plenum of the Latvian Writers Union. Several months later, the idea of a popular front was brought to fruition, with a formal first congress organized on October 8–9, 1988.

The LTF had more than 100,000 dues-paying members and chapters in almost every locality in Latvia. These members slowly took the initiative in politics and became a de facto second government, pushing the Latvian Supreme Soviet to adopt a declaration of sovereignty and economic independence in July 1989. They also helped elect a majority of their approved candidates for the all-union Congress of People's Deputies in the spring of 1989; for the municipal local elections in December of that year; and for the critical parliamentary elections of March–April 1990. Slightly more than two-thirds of the delegates in the new parliament, now known as the Supreme Council, voted in favor of a transition to a democratic and independent Latvia on May 4, 1990. This process was marred by several instances of Soviet aggression, most notably in January 1991, when five people were killed during an attack on the Latvian Ministry of Interior in Riga by units of the Soviet Ministry of Internal Affairs Special Forces Detachment (Otryad militsii osobogo naznacheniya—OMON), commonly known as the Black Berets. The transition turned out to be much briefer than anyone could have expected, however, because of the failed Soviet coup of August 1991. Latvia declared independence on August 21, 1991. Soon thereafter, the Soviet Union recognized Latvia's independence, and once again Latvia was able to join the world community of nations.

Physical Environment

Latvia is traditionally seen as a tiny country. In terms of its population of about 2.6 million, it deserves this designation. Geographically, however, Latvia encompasses 64,589 square kilometers, a size surpassing that of better-known European states such as Belgium, the Netherlands, Switzerland, and Denmark. Seen from the air, Latvia is an extension of the East European Plain. Its flat terrain differs little from that of its surrounding neighbors. Latvia's only distinct border is the Baltic Sea coast, which extends for 531 kilometers. Its neighbors include Estonia on the north (267 kilometers of common border), Lithuania on the south (453 kilometers), Belarus on the southeast (141 kilometers), and Russia on the east (217 kilometers). Prior to World War II, Latvia bordered eastern Poland, but as a result of boundary changes by the Soviet Union, this territory was attached to Belorussia. Also, in 1944 Russia annexed the northeastern border district of Latvia, known as Abrene, including the town of Pytalovo (see fig. 2).

Geographic Features

The physiography of Latvia and its neighboring areas was formed, to a large degree, during the Quartenary period and the Pleistocene ice age, when soil and debris were pushed by glaciers into mounds and hills. Undulating plains cover 75 percent of Latvia's territory and provide the main areas for farming; 25 percent of the territory lies in uplands of moderate-sized hills. About 27 percent of the total territory is cultivable, with the central Zemgale Plain south of Riga being the most fertile and profitable. The three main upland areas—in the provinces of Kurzeme (western Latvia), Vidzeme (central Latvia), and Latgale (eastern Latvia)—provide a picturesque pattern of fields interspersed with forests and numerous lakes and rivers. In this area, the extensive glacial moraines, eskers, and drumlins have limited the profitability of agriculture by fragmenting fields and presenting serious erosion problems.

About 10 percent of Latvian territory consists of peat bogs, swamps, and marshes, some of which are covered by stunted forest growth. Forests are the outstanding feature of Latvia, claiming 42 percent of the territory. Lumber and wood products are among the country's most important exports. Two-thirds of the forests consist of Scotch pine or Norway spruce. Latvian forests differ from those of North America primarily because of their relatively brush-free understory. The forest floor, however, is far from a biological desert, as is often the case in tree plantations. Indeed, one of the most widespread pastimes of the population is picking blueberries, mushrooms, cranberries, and other bounties of the natural environment.

Few of the forests are fully mature because of previous overcutting and also because of several violent storms during the 1960s, which snapped or uprooted millions of trees. As a consequence, most of the wood today is derived from thinning and improvement cuts, forming 50 percent of the annual total growth increment of 8 million cubic meters of wood.

For a long time, wood has been a basic source of energy. The utilization of wood as fuel has increased dramatically in the 1990s, even in cities, because of the numbing price hikes on other forms of energy. Local wood is also an important resource for the pulp and paper industry and for specialized plywood and furniture manufacturers. A great concern today is the unregulated cutting of timber for the foreign market. Prices paid by European wood buyers are phenomenally high by local standards, and there is much pressure to utilize this opportunity for cash accumulation, even without legal permits. By 1992 the problem had become so serious that Latvian forestry officials were given the right to carry firearms.

Not all forests are productive. Many areas, especially abandoned, formerly private farms, have become overgrown with low-value alders and other scrub trees. With the return of private farming, these areas are once again being reclaimed for agriculture. In the process, however, there is a danger that these areas, which are ideal for wildlife, will become threatened. The decades-long neglect of extensive areas of marginal farmland was a boon for the establishment of unique ecological conditions favorable for the survival of animal species rarely found in other parts of Europe. According to a World Wildlife Fund study in 1992, Latvia has unusual populations of black storks, small eagles, otters, beaver, lynx, and wolves. There are also great concentrations of deer (86,000), wild boar (32,000), elk (25,000), moose (13,000), and fox (13,000). Many Latvians today are planning to exploit this resource by catering to foreign hunters.

The variegated and rapidly changing physiography of glacial moraines and lowlands has also allowed temperate flora, such as oaks, to grow within a few hundred meters of northern flora, such as bog cotton and cloudberries. This variety and the rapid change in natural ecosystems are among the unique features of the republic.

The Soviet system left behind another windfall for naturalists. The Latvian western seacoast was a carefully guarded border region. Almost all houses near the sea were razed or evacuated. As a result, about 300 kilometers of undeveloped seashore are graced only by forests of pine and spruce and ecologically unique sand dunes. The temptation for fast profit, however, may foster violation of laws that clearly forbid any construction within one kilometer of the sea. Unless the government takes vigorous action, one of the last remaining wild shorelines in Europe may become just a memory.

The seashore adjoining the population centers around Riga was a major focus of tourism during the Soviet era. Jurmala, with its many sanatoriums and tourist accommodations, its tall pines, sandy beaches, and antique architecture, is now experiencing a wrenching readjustment. East European tourists can no longer afford to come here, and Western tourists have not yet discovered the area and its relatively low prices. West Europeans may be loath to come, however, because excessive pollution has closed Jurmala beaches to swimming since 1988. Moreover, facilities and accommodations adequate for Soviet tastes fall far short of minimal standards expected in the West.

Latvia has an abundant network of rivers, contributing to the visual beauty and the economy of the country. The largest river is the Daugava, which has been an important route for several thousand years. It has been used by local tribes as well as by Vikings, Russians, and other Europeans for trade, war, and conquest. With a total length of 1,020 kilometers, the Daugava (or Zapadnaya Dvina in its upper reaches) originates in the Valday Hills in Russia's Tver' Oblast, meanders through northern Belarus, and then winds through Latvia for 370 kilometers before emptying into the Gulf of Riga. It is about 200 meters wide when it enters Latvia, increasing to between 650 and 750 meters at Riga and to 1.5 kilometers at its mouth.

The river carries an average annual flow of twenty-one cubic kilometers. Its total descent within Latvia of ninety-eight meters has made it an attractive source of hydroelectric power production. The first hydroelectric station, at Kegums, was built during Latvia's independence period. The second dam, at Plavinas, aroused an unusual wave of protest in 1958. Most Latvians opposed the flooding of historical sites and a particularly scenic gorge with rare plants and natural features, such as the Staburags, a cliff comparable in cultural significance to the Lorelei in Germany. The construction of the dam was endorsed in 1959, however, after the purge of relatively liberal and nationally oriented leaders under Berklavs and their replacement by Moscow-oriented, ideologically conservative cadres led by Pelse. The third dam, just above Riga, did not provoke much protest because of the seeming hopelessness of the cause. The proposed fourth dam, at the town of Daugavpils on the Daugava River, became the rallying point for protest in 1986–87 by hundreds of thousands of Latvians. This dam was not constructed, in spite of the vast expenditures already poured into the project.

Smaller rivers include the Lielupe, in central Latvia, with an average annual flow of 3.6 cubic kilometers; the Venta, in the west, with 2.9 cubic kilometers; the Gauja, in the northeast, with 2.5 cubic kilometers; and the Aivikste, in the east, with 2.1 cubic kilometers. Very little hydroelectric power is generated by their waters, although planners are now thinking of reactivating some of the abandoned older dams and turbines. The Gauja is one of Latvia's most attractive, relatively clean rivers and has an adjoining large national park along both of its banks as one of its notable features. Its cold waters attract trout and salmon, and its sandstone cliff and forest setting are increasingly a magnet for tourists interested in the environment.

More than 60 percent of the annual water volume of Latvia's six largest rivers comes from neighboring countries, mainly from Belarus and Lithuania. These adjoining resources create obvious needs for cooperation, especially in pollution control. The dangers from a lack of cooperation were brought home to Latvians in November 1990, when a polymer complex in Navapolatsk, Belarus, accidentally spilled 128 tons of cyanide derivatives into the Daugava River with no warning to downstream users in Latvia. Only the presence of numerous dead fish alerted Latvian inhabitants to the danger.

Climate

Latvia's northern location matches Labrador's latitude. In the summer, daylight hours are much longer and in the winter much shorter than in New York City, for example. In December it is still pitch dark at 9:00 A.M., and daylight disappears before 4:00 P.M. This light deprivation may be an important ingredient in deciphering certain aspects of Latvian collective behavior. It may account for the general exuberance and joie de vivre in spring and summer, and the relative taciturnity and melancholy the rest of the year. The climate is far different from that of Labrador, however, because of the effect of the Gulf Stream flowing across the Atlantic Ocean from Mexico. Average temperatures in winter are reasonably mild, ranging in January from −2.8°C in Liepaja, on the western coast, to −6.6°C in the southeastern town of Daugavpils. July temperatures range from 16.7°C in Liepaja to 17.6°C in Daugavpils. Latvia's proximity to the sea brings high levels of humidity and precipitation, with average annual precipitation of 566 millimeters in Riga. There, an average of 180 days per year have precipitation, forty-four days have fog, and only seventy-two days are sunny. Continuous snow cover lasts eighty-two days, and the frost-free period lasts 177 days.

This precipitation has helped provide the abundant water for Latvia's many rivers and lakes, but it has created many problems as well. A large part of agricultural land requires drainage. Much money has been spent for amelioration projects involving the installation of drainage pipes, the straightening and deepening of natural streams, the digging of drainage ditches, and the construction of polder dams. During the 1960s and 1970s, drainage work absorbed about one-third of all agricultural investments in Latvia. Although accounting for only one-third of 1 percent of the territory, Latvia was responsible for 11 percent of all artificially drained land in the Soviet Union.

An additional problem associated with precipitation is the difficulty of early mechanized sowing and harvesting because of waterlogged fields. Heavy precipitation occurs, especially during harvest time in August and September, requiring heavy investment outlays in grain-drying structures and ventilation systems. In 1992, ironically, Latvia experienced the driest summer in recorded weather history, but unusually heavy rains in the preceding spring kept crop damage below the extent expected. The moist climate has been a major factor orienting Latvian agriculture toward animal husbandry and dairying. Even most of the field crops, such as barley, oats, and potatoes, are grown for animal feed.

View of Riga, with pavilions of the central market in center and the
Daugava River in rear
Courtesy Roland Sudmalis
Street in Liepaja
Courtesy Linda Sudmalis

Natural Resources

Latvia cannot claim valuable natural resources. Nevertheless, the abundant presence of such materials as limestone for cement (6 billion cubic meters), gypsum (165 million cubic meters), high-quality clay (375 million cubic meters), dolomite (615 million cubic meters), peat (480 million tons), and construction materials, including gravel and sand, satisfy local needs. Fish from the Baltic Sea is another potential export resource export. Amber, million-year-old chunks of petrified pine pitch, is often found on the beaches of the Baltic Sea and is in high demand for jewelry. It has also had a symbolic impact on the country, which is often called Dzimtarzeme, or Amberland. The future may hold potentially more valuable resources if oil fields are discovered in Latvian territorial waters, as some geologists have predicted.

Society

Population

Latvia's population has been multiethnic for centuries. In 1897 the first official census in this area indicated that Latvians formed 68.3 percent of the total population of 1.93 million; Russians accounted for 12.0 percent, Jews for 7.4 percent, Germans for 6.2 percent, and Poles for 3.4 percent. The remainder were Lithuanians, Estonians, Gypsies, and various other nationalities.

World War I and the emergence of an independent Latvia led to shifts in ethnic composition. By 1935, when the total population was about 1.9 million, the proportion of Latvians had increased to 77.0 percent of the population, and the percentages for all other groups had decreased. In spite of heavy war casualties and the exodus of many Latvians to Russia, in absolute terms the number of Latvians had grown by 155,000 from 1897 to 1935, marking the highest historical level of Latvian presence in the republic. Other groups, however, declined, mostly as a result of emigration. The largest change occurred among Germans (from 121,000 to 62,100) and Jews (from 142,000 to 93,400). During World War II, most Germans in Latvia were forced by Adolf Hitler's government to leave for Germany as a result of the expected occupation of Latvia by Stalin's troops. The Jews suffered the greatest tragedy, however, when between 70,000 and 80,000 of them were executed by the

Nazi occupation forces between 1941 and 1944. Latvians also suffered population losses during this period as a result of deportations, executions, and the flight of refugees to the West. By 1959 there were 169,100 fewer Latvians in absolute terms than in 1935, in spite of the accumulated natural increase of twenty-four years and the return of many Latvians from other parts of the Soviet Union after 1945.

The balance of ethnic groups in 1959 reflected the vagaries of war and the interests of the occupying power. The Latvian share of the population had decreased to 62.0 percent, but that of the Russians had jumped from 8.8 percent to 26.6 percent. The other Slavic groups—Belorussians, Ukrainians, and Poles—together accounted for 7.2 percent, and the Jews formed 1.7 percent. Indeed, one of the greatest concerns Latvians had during the almost half-century under Soviet rule was the immigration of hundreds of non-Latvians, which drastically changed the ethnic complexion of the republic. Even more, with each successive census Latvians saw their share of the population diminish, from 56.8 percent in 1970 to 54.0 percent in 1979 and to 52.0 percent in 1989 (see table 15, Appendix). With each year, a net average of 11,000 to 15,000 non-Latvian settlers came to the republic, and such migration accounted for close to 60 percent of the annual population growth. The newcomers were generally younger, and hence their higher rates of natural increase helped to diminish the Latvian proportion even more.

The threat of becoming a minority in their own land was one of the most important elements animating the forces of political rebirth. There was a widespread feeling that once Latvians lost their majority status, they would be on the road to extinction. During the period of the national awakening in the late 1980s, this sentiment produced a pervasive mood of intense anxiety, perhaps best expressed by the popular slogan "Now or Never." It also came across very bluntly in "The Latvian Nation and the Genocide of Immigration," the title of a paper prepared by an official of the Popular Front of Latvia in 1990. By then, largely as a result of the great influx of new settlers encouraged by Soviet authorities, Latvians were a minority in six of the largest cities in Latvia (see table 16, Appendix). Even in the capital city of Riga, Latvians had shrunk to only about a third of the population. Thus, they were forced to adapt to a Russian-speaking majority, with all of its attendant cultural and social patterns. There was not a single city district in Riga where Latvians could hope to transact business using only Latvian. This predominantly Russian atmosphere has proved difficult to change, in spite of the formal declaration of Latvian independence and the passing of several Latvianization laws.

Even in the countryside of certain regions, Latvians are under cultural and linguistic stress from their unilingual neighbors. The most multinational area outside of cities can be found in the province of Latgale in the southeastern part of Latvia. There the Daugavpils district (excluding the city) in 1989 was 35.9 percent Latvian, Kraslava district 43.1 percent, Rezekne district (excluding the city) 53.3 percent, and Ludza district 53.4 percent. For several decades, Latvians in these districts were forced to attend Russian-language schools because of the dearth or absence of Latvian schools. Not surprisingly, during the Soviet period there was a process of assimilation to the Russian-language group. With the advent of independence, Latgale has become a focal point for official and unofficial programs of Latvianization, which include the opening of new Latvian schools, the printing of new Latvian local newspapers, and the opening of a Latvian television station for Latgalians. A major thrust in Latvianization is also provided by the resurgent Roman Catholic Church and its clergy.

Most Latvians themselves are not aware that by 1989 they had become a minority of the population in the usually most active age-group of twenty to forty-four (see table 17, Appendix). In the age category of thirty-five to thirty-nine, Latvians were down to 43.0 percent of the total. The period spanning the years from the late teens to middle age usually provides the most important pool of people for innovation and entrepreneurship (see fig. 8). The relatively low Latvian demographic presence in this group could partly account for the much smaller visibility of Latvians in the privatization and business entrepreneurship process within the republic.

Population Changes since Independence

In 1994, according to official estimates, Latvia had a population of 2,565,854 people. This figure was smaller than for the 1989 census (2,666,567), reflecting a fundamental change in the demography of Latvia. The population in the republic decreased for the first time since 1945, except in 1949 when more than 40,000 Latvians were deported. Between January 1989 and January 1994, the total decrease was more than 100,000.

Two important factors have contributed to this change. During 1991, 1992, and 1993, the natural increase was negative; in other words, more people died than were born. The moving variable has been the number of births. In 1991 the total number born was only 34,633, which was 8.7 percent less than in the previous year and 18 percent less than in 1987 (see table 18, Appendix). The number of deaths remained about constant. For the first time since 1946, more deaths than births occurred in 1991—by a margin of 116. This gap increased significantly in 1992, when 3,851 more deaths than births were recorded. The death rate increased from 13.5 per 1,000 in 1992 to 16.3 per 1,000 in 1994, and the birth rate fell from 12.9 per 1,000 in 1992 to 9.5 per 1,000 in 1994. The postponement by many families of procreation is not surprising in view of the economic traumas suffered by most people and the general political and economic uncertainties prevailing in the country.

An even more important factor at work in the overall decrease of population has been the net out-migration of mostly nonindigenous individuals (see table 19, Appendix). The principal factors affecting the direction of migration included Latvia's declaration of independence and its laws checking uncontrolled immigration into the country. Independence brought a shift in political power to the Latvian group. Many individuals who could not adjust to living in a newly "foreign" country or who did not want to accommodate the new Latvian language requirements in certain categories of employment decided to leave.

A sociological poll published in November 1992 indicated that 55 percent of non-Latvians would not move east (that is, to other parts of the former Soviet Union) even if they were offered a job and living accommodations; 19 percent expressed a willingness to do so (3 percent only temporarily); and 26 percent said they did not know whether they would move. Only about 205,000 non-Latvians out of 1.3 million living in Latvia were willing to leave permanently if offered jobs and roofs over their heads. Aside from economic considerations, this surprisingly strong attachment to Latvia by non-Latvian ethnic groups is attributable to the fact that many of them were born in Latvia and have had little if any contact with their forebears' geographical areas of origin. According to the 1989 census, of the non-Latvian ethnic groups in the country, about 66 percent of Poles, 55 percent of Russians, 53 percent of Jews, 36 percent of

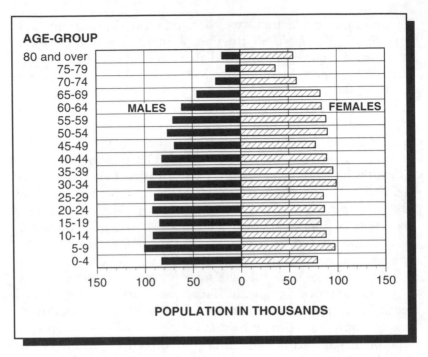

Source: Based on information from Latvia, Valsts Statistikas Komiteja, *Latvija Skaitlos,*
    1993 (*Latvia in Figures, 1993*), Riga, 1994, 16.

Figure 8. Population of Latvia by Age and Gender, 1993

Lithuanians, 31 percent of Belorussians, and 19 percent of
Ukrainians had been born in Latvia (see table 20, Appendix).

Marriage and Divorce

In spite of Latvians' fears of becoming a minority and in
spite of the strains caused by Russification and language ineq-
uities, a relatively high proportion of Latvians have married
members of other ethnic groups. Some 30 percent of marriages involving Latvians were of mixed nationality in 1988
(although only 17 percent of all marrying Latvians in 1988
entered into mixed marriages). This rate of intermarriage was
one of the highest of any titular nationality in the republics of
the Soviet Union. Comparable rates were found in Belorussia
(34.6 percent) and Ukraine (35.6 percent); a much lower rate
was found in Estonia (16.1 percent). The marriage statistics of
1991 do not indicate any significant changes in this respect,

with just under 18 percent of all Latvians marrying members of other ethnic groups.

Latvia has an extremely high divorce rate, but there is no adequate explanation for it. In 1991 Latvia registered 22,337 weddings and 11,070 divorces, for a divorce rate of 49.6 percent. Among various ethnic groups, these rates vary: Latvian males, 39.1 percent, and females, 39.9 percent; Lithuanian males, 52.7 percent, and females, 45.0 percent; Polish males, 43.7 percent, and females, 54.5 percent; Russian males, 60.2 percent, and females, 58.3 percent; Belarusian males, 58.8 percent, and females, 61.0 percent; Ukrainian males, 64.4 percent, and females, 65.2 percent; Jewish males, 67.6 percent, and females, 65.9 percent; and males of other ethnic groups, 64.8 percent, and females, 70.0 percent. During the first nine months of 1992, as compared with the same period in 1991, marriages decreased by 10 percent, but divorces increased by 24 percent. For every 1,000 marriages, there were 683 divorces.

Perhaps the instability of marriage accounts for the relatively high percentage of births outside of marriage. In 1989 in Latvia, 15.9 percent of infants were born to women who were not married. In Lithuania the comparative rate was 6.5 percent, but in Estonia the rate was 25.2 percent. In the Soviet Union as a whole in 1988, the rate was 10.2 percent.

Urbanization, Employment, and Education

Latvia was one of the most urbanized republics of the former Soviet Union, reaching an urbanization rate of 71 percent in 1990. Subsequently, the rate of urbanization decreased and was estimated to be 69.5 percent in 1992. Part of the reason for the decline no doubt can be found in the out-migration of non-Latvians to other republics. It seems probable, as well, that a slight shift back to rural areas occurred as a result of the start-up of some 50,000 private farms.

The rapid economic changes of the early 1990s have brought about an employment reorientation by various ethnic groups. The division of labor between Latvians and non-Latvians that prevailed in 1987, the most recent year for which such data are available, offers a general indication of where the groups work. The Latvian share was above average in culture and art (74.6 percent), agriculture (69.5 percent), public education (58.8 percent), communications (56.7 percent), administration (56.4 percent), credit and state insurance (55.1 percent), and health care and social security (53.5 percent).

Latvians were significantly underrepresented in heavy industry (36.3 percent), light industry (33.6 percent), machine building (31.0 percent), the chemical industry (30.1 percent), railroad transport (26.5 percent), and water transport (11.5 percent). The work categories facing the greatest threat of unemployment are those with the fewest Latvians. This may create future strains and possible confrontations between Latvians and non-Latvians if solutions are not found.

In the long run, however, higher education might be an important variable in advancement and adjustment to new economic situations. In 1989 only ninety-six out of 1,000 Latvians completed higher education, compared with 115 out of 1,000 for the entire population. The most educated were Jews, with a rate of 407 per 1,000 completing higher education, followed by Ukrainians with 163 and Russians with 143. Belorussians, Poles, and Lithuanians had a rate below that of the Latvians. One of the key variables accounting for this spread in educational achievements is rural-urban location. Jews and Russians are much more urban than Latvians or Poles. It is difficult to compete in entrance examinations after attending schools in rural areas where there are regular official interruptions in the fall for harvesting and in the spring for planting. Distances and poor transportation networks provide another obstacle to completing secondary school. Most institutions of higher learning are located in Riga. Unless one has relatives or friends there, it is difficult to find living accommodations. Student residences can cater to only a small proportion of applicants.

One of the unique aspects of the Latvian education system was the introduction during the 1960s of schools with two languages of instruction, Latvian and Russian, in which each group held classes in its own language. About a third of all schoolchildren went to these schools, and the others attended the purely Latvian or Russian schools. Extracurricular activities and parent-teacher events were expected to be held together, and almost inevitably they were conducted in Russian because of the imbalance in language knowledge. These schools did not foster interethnic friendship, as originally hoped, and they were being phased out in post-Soviet Latvia. In the 1993–94 school year, sixty-nine out of 574 such primary schools remained.

All children, from about the age of six, must complete nine years of primary schooling, which may be followed by three years of secondary education or one to six years in technical,

*Dinner preparations in
households in Riga and
Priekule, near Liepaja
Courtesy Linda Sudmalis*

vocational, or art schools. In the 1993–94 school year, a total of 76,619 students were enrolled in primary schools, 242,677 in secondary schools, 27,881 in vocational schools, 19,476 in special secondary institutions, and 7,211 in special schools for the physically and mentally handicapped. There were eighteen universities and other institutions of higher education, with 36,428 students. The literacy rate approached 100 percent.

One of the innovations introduced with independence was the reestablishment of schools or programs for other ethnic groups. Before the Soviet occupation in 1940, Latvia had more than 300 state-supported schools offering instruction for different ethnic groups: 144 Russian, sixty Jewish, sixteen Polish, thirteen Lithuanian, four Estonian, one Belorussian, and eighty-five with several languages of instruction. All of these except the Russian schools were closed after 1945. After 1990 various ethnic groups were offered the opportunity of again maintaining schools in their own language of instruction, and by the 1993–94 school year some 210 schools were in operation: more than 200 Russian, four Polish, one Estonian, one Lithuanian, one Ukrainian, and one Jewish. Latvia had the first Jewish secondary school in the entire Soviet Union. It should be noted that most of the non-Latvian groups had largely assimilated with the Russians, and many of their members did not speak their native tongue.

Health and Welfare

In the early 1990s, the health care system that Latvia inherited from the Soviet regime had yet to meet Western standards. It continued to be hampered by shortages of basic medical supplies, including disposable needles, anesthetics, and antibiotics. In 1992 there were some 176 hospitals, with 130 beds per 10,000 inhabitants—more than in Estonia and Lithuania—but they were old, lacked modern facilities, and were concentrated in urban areas. The number of physicians, forty-one per 10,000 inhabitants, was high by international standards, but there were too few nurses and other paramedical personnel.

At a time when most of the modern world was experiencing rapid strides in the extension of average life span, the Soviet Union and Latvia were going backward. Between 1965 and 1990, the male life span in Latvia decreased 2.4 years, from 66.6 to 64.2 years. For females, there was a decrease between 1965 and 1979 from 74.4 to 73.9 years, but the average life span rose to 74.6 by 1990. In comparison, in 1989 the average life expect-

Polyclinic in Priekule, with ambulance in front
Courtesy Roland Sudmalis

ancy in the Soviet Union was 64.6 for males and 74.0 years for
females. Overall, Latvia then ranked eighth among the Soviet
republics. For males, however, Latvia was eleventh, ahead of
three Soviet Central Asian republics and Russia. Among
females, Latvia did better, sharing fourth ranking with Ukraine.

According to the calculations of a Latvian demographer in
1938–39, Latvia was about thirteen years ahead of the Soviet
Union in life expectancy. No doubt, an important role in less-
ening the average life span statistics was played by the massive
in-migration of people after 1945 from mostly rural and pov-
erty-stricken parts of the Soviet Union. Even in 1988–89, within
Latvia there was a difference of 0.8 year between Latvian and
Russian life expectancy. Standardized rates that account for
urban and rural differences show that Latvians live 1.7 years
longer than Russians.

Perhaps no other index of the role of Sovietization is as indicative as the gap in life expectancy between Latvia and Finland, the Baltic states' northern neighbor. In 1988 Finland registered life span rates of 70.7 years for males and 78.7 for females, which were 6.5 and 4.1 years higher than the respective rates in Latvia. By 1994 life expectancy in Latvia had increased only marginally: 64.4 years for males and 74.8 years for females, compared with Finland's rates of 72.1 years for males and 79.9 years for females. During the 1930s, Latvia's rates had been higher than those in Finland and on a par with those of Austria, Belgium, France, and Scotland.

The infant mortality rate rose to 17.4 deaths per 1,000 live births in 1992, after a steady decline beginning in 1970 and an estimated eleven deaths per 1,000 live births in 1988. Its rate was higher than that of Estonia and Lithuania and almost three times the rate of infant mortality in Finland. In 1994 there were 16.3 deaths per 1,000 population in Latvia. The primary causes of infant deaths in Latvia are perinatal diseases; congenital anomalies; infectious, parasitic, or intestinal diseases; respiratory diseases; and accidents and poisonings. Environmental factors and alcoholism and drug abuse also contribute to infant mortality.

Latvia outpaced most of the other republics in the Soviet Union in deaths from accidents, poisonings, and traumas. In 1989 some 16 percent of males and 5.6 percent of females died from these causes. The suicide rate of 25.9 per 100,000 in 1990, or a total of 695, was more than twice that of the United States. In 1992 the number of suicides increased to 883. Other major causes of death include cancer, respiratory conditions, and such stress-related afflictions as heart disease and stroke. Although drug addiction and acquired immune deficiency syndrome (AIDS) are on the increase, their incidences are not yet close to those in many Western countries.

Traffic deaths in 1990 reached a rate of 43.5 per 100,000 population, or a total of 1,167. There were 245 homicides in 1990, a rate of 9.1 per 100,000. This increase represented a dramatic jump from 1988, when the rate was 5.8, and from 1985, when it was 5.2. The greater availability of weapons has been one cause. More important, Riga and other cities have been targeted by mafia-style criminal gangs intent on carving up and stabilizing their areas of operation against other gangs. Still another cause is the decrease in the efficiency of law enforcement organs because of low pay, rapid turnover of cadres, lack of gasoline for automobiles, and language problems. The rise in criminal activity has increased Latvians' stress, interfered with their enjoyment of life, and impaired their well-being, health, and physical survival.

Another important ingredient affecting the survival of people in Latvia includes dangerous life-styles and substance abuse. Alcohol consumption rose from an average per capita rate of 1.9 liters per year in the 1920–34 period to 11.7 liters per year in 1985. This sixfold increase in alcohol consumption has had deleterious effects in many other areas of life and health and is one of the main causes of traffic deaths, drownings, fires, and crime.

Most Latvian males are inveterate smokers. A study of six cities in the mid-1980s discovered that 63 percent of men were active smokers, 13 percent had quit, and only 24 percent had never smoked. Smoking takes a particularly heavy toll in Latvia because the allowable tar content in cigarettes is high (three times as great as in Finland), most of the cheaper brands do not have a filter, and most men prefer to inhale deeply. There is a high incidence of illnesses related to smoking and environmental pollution, such as emphysema, lung cancer, bronchial asthma, and bronchitis.

Another habit dangerous to health is the preference for fatty diets and minimal attention to exercise. The economic hardships of recent years appear to have decreased the number of grossly overweight people. This may be one of the few unintended benefits of the reconstruction period.

The total number of pension recipients in Latvia grew from 603,600 in 1990 to 657,700 in 1993. Old-age pensions accounted for the largest number of awards (500,300), followed by disability pensions (104,200) and survivor's pensions (26,300). Old-age pensions remained very low, ranging from LVL15 to LVL23.5 (for value of the lats—see Glossary) per month, depending on the number of years of work.

Religion

In 1935, before Latvia's occupation, official statistics indicated a fairly broad spectrum of religious traditions. Evangelical Lutheranism was the single most widespread creed, claiming the attachment of 55.2 percent of the population and 68.3 percent of ethnic Latvians. Roman Catholicism was the second most popular choice, preferred by 24.5 percent of the population and 26.4 percent of ethnic Latvians. Because it was especially entrenched in the economically less-developed southeastern province of Latgale (70 percent in this region) and was commonly seen as being regional rather than national, Roman Catholicism's impact on the secular world of politics and culture appeared muted in comparison with that of Lutheranism. The Orthodox Church of Latvia had a following of 9 percent of the population, with its greatest concentration among Russians and other Slavs but with 33 percent of its support also coming from ethnic Latvians. Old Believers (see Glossary), constituting 5.5 percent of the population, are a unique Russian fundamentalist sect whose forebears had fled persecution from the tsarist empire in the seventeenth century and had found refuge in then Swedish- and Polish-controlled Latvia. About 5 percent of Latvia's citizens were Jewish. The rest of the pre-World War II population was scattered among an array of Protestant denominations.

World War II and a half-century of Soviet occupation and persecution of believers fundamentally changed the religious spectrum. The Evangelical Lutheran Church, with an estimated 600,000 members in 1956, was affected most adversely. An internal document of March 18, 1987, spoke of an active membership that had shrunk to only 25,000. By 1994 religious congregations in Latvia numbered 819, of which 291 were Lutheran, 192 Roman Catholic, 100 Orthodox, fifty-six Old Believer, seventy Baptist, forty-nine Pentecostal, thirty-three Seventh-Day Adventist, five Jewish, three Methodist, and two Reformed.

Part of the explanation of the diminished status of Latvia's Lutheran Church is to be found in its relative weakness as an institution, unable to withstand the pressures of occupation as robustly as the Roman Catholic Church. For centuries Latvian attachment to Lutheranism was rather tepid, in part because this religion had been brought by the Baltic barons and German-speaking clergy. During Latvia's earlier independence period (1920–40), efforts were made to Latvianize this church. Original Latvian hymns were composed, Latvian clergy became predominant, and the New Testament was translated into modern Latvian. During the tribulations of World War II, Latvians intensified their religiosity, but at the same time the Lutheran Church suffered serious losses. Many of the most religious and talented individuals and clergy fled as refugees to the West or were deported to Siberia. A large number of church buildings were demolished by war action.

Day care center in Priekule
Courtesy Linda Sudmalis

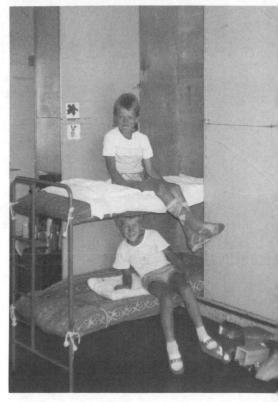

The Roman Catholic Church had a much closer historical bonding with its flock. During the period of national revival through the latter part of the nineteenth century in Latgale, the clergy were among the leaders of enlightenment and an important bastion against Russification. They nurtured and were themselves members of the Latgalian intelligentsia. During the years of communist occupation, the greater commitment demanded by the Roman Catholic Church helped maintain a higher degree of solidarity against atheist incursions. For the church, the practice of confession was a useful method for monitoring the mood of the population and for organizing initiatives to counter or prevent serious cleavages or even surreptitious activities by the communist leadership. Direct guidance from Rome offered some protection against the manipulation of clergy by state functionaries. Finally, the population of Latgale did not have the same opportunity to flee from Latvia because it was cut off earlier from access to the seacoast by the Red Army. Roman Catholic clergy, who were unmarried, were also more inclined to remain with their religious charges, whereas Lutheran clergy had to take into account the safety of their families.

Most Latvian Jews were annihilated by the Nazis during World War II. After the war, a certain number of Jews from other parts of the Soviet Union settled in Latvia. Many of them had already endured antireligious campaigns under Stalin, and there were many obstacles placed in the way of reviving Jewish religious activity. Most former Latvian synagogues were confiscated by the state for other uses, and nowhere in the entire Soviet Union did there exist any centers for rabbinical education. After Latvia's independence in 1991, there was a resurgence of interest in religious affairs. Five Jewish congregations served the growth in demand for services.

The statistics for 1991 point to an interesting pattern (see table 21, Appendix). At that time, far more people were baptized than married in church. Part of the explanation can be found in the requirement by some religions, including Lutheranism, that people must be first baptized and confirmed before having a religious wedding. Another possible explanation for this phenomenon is that the communist state was quite successful in sowing doubts about religion among the young and the middle-aged. Many, especially former members of the Komsomol and the communist party, feel uncomfortable in their personal relationship with the church but also have a desire to open more options for their offspring. Indeed, it is a common phenomenon to see nonreligious parents sending their children to Sunday school for the sake of "character building." In the process, however, some of the parents have become tied to a church and have joined the congregation.

During communist rule, every effort was made to curtail the influence of religion. All potential avenues of contact with the population were cut off. Schools, media, books, and workplaces were all off-limits to religious organizations. Even charity work was forbidden. Indeed, the family itself was not at liberty to guide children into active church work until the age of eighteen. Thus, no Sunday schools, religious choirs, or camps were open to young people. Religious publications, with a few exceptions, were limited to yearbooks and song sheets for Sunday services. Regular churchgoers were subject to various pressures, including harassment at work and comradely visits by local atheists. Anyone with career ambitions had to forgo visible links with religion. The state successfully preempted the most important church ceremonies of baptism, confirmation, weddings, and funerals by secular ceremonies. In 1986 the Lutheran Church registered 1,290 baptisms, 212 confirmations, 142 marriages, and 605 funerals—a fraction of the activity that was to occur in 1991. Evidently, a revolution in the status of the church occurred within that brief period.

Starting with 1987, the Lutheran Church experienced a revival pioneered by a group of young, rebellious, and very well-educated clergy who formed the organization Rebirth and Renewal (Atdzimsana un Atjaunosana). There were confrontations with communist authorities and with the ossified hierarchy of the Lutheran Church itself, which had become somnolent and very accommodating to the demands of secular powers. With the advent of political plurality, the Lutheran Church was able to expand its role and its activities. Church buildings were refurbished, demolished churches were renewed, Sunday schools were opened, religious education was provided in day schools, and the media reported sermons and religious discussions. For several years after the liberalization of church activities, religion became extremely fashionable. Part of this boom, as acknowledged by the Lutheran clergy, was a rebellion against authorities that coincided with the general political effervescence.

The Roman Catholic Church also went through a process of renewal, but its changes were not as marked because it had been able to maintain a strong presence in the population even under the most adverse conditions. Thus, in 1985 the Roman Catholics performed 5,167 baptisms, about five times as many as the Lutherans. In 1991 the Roman Catholics performed 10,661 baptisms, more than double the number in 1985. Among the Roman Catholics baptized in 1991, only 40 percent had been born in families in which the parents had married in church.

A major change in the geography of the Roman Catholic Church also presented problems. Whereas in 1935 more than 70 percent of Roman Catholics resided in the southeastern province of Latgale, by 1990 only 42 percent lived there. Thus, many Roman Catholics lived throughout Latvia, where often no churches of their creed existed. There has been much ecumenical goodwill, and the more numerous Lutheran churches are being used by Roman Catholics and by other religious groups. Administratively, the Roman Catholic Church comprises the Archdiocese of Riga and the Diocese of Liepaja.

Latvia's Roman Catholic Church received a great moral boost in February 1983 when Bishop Julijans Vaivods was made a cardinal. This was the first such appointment in the history of Latvia and the first within the Soviet Union. No doubt part of the willingness of the communist party to accommodate the Roman Catholic Church in this way was the fact that Vaivods was eighty-seven years old in 1983. Yet, he confounded the communists by living until May 1990, thus providing more than seven years of leadership.

Vaivods, who studied theology in St. Petersburg and was an eyewitness to the Bolshevik Revolution, was also an extremely able tactician. His efforts on behalf of the Roman Catholic Church in the Soviet Union are a classic case of stubborn, low-key, but effective opposition to party pressure. The Soviet regime had decided to allow Roman Catholic congregations outside Latvia and Lithuania to die by not allowing them new clergy. Almost daily, delegations of Roman Catholic faithful from various parts of the Soviet Union came to Vaivods during the 1960s pleading for help. He sent Latvian priests to Leningrad (St. Petersburg), Tallinn, and other cities, in spite of local shortages. When pressed by the delegations to allow their own people to enroll in Latvia's Roman Catholic seminary, Vaivods made it clear that the obstacle was not the church but rather state authorities who had given him instructions to claim that the seminary was too small. Under pressure, the authorities

St. Gertrude's Church in Riga
Courtesy Debbie Horrell

relented and allowed a trickle of seminarians from outside Latvia, but as punishment they took away almost half of the seminary's rooms. The church skimped and struggled but did not change its policy. By 1978 the expropriated space was returned, and three years later permission was granted for the construction of a new seminary. Thereafter, seminarian numbers increased rapidly from eighteen in 1980 to 107 in 1989. Most of the students were non-Latvians slated for service in other areas of the Soviet Union.

Latvian Lutherans also provided help to their brethren in other Soviet republics. Lutheran clergy were trained in Latvia for Lithuania. More important, Bishop Haralds Kalnins single-handedly took care of scattered German Lutherans outside the Baltic region. Besides ministering and preaching, he was empowered to ordain religious workers and to settle questions of theological education. In one six-day trip to Kazakhstan in 1976, the bishop held seven services in which 400 people received Holy Communion, twenty children were christened, thirty-five youths were confirmed, and ten couples were married. He was able to carry this load in spite of his advanced age.

The pre-World War II independent Orthodox Church of Latvia was subordinated to the Moscow Patriarchate after the war, and its new clergy were trained in seminaries in Russia. It remained a major religious organization in Latvia because of the heavy influx of Russians and other Orthodox Slavs after the war. Only in 1992 did the Orthodox Church of Latvia become administratively independent once again. Its cathedral in the center of Riga had been transformed by the communists into a planetarium with an adjoining coffee shop popularly dubbed "In God's Ear." The cathedral is now being restored to its original architecture and purpose.

With the advent of independence, several other changes were introduced as well. Potential Lutheran pastors could now receive their training through the Faculty of Theology, which is affiliated with the University of Latvia. The Roman Catholics acquired a modern new seminary, but they had problems recruiting able scholars and teachers as well as students. Most Roman Catholic seminarians from outside Latvia have returned to their respective republics, and new seminarians are being trained locally. The new freedoms have allowed many other religious groups to proselytize and recruit members. Under conditions of economic and political uncertainty, their efforts are bearing fruit. Such denominations as the Baptists,

Pentecostals, and Seventh-Day Adventists have made significant inroads. Charismatic movements, animists, Hare Krishna, and the Salvation Army have all attempted to fill a void in Latvia's spiritual life. Undoubtedly, there is great interest among Latvians in spiritual matters, but it is difficult to know how much of it is genuine and how much reflects the ebb and flow of fashion and will be replaced by other trends.

Language and Culture

The Latvian language, like Lithuanian, belongs to the Baltic branch of the Indo-European family of languages. Latvian is an inflective language, written in the Latin script and influenced syntactically by German. The oldest known examples of written Latvian are from catechisms published in 1585. Because of the heavy influx of ethnic Russians and other Slavs after World War II, nearly one-half of the country's population does not speak Latvian (see table 22, Appendix). Most ethnic Latvians speak Russian, however, and many also know German (see table 23, Appendix).

Latvian culture is strongly influenced by folklore and by the people's attachment to their land. Christian rituals often are intermingled with ancient customs, and pagan geometric symbols remain evident in the applied arts. Ancient folksongs, or *dainas*, that were first collected and published in the mid-nineteenth century, most notably by Krisjanis Barons, are a cultural treasure. In 1888 the great epic poem *Lacplesis* (Bear Slayer) by Andrejs Pumpurs was published, marking the dawn of modern Latvian literature. Janis Rainis (1865–1929) usually tops the list of Latvia's greatest writers. One of the most prominent figures in Latvian literature today is the poet Imants Ziedonis, who also has established a fund to promote the development of Latvian culture.

Latvia has a number of theaters (mostly in Riga), an opera, a symphony orchestra, and a permanent circus. Riga's Dome Cathedral houses one of the largest and most famous organs in the world. The works of many prominent Latvian artists are displayed at the National Fine Arts Museum and at the many art galleries in Riga. Other museums include the Museum of History and Navigation and the Museum of Natural History. There are 168 public libraries in the capital. Books and periodicals are published in Latvian and in other languages.

Economy

The Latvian economy, much like that of other former Soviet republics in the 1990s, is going through an extremely difficult period of adjustment and rapid change. Hence, all statistics and assessments are subject to dramatic change.

Historical Legacy

For Latvia and the other two Baltic republics, the period of development between 1920 and 1940 is regarded as a guide and a morale booster. Latvians know how wrenching the sudden changes were after World War I. Russia had removed almost all factory equipment, railroad rolling stock, raw materials, bank savings, and valuables to the interior. Almost none of these assets were returned. With the victory of Stalin and the sealing of the Soviet Union to the outside world, Latvia had to change its entire pattern of trade and resource buying. In other words, the Russian market, which had been the basis of the manufacturing industry, was no longer accessible. Moreover, the war had left deep demographic wounds and incalculable material damage. In six years of continuous war, with front lines changing from year to year and even month to month, more than one-quarter of all farm buildings had been devastated; most farm animals had been requisitioned for army supplies; and the land had been lacerated by trenches, barbed wire, and artillery craters. Even trees retained the legacy of war; Latvian timber was dangerous for sawmills because of the heavy concentration of bullets and shrapnel.

Independent Latvia received no foreign aid for rebuilding. On the contrary, it had to squeeze the low incomes of its population to repay war debts incurred by the troops fighting for Latvian independence. In spite of all these obstacles, the economic record of the twenty years is truly impressive. Latvia successfully effected agrarian reform and provided land for hundreds of thousands of the dispossessed. Many of these farmsteads pooled their resources through an extensive system of cooperatives that provided loans, marketing boards, and export credits. The currency was stabilized, inflation was low, unemployment was much better than in West European countries even during the Great Depression years, and foreign debt was not excessive. Perhaps the most objective index of Latvia's economic status is evident from the 10.6 tons of gold that it placed in foreign banks before the invasion of the Red Army.

Most Latvians who remember the period consider it a golden era. Many of its successful economic approaches are being raised in debates today.

The Soviet Period

The half-century of Soviet occupation started with the expropriation without compensation of almost all private property by the state. Within a few years, farms, which had not been nationalized immediately, were forced into collectives in the wake of the deportation of more than 40,000 mostly rural inhabitants in 1949. For many decades, in the struggle between rationality and ideological conformity, or between the so-called "expert" and "red," the latter consideration usually prevailed.

Between 1957 and 1959, a group of Latvian communist functionaries under Eduards Berklavs tried to reorient Latvia toward industries requiring less labor and fewer imports of raw materials. At this time, Pauls Dzerve, an economist and an academician, raised the idea of republican self-accounting and sovereignty. The purges of 1959 replaced these experimenters, and Latvia continued in the race to become the most industrialized republic in the Soviet Union, with a production profile that was almost wholly determined in Moscow. Latvia lost its ability to make economic decisions and to choose optimum directions for local needs. A broad-based division of labor, as seen by Moscow central planners, became the determining guide for production. This division of labor was highly extolled by the Soviet leadership of Latvia. For example, Augusts Voss, first secretary of the Communist Party of Latvia (CPL), summarized this common theme in 1978: "Today, nobody in the whole world, not even our opponents or enemies, can assert that the separate nations of our land working in isolation could have achieved such significant gains in economic and cultural development in the past few decades. The pooling of efforts is a powerful factor in increased development." The extolling of the virtues of a Soviet-style economy included an entire refrain of "self-evident truths," which were aimed at reinforcing the desire of Latvians not just to accept their participation in the division of labor within the Soviet Union but also to support it with enthusiasm.

People in the West often underestimated the effectiveness of the Soviet propaganda machine. The media reinforced the popular images of the decadent and crumbling capitalist economies by portraying scenes of poverty, bag ladies, racial tensions, armies of the unemployed, and luxury dwellings in contrast to slums. The discovery by Russians, and especially by their elites, of the much more nuanced realities of the outer world were important incentives for change and even abandonment of communism. Before that discovery, though, the barrage of propaganda had considerable effect in Latvia. But other factors tended to mitigate or counter its impact. One of these was the collective memory of Latvia's economic achievements during its period of independence. Another was the credible information about the outside world that Latvians received from their many relatives abroad, who began to visit their homeland in the 1960s. Twenty years later, many visitors from Latvia, often going to stay with relatives in the West, were able to see firsthand the life-styles in capitalist countries. During this period of awakening, the argument was clearly made and understood: if Latvia had remained independent, its standard of living would have been similar to that of the Baltic states' northern neighbor, Finland, a standard that was obviously significantly higher than that of Latvia.

By the late 1980s, the virtues of a division of labor within the Soviet Union were no longer articulated even by the CPL leadership. Together with the communist leaders in the other Baltic republics, the CPL leaders desired to distance themselves from a relationship that they were beginning to see as exploitative. Thus, on July 27, 1989, Latvia passed a law on economic sovereignty that was somewhat nebulous but whose direction was clear—away from the centralizing embrace of Moscow.

The shift toward Latvian control of the economy can be seen from the changes in jurisdiction between 1987 and 1990. Although the percentage of the Latvian economy controlled exclusively by Moscow remained about the same (37 percent), the share of the economy controlled jointly declined from 46 to 21 percent, and the share exclusively under Latvia's jurisdiction increased from 17 to 42 percent during this period.

The Soviet division of labor entailed, in the Latvian case, significant imports of raw materials, energy, and workers, as well as exports of finished products. Exports as a proportion of the gross national product (GNP—see Glossary) accounted for 50 percent in 1988, a level similar to that of ten of the other republics but not Russia, which had only a 15 percent export dependency. After the disintegration of the Soviet Union, rising energy prices and the lifting of price controls on many Latvian goods often made them too expensive for the markets of the former Soviet Union, but the technological inferiority of these goods limited their marketability in the West (see Postindependence Economic Difficulties, this ch.).

Economic Sectors

During the postwar era, industry supplanted agriculture as the foremost economic sector. By 1990 industry accounted for almost 43 percent of the gross domestic product (GDP—see Glossary) and for more than 30 percent of the labor force (see table 24, Appendix). Aggressive industrialization and forced relocation of labor, particularly in the 1950s and 1960s, reduced agriculture's share of the labor force from 66 percent in 1930 to about 16 percent in 1990. Agriculture accounted for 20 percent of GDP in 1990; transportation and communications, about 8 percent; construction, less than 6 percent; and trade, services, and other branches, about 20 percent.

Industry

In 1990, 38.9 percent of all industrial personnel in Latvia were employed by the engineering industry (including machine building and electronics) and 17 percent by the textile industry. Other important industries included food (12.7 percent), wood and paper (9.6 percent), chemicals (5.7 percent), and building materials (4.6 percent). Latvia, the most industrialized Baltic state, accounted for all electric and diesel trains produced in the Soviet Union, more than one-half of the telephones, and more than 20 percent of the automatic telephone exchanges, refrigeration systems, and buses.

Because of its deficiency in natural resources, Latvia relies heavily on imports of fuels, electric power, and industrial raw materials. Energy is generated domestically by three hydroelectric power plants on the Daugava River, which have a total capacity of 1,500 megawatts, and by two thermal power plants near Riga, which have a total capacity of 500 megawatts (see fig. 9). In 1991 about 43 percent of total electricity consumed was imported from neighboring states. The country's natural resources are primarily raw construction materials, including dolomite, limestone, clay, gravel, and sand.

Agriculture

In 1990 Latvia had 2,567,000 hectares of agricultural land, 32 percent less than in 1935. More than 1 million hectares of agricultural land, much of it abandoned, were converted to for-

Figure 9. Economic Activity in Latvia, 1995

est under Soviet rule. Of its nearly 1.7 million hectares of arable land, about one-half was used for growing fodder crops,
more than 40 percent for grain, 5 percent for potatoes, and
approximately 2 percent for flax and sugar beets together.

The Soviet authorities socialized agriculture, permitting only
small private plots and animal holdings on the vast state and
collective farms. By 1991, when Latvia regained its independence, a network of more than 400 collective farms, with an

average size of almost 6,000 hectares, and more than 200 state farms, averaging about 7,300 hectares in size, had been created. Private household plots, despite their small size (0.5 hectare, maximum), played a significant role in the agricultural sector by supplementing the output of the notoriously inefficient state and collective farms. In 1991 some 87 percent of all sheep and goats were held on private plots, as were approximately 33 percent of dairy cows and more than 25 percent of cattle.

Under Soviet rule, Latvia became a major supplier of meat and dairy products to the Soviet Union. From 1940 to 1990, livestock production nearly doubled; by contrast, crop cultivation increased by only 14 percent, despite major investments in soil drainage and fertilization projects. In 1990 Latvia exported 10 percent of its meat and 20 percent of its dairy products to other Soviet republics, in return for which it obtained agricultural equipment, fuel, feed grains, and fertilizer. As the centralized Soviet system collapsed, however, a shortage of feed and the rising costs of farm equipment took a toll. From 1990 to 1991, the number of animals on state and collective farms in Latvia fell by up to 23 percent. Consequently, the output of meat, milk products, and eggs from these farms declined by 6 to 7 percent (see table 25, Appendix).

Transportation and Telecommunications

Transportation is a relatively small but important branch of Latvia's economy. The infrastructure is geared heavily toward foreign trade, which is conducted mainly by rail and water. Roads are used for most domestic freight transport.

In 1992 Latvia had 2,406 kilometers of railroads, of which 270 kilometers were electrified. The railroads carried 31.8 million tons of freight and 83.1 million passengers. Most railcars are old, with some having been in service for twenty or more years. Train service is available to Moscow, St. Petersburg, and Warsaw.

Of the 64,693 kilometers of public roads, 7,036 kilometers were highways or national roads and 13,502 kilometers were secondary or regional roads in 1994. Latvia had a fleet of 60,454 trucks and 11,604 buses; private passenger automobiles numbered 367,475. Many, if not most, trucks were more than ten years old. Despite the growing number of automobiles, commuters continued to rely mainly on trains and buses, each of which accounted for 5 billion to 6 billion passenger-kilome-

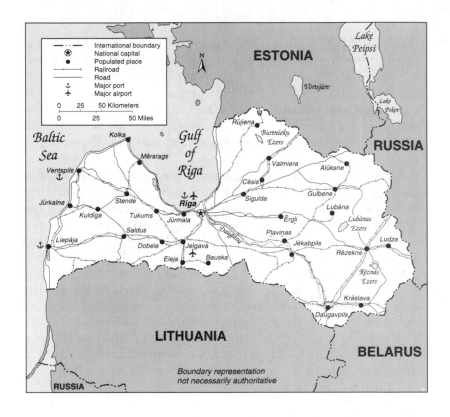

Figure 10. Transportation System of Latvia, 1995

ters per year in the early 1990s. Bus service was provided between Riga and Warsaw.

Latvia's location on the Baltic Sea has provided the country with one of its major economic moneymakers for the future. The three large seaports of Riga, Ventspils, and Liepaja are particularly promising for future trade because they can be used during all seasons and because a dense network of railroads and roads links them with many of the landlocked regions of neighboring countries (see fig. 10). For many years, Riga was the end point for Japanese container traffic originating in the Russian Far East, primarily the port of Nakhodka. This traffic was mostly unidirectional from east to west. With the expected opening up of Japan to incoming world trade, however, European exporters may find that Riga is the best route for their containers bound for Japan or even China.

Ventspils is the end terminal for a Volga Urals crude oil pipe-line built in 1968. Its port has the capacity to service three large ocean tankers simultaneously. The American Occidental Petro-leum Company constructed an industrial chemical complex there providing for the processing and export of raw materials coming from Russia and Belarus.

The port of Liepaja has not yet been involved in major eco-nomic activity because until May 1992 it was still in the hands of the Russian armed forces. The port, which ranks as one of the Baltic Sea's deepest, was restricted for many decades because of its military orientation. Much capital investment will be required to adapt this port for commercial use. With careful development, Liepaja could become an active commercial port. A dozen or so smaller ports that have been used mainly for fishing vessels could also be exploited for the distribution of commercial products.

Riga, Ventspils, and Liepaja together handled about 27.2 million tons of cargo in 1993. That year 16.3 million tons of petroleum exports from Russia passed through Ventspils, one of the former Soviet Union's most important ports. Grain imports account for most of the freight turnover at the port of Riga, also a Baltic terminus of the petroleum pipeline network of the former Soviet Union. Liepaja, a former Soviet naval port, became a trade port in the early 1990s. Also during this period, steps were taken to privatize the Latvian Shipping Com-pany, formally separated from the former Soviet Union's Minis-try of the Maritime Fleet. The Maras Line, a joint venture with British interests, began to operate between Riga and Western Europe. Latvia's fleet consisted of ninety-six ships, totaling nearly 1.2 million deadweight tons: fourteen cargo, twenty-seven refrigerated cargo, two container, nine roll-on/roll-off, and forty-four oil tanker vessels.

The country's main airport is in Riga. Latvian Airlines, the national carrier, provides service to Copenhagen, Düsseldorf, Frankfurt, Helsinki, Kiev, Minsk, Moscow, St. Petersburg, and Stockholm. Baltic International Airlines, a joint Latvian-United States company, operates flights to Frankfurt and London. Ser-vice to Oslo, Berlin, and Amsterdam is offered by Riga Airlines Express, a joint venture between two Latvian joint-stock compa-nies and a Swiss enterprise. Other carriers include Finnair, Lufthansa, SAS (Scandinavian Airlines), LOT (Polish Airlines), and Estonian Air.

The country's telecommunications network is undergoing reconstruction as a result of the privatization of the telecommunications system in 1993 and the sale of a 49 percent share to a British-Finnish telecommunications consortium in 1994. A new international automatic telephone exchange was installed in Riga, and improved telephone and telegraph services became available at standard international rates. The long-term development plan of Lattelcom, the privatized telecommunications company, calls for the creation of a fully digitized network by the year 2012. In 1992 Lattelcom had about 700,000 telephone subscribers, over half of whom were in Riga. Unmet demand because of a shortage of lines was officially 190,000. The unofficial figure, that of potential customers not on the waiting list, was believed to be much larger. There were an estimated 1.4 million radio receivers and 1.1 million television receivers in use in 1992. By early 1995, Latvia had more than twenty-five radio stations and thirty television broadcasting companies. Radio programs are broadcast in Russian, Ukrainian, Estonian, Lithuanian, German, Hebrew, and other foreign languages.

Foreign Trade

In the early 1990s, Latvia succeeded only partially in reorienting foreign trade to the West. Russia continued to be its main trading partner, accounting for nearly 30 percent of the country's exports and more than 33 percent of its imports in 1993 and for about 28 percent of its exports and nearly 24 percent of its imports in 1994. Overall, more than 45 percent of Latvia's exports were destined for the former Soviet republics (mainly Russia, Ukraine, and Belarus), and about 38 percent of its imports came from the former Soviet Union in 1993. Among Western countries, the Netherlands received the largest volume of Latvia's exports (8.2 percent), followed by Germany (6.6 percent) and Sweden (6.5 percent). The primary sources of imports from the West were Germany (11.6 percent) and Sweden (6.2 percent).

The main import was oil, followed by natural gas, machinery, electric power, and automobiles. Oil products, wood and timber, food products, metals, and buses were the main exports (or, in the case of oil products and metals, reexports). In 1994, according to Western estimates, Latvia's foreign trade deficit was LVL141.1 million, about three times higher than that in 1993. The balance of trade deteriorated in 1994, particularly because the strength of the lats made Latvia's exports too expensive.

A total of about US$73 million in humanitarian aid was received in 1992. (Reliable estimates of total aid flows in 1993 were unavailable.) In 1993 Latvia received aid in the amount of ECU18 million (for value of the European currency unit—see Glossary) from the European Union (see Glossary) through its Poland/Hungary Aid for Restructuring of Economies (PHARE) program. Of a US$45 million import rehabilitation loan from the World Bank (see Glossary), about US$21 million had been used in 1993. In 1994 the European Investment Bank (EIB) granted loans of US$6.4 million for financing small- and medium-sized companies. For this purpose Latvia also received a US$10 million loan from Taiwan. In addition, Latvia obtained a US$100 million joint financing credit from the European Bank for Reconstruction and Development (EBRD) and the Export-Import Bank of Japan.

Postindependence Economic Difficulties

The Latvian economy began to falter in 1991 and took a nosedive in 1992. Industrial production declined by 31 percent in 1993, a relative improvement compared with the previous year's decline of 35 percent. Especially hard hit was the engineering industry, which was not able to sell most of its production. By January 1994, the official unemployment rate had reached a high of 5.9 percent. (The actual rate of unemployment, including the long-term unemployed, approached 14 percent.)

International trade also plummeted. Most of the trade with the former Soviet republics is conducted using world prices. One of the key areas of change is in the price of energy, which increased seventy-five times between 1990 and 1992. The average prices of imports in these two years increased forty-five times, whereas prices of exports increased only about thirty-three times. With such price hikes and the general economic chaos prevailing in the whole post-Soviet region, exports in the 1990–92 period decreased by 44 percent, imports by 59 percent, and energy imports by 52 percent. Despite moderate improvement in 1993, Latvia continued to face the challenge of modernizing its production equipment and improving the quality and qualifications of its work force. To do that, it needed international credit and investment. Foreign investment, estimated to be about US$130 million in November

1993, was still small, mainly because of political uncertainty. The greatest influx of foreign investment was from Germany (US$31 million), followed by the United States, Sweden, Russia, Switzerland, and Austria.

There is, nonetheless, evidence of considerable progress in economic reform. In 1991 most, or 88.2 percent, of Latvian exports went to the former Soviet Union, and 3.2 percent went to Western countries. One year later, more than 20 percent of exports went to the West. In 1993 West European countries accounted for about 25 percent of Latvia's exports and 17 percent of its imports. Moreover, there has been a positive shift in the distribution of economic sectors, away from industry and toward services. By 1994 the services sector accounted for more than 50 percent of Latvia's GDP; industry, about 22 percent; and agriculture, 15 percent. Another major achievement has been in the stabilization of the Latvian currency. Latvia used the Russian ruble as legal tender until May 7, 1992, when it introduced the Latvian ruble as a coequal currency. On July 20, it made the Latvian ruble the sole official mode of payment. On March 5, 1993, the new Latvian currency, the lats, was introduced to be used with the Latvian ruble. The lats became the sole legal tender in October 1993. The Bank of Latvia has scrupulously followed the directions of the International Monetary Fund (IMF—see Glossary) by restricting the printing of money and credits. By strictly controlling the money supply, it was able to wrestle inflation down to 2.6 percent in December 1992 and to keep it at an average of less than 3 percent a month through December 1993. The annual inflation rate was reduced from more than 958 percent in 1992 to 35 percent in 1993 and 28 percent in 1994.

In Latvia, as in Russia, managers of state-owned production plants pressed the government through early 1992 to increase credits, but failed. The strength of the Latvian currency has contributed to price increases, making it difficult to export Latvian products to the former Soviet Union. Exporters called for a devaluation of the currency and a lowering of interest rates. Despite low inflation and a strong currency, annual interest rates exceeded 100 percent, making it difficult for enterprises to obtain loans.

It is indicative of the struggles waged by different sectors of the economy, state structures, and other institutions that the 1993 state budget was introduced and accepted only in February 1993. At almost 29 percent, the biggest item in the pro-

Traffic in downtown Riga
Courtesy Chester Pavlovski

jected budget was pensions. Unpaid taxes and unanticipated expenditures on pensions and other social benefits that year contributed to a deficit of LVL54 to LVL55 million (3.2 percent of GDP). To raise additional revenue, the value-added tax (VAT—see Glossary) was increased from 12 percent to 18 percent in November. In December the government also began to issue short-term promissory notes. The budget crisis abated in 1994, with an estimated deficit of LVL36.7 million (1.6 percent of estimated GDP). According to the Economist Intelligence Unit, with a projected revenue of LVL476 million and expenditures of LVL516 million the 1995 budget would run a deficit of about LVL40 million (1.5 percent of estimated GDP).

Privatization

One of the most difficult aspects of economic reform in Latvia is the process of privatization. By the end of 1992, only six out of the more than 2,000 state-run enterprises had been privatized. Of the 703 enterprises slated for privatization in 1993, only nineteen had been privatized by mid-October. An agency charged with the privatization of enterprises was not established until November 1993. By January 1994, about thirty state-owned firms had been sold. It had been widely assumed that Latvia would be one of the leaders in privatization because of its experience with a market economy as an independent state from 1920 to 1940 and because of a latent antipathy to communism. Many factors have hindered the privatization process, however.

Until the early 1990s, no major initiatives in this realm could be made because of unclear jurisdiction. As early as 1990, Moscow had prepared a privatization plan for Latvia, which assigned 51 percent of the shares of industries to their workers, with the remainder to be divided between Latvia and the rest of the Soviet Union. Such a move was vetoed by Latvia. One of the primary reasons for the slow pace of privatization was the attempt to honor the claims of previous owners or their descendants. The right to make such claims was extended to the end of 1993. By January 1, 1993, there had been 14,958 requests for buildings, of which only 2,614 had been reviewed. In addition, more than 10,000 apartments had been denationalized, and more than 50,000 claims to city land had been received. A number of owners have been reluctant to make early claims because they would be liable for large costs, especially in buildings with high tax, heating, lighting, and repair bills. Mean-

Riga Airport
Courtesy Juris Ubans
Coal-loading area at the port in Riga

while, rents have been strictly controlled, and tenants cannot be evicted for seven years unless an equivalent apartment is provided elsewhere.

Potential private owners reclaiming their rightful properties face other obstacles as well. There are legal confrontations between previous owners and a variety of squatters or other claimants. Before independence, many properties were leased or sold to cooperatives. Property law in Latvia has a curious clause that allows so-called "jurisdictional persons" to keep their contracts or properties if the acquisitions were made out of ignorance or "goodwill." In most of these cases, the former owner is then granted compensation by the state, which is usually a small fraction of the worth of a property.

An important psychological aspect of privatization is that many Latvian citizens are afraid of selling off Latvia for a pittance. On the one hand, a belief widely held by leftists—former communists—is that the IMF is trying to wreck the Latvian economy in order to lower purchase prices for foreign firms. On the other hand, rightists charge that the old managers are sabotaging production to lower the value of firms and allow themselves and their Moscow-based mafia allies to once again dominate the Latvian economy. Of particular note is the widespread belief among ethnic Latvians that the main beneficiaries of privatization will be non-Latvians. There is a common perception that about 80 percent of private economic activity is in the hands of other ethnic groups. In private interviews, many reasons are given for this economic breakdown: other groups are more active and willing to take risks; they have better contacts in the old party *nomenklatura* (see Glossary); they have more links with organized crime; they live mostly in cities where the economic action is; and business has not traditionally been highly regarded in Latvian culture. The predominantly Latvian state bureaucracy, which can affect the rate of privatization, is afraid of losing its power and the concomitant benefits involved in the control of industries.

As in other formerly socialist states, there has been an innate difficulty in estimating the value of industries or buildings. An auction could help overcome this problem, but other considerations, such as job retention and the ability of different bidders to compete in future markets, have become important. In effect, only 9.5 percent of the 295 privatization sales held in Latvia by January 1, 1993, had been accomplished through auction. Most of the privatization undertakings were bids to lease commercial sales establishments for up to five years. In most cases, the leasing of commercial sales establishments requires that the newly private entrepreneurs continue the same line of business as before. Even this kind of relatively mundane transaction was plagued by jurisdictional squabbles. For example, in the lease of the Minsk, one of the largest department stores in Riga, it was discovered after the contract had been signed that the city district that organized the lease had no right to do so because the Minsk is actually under the jurisdiction of the city of Riga. This case illustrates just one problem such initiatives can engender. There were also public charges about favoritism, the involvement of family members of the Cabinet of Ministers, the undervaluation of existing stock, and so on.

A few foreign investors had started up new firms or enterprises, but initial investments were cautiously small—in most cases well below US$1 million. In 1992, for example, total capital investments involving United States enterprises amounted to less than US$13 million. The many problems slowing down foreign investment include the limited title to land (at best a ninety-nine-year lease); the unreliability of contracts with government representatives or ministries, which can be broken; the expectation in some instances of favors or bribes by government contracting or signing parties; the presence of organized crime and, in some localities, its demands for protection money; the widely reported stealing and pillaging of private property; and the variable quality of workers. Other problems involve communications difficulties, a dearth of adequate housing for Western staff, the deficit in knowledge of foreign business language, the lack of Western-trained management, and even the question of safety in the streets. These problems are also reflected in other former Soviet republics. Latvia appears to be tackling them with vigor and determination, however, and major improvements in the investment climate have already been achieved.

Until 1993 one of the key variables blocking a resurgence in economic activity was the erratic and unstable local banking and financing system. More than forty banks in Latvia had an average capitalization of less than US$1 million. Interest rates varied considerably, and services had yet to meet Western standards. The Bank of Latvia, which is the country's central bank, operated forty-eight branches and a specialized foreign branch.

Although much remains to be done, some progress has been made in reforming the financial sector, particularly in privatizing commercial operations. Twenty-one former branches of the Bank of Latvia were merged in 1993 to establish the Universal Bank of Latvia, the privatization of which was to be completed in 1995. The Latvian Savings Bank also was to be restructured and privatized by the end of 1995. As the central bank, the Bank of Latvia assumed a supervisory role, guiding and monitoring the country's banks. To facilitate payments, many banks have joined the Society of Worldwide Interbank Telecommunication (SWIFT), the international fund transfer system, and some have begun to offer credit cards, cash advances, and other services.

Progress toward privatization has been made in agriculture as well. By January 1, 1993, some 50,200 farmsteads encompassing 21 percent of farmland had been given over to individual ownership. By late 1993, the number of private farms had grown to 57,510, compared with 3,931 at the end of 1989 (see table 26, Appendix). At the same time, another 99,400 families were assigned private plots averaging 4.4 hectares, which provided a significant buttress to their economic survival. The major thrust for this privatization came from the program of denationalization, which returned farms and land to former owners or their relatives. Aspects of this privatization could cause problems in the future, however. Although imbued with idealistic expectations, the new farmers have little equipment and inadequate housing for themselves and their animals. Also, many of them have never farmed before. Their farms are usually small, averaging seventeen hectares each. Not all collective farms were dismembered, but where they did split up, the leadership of these farms was able in many instances to buy out equipment and animals at preinflation prices. This apparent unfairness has left a legacy of bitterness.

In November 1992, a law providing vouchers for privatization was passed. The law came into effect on May 1, 1993, and the distribution of vouchers began in September. The law provides for the distribution of vouchers according to one's length of residence in Latvia, with one year worth one voucher, or about US$42. Other factors are also taken into account. For example, those who can lay claim to Latvian citizenship prior to the Soviet occupation in June 1940 and their progeny are entitled to an additional fifteen vouchers as compensation for so-called "ancestral investments." Refugees who left Latvia because of World War II may also obtain one voucher for each year lived in Latvia before December 31, 1944. Those forcibly deported from Latvia in the past receive a differentiated number for each year of confinement in prison camps or in exile. Finally, people are allotted vouchers on those occasions where private claims on property cannot be realized because of conflicts with squatters or because compensation is chosen in lieu of property. An estimated 87 percent of vouchers are to be granted to Latvian citizens. Of the total of 113 million vouchers in circulation, an estimated 2 million are expected to be used for purchasing farmland, 40 million for city land, 43 million for apartments, and 28 million for state enterprises.

Public opinion is an important consideration in policy making. Popular attitudes toward privatization differ somewhat between Latvians and others but not between men and women or between urban and rural areas. A random poll revealed the greatest split between individuals thirty-four years and younger and those thirty-five and older, and this difference may portend increased support for privatization.

Consumption Patterns

One of the main effects of the 1991–92 economic changes and dislocations has been a change in the pattern of consumption. According to family budget studies, food claimed only 29.4 percent of expenditures in 1990 but rose to 37.8 percent in 1991 and to 48.8 percent in 1992 (January–September). (In the United States, an average of 15 percent of income goes to food purchases.) The share of other commodities in the budget decreased from 37.6 percent in 1990 to 24.1 percent in 1992. Services, taxes, and other expenses declined only marginally as a proportion of total spending.

In the third quarter of 1992, the average monthly wage was 5,054 Latvian rubles, and the minimum wage was set at 1,500. According to the calculations of the Ministry of Welfare, the minimum "crisis survival basket" was determined to cost 3,010 Latvian rubles, and a minimum noncrisis basket of food and services cost 4,120 Latvian rubles. To purchase one kilogram of beef in September 1992, a person employed in the state sector had to work 180 minutes; for one kilogram of pork, 309 minutes; one liter of milk, thirty-six minutes; ten eggs, 110 minutes; one kilogram of sugar, 159 minutes; a man's suit, ninety-four hours; a man's shirt, 520 minutes; one pair of men's socks, fifty-two minutes; one pair of pantyhose, 110 minutes; and a pair of women's shoes, twenty-four hours. The price of one kilogram of bread was equivalent to 15 percent of a day's wages.

The decrease in real wages and the increase in the cost of goods resulted in a decrease of 45 percent in retail sales between January and September 1991. The volume of purchases of many items decreased by well over 50 percent.

However, retail sales do not reflect total consumption. Many individuals started their own garden patches; relatives availed themselves of their farm connections; and farmers, of course, grew their own food and exchanged it for other goods and services. A survey of family budgets found that in comparing the first nine months of 1991 and 1992, meat consumption decreased by 13 percent, milk and milk products by 18 percent, fish and fish products by 24 percent, and sugar by 19 percent. Bread products consumption increased by more than 10 percent, however. Total calorie intake decreased by 5.9 percent, and fat intake fell by 11 percent.

Although the purchase of new manufactured goods decreased significantly, there is still a considerable availability of household goods likely to last well into the 1990s. In 1991, for example, for every 100 families there were 143 radios, 110 televisions, ninety-nine refrigerators, eighty-nine washing machines, seventy vacuum cleaners, and thirty-seven automobiles.

Government and Politics

Transition to Independence

The decision of the Latvian Supreme Soviet in December 1989 to end the communist party's monopoly on political power in Latvia cleared the way for the rise of independent political parties and for the country's first free parliamentary elections since 1940. Of the 201 deputies elected to the new Supreme Council, the transitional parliament, in March and April 1990, only fifteen had served in any of the previous Soviet Latvian legislative assemblies, and about two-thirds belonged to the proindependence Popular Front of Latvia (see Historical Setting, this ch.).

On May 4, 1990, a declaration renewing the independence of the Republic of Latvia was adopted by the Supreme Council. A de facto transition period for the renewal of independence was to culminate in elections to a restored Saeima (Latvia's pre-1940 legislature). The Supreme Council declared the Soviet annexation of Latvia illegal and restored certain articles of the constitution of February 15, 1922, pertaining to the election of the Saeima and to Latvia's status as an independent and democratic state whose sovereign power rests with the Latvian people.

To pass this declaration, according to Soviet Latvian law, it was necessary to have at least a two-thirds majority of the total number of deputies—134 out of 201. The vote was close, but the declaration passed with 138 votes. The Russophone Ravnopraviye (Equal Rights Movement) boycotted this resolution by walking out of parliament.

On August 21, 1991, in an emergency session following the Soviet coup in Moscow, the Supreme Council declared Latvia's full independence, ending the transition period. Several parts of the May 4, 1990, declaration, however, were not affected. Of particular importance was the inaction on the creation of a revised constitution to reflect "new" realities. A particularly vigorous opposition to this clause was mounted by the Latvian Citizens' Committee (Latvijas Pilsonu Komiteja), which was opposed to the legitimacy of the newly elected Supreme Council and did not see how an illegitimate body could create a legitimate new constitution. The committee fought to retain the entire package of the 1922 constitution without any amendments. Its initiative was endorsed by numerous deputies within the Popular Front of Latvia, who were so opposed to any compromises on this issue that they created a separate parliamentary faction called Satversme (Constitution). Their reluctance to tamper with the 1922 constitution and the basics of the 1918 republic extended to a refusal to change Latvia's electoral law, which technically was not even part of the constitution. Minor changes in the electoral law were accepted, however, including the right to vote at age eighteen.

In view of the fact that elections to the Supreme Council were competitive and democratic, why was there so much opposition to the right of this council to deal with constitutional questions? The elections in 1990, critics said, were still held in occupied Latvia in accordance with the rules agreed upon by the communist-led Supreme Soviet of Latvia. One of the greatest points of contention was participation by the Soviet army, which refused to provide for any valid enumeration of voters and was allowed to vote using different rules from the rest of the population. Many of the opponents also contended that, according to international law, people who were resettled in an occupied territory had no automatic right to citizenship or the right to vote. Thus, only those with Latvian citizenship prior to Soviet occupation on June 17, 1940, and their progeny were entitled to determine Latvia's future. This point of view prevailed in the determination of the electorate for the June 5–6, 1993, elections to the restored Saeima. About 25 percent of the permanent residents of Latvia, mainly ethnic Russians, were not allowed to vote in those elections.

Political System

The current electoral system is based on that which existed in Latvia before its annexation by the Soviet Union. One hundred representatives are elected by all citizens at least eighteen years of age, on the basis of proportional representation, for a period of three years. The Saeima elects a board, consisting of a chairman, two deputies, and two secretaries. The chairman or a deputy acts as speaker of the legislature. By secret ballot, the Saeima also elects the president, who must be at least forty years of age and have an absolute majority of votes. The president then appoints the prime minister, who nominates the other cabinet ministers. The entire Cabinet of Ministers must resign if the Saeima votes to express no confidence in the prime minister.

The Saeima has ten permanent committees with a total of 100 positions, so every deputy may sit on one committee. There are five other committees with a total of thirty-four positions. Committee chairmen, elected by committee members, often belong to minority parties not represented in the Saeima's ruling coalition. Draft laws for consideration by the Saeima may be submitted by its committees, by no fewer than five representatives, by the Cabinet of Ministers, by the president, or, in rare instances, by one-tenth of all citizens eligible to vote.

The president is elected for a period of three years and may not serve for more than two consecutive terms. As head of state and head of the armed forces, the president implements the Saeima's decisions regarding the ratification of international treaties; appoints Latvia's representatives to foreign states and receives representatives of foreign states in Latvia; may declare war, in accordance with the Saeima's decisions; and appoints a commander in chief in time of war. The president has the right to convene extraordinary meetings of the Cabinet of Ministers, to return draft laws to the Saeima for reconsideration, and to propose the dissolution of the Saeima.

Latvia's judicial system, inherited from the Soviet regime, is being reorganized. There are regional, district, and administrative courts as well as a Supreme Court. Final appeals in criminal and civil cases are made to the Supreme Court, which sits in Riga.

Latvia's four provinces (Vidzeme, Latgale, Kurzeme, and Zemgale) are subdivided into twenty-six districts, seven municipalities, fifty-six towns, and thirty-seven urban settlements. The highest decision-making body at the local level of government is the council, elected directly by the locality's permanent population for five-year terms and consisting of fifteen to 120 members. Members elect a board, which serves as the council's executive organ and is headed by the council chairman. In May 1994, in their first local elections since regaining independence, Latvian citizens elected more than 3,500 representatives, most belonging to right-of-center, pro-Latvian-rights parties and organizations. Candidates from the Latvian National Independence Movement were the most successful, and those from organizations succeeding the once-dominant Communist Party of Latvia fared worst.

Current Politics

More than twenty political parties or coalitions contended for seats in the June 1993 general elections, including Latvia's Way (Latvijas Cels), the Popular Front of Latvia, the Latvian National Independence Movement, Harmony for Latvia, the Latvian Democratic Labor Party, the Latvian Farmers Union, the Latvian Social Democratic Workers' Party, the Green Party, and Ravnopraviye. Latvians who fled as refugees to the West during World War II were granted the right to vote, even if they had become citizens of other countries. Of the estimated 120,000 such émigrés, however, barely 10,000 had bothered to register by May 1993.

With 32.4 percent of the vote, Latvia's Way, a centrist coalition founded three months before the election, won the largest number of seats—thirty-six. It succeeded in uniting a wide range of prominent advocates of democratization, a free-market economy, and closer cooperation among the Baltic states. The Latvian National Independence Movement, which was further to the right on the political spectrum, won fifteen seats; the moderate-left Harmony for Latvia, which took a liberal stance toward the issue of citizenship, won thirteen seats; and the center-right Latvian Farmers Union won twelve seats. Four smaller groups—Ravnopraviye, the Fatherland and Freedom Union, the Christian Democratic Union, and the Democratic Center Party (subsequently renamed the Democratic Party)—won fewer than ten seats each. The Popular Front of Latvia, despite its large following before independence, fell short of the 4 percent threshold required for representation.

At the start of its first session in July 1993, the Saeima's major acts included election of Anatolijs Gorbunovs of Latvia's Way as its chairman, full restoration of the 1922 constitution, and election of a president. Three candidates ran for president: Gunars Meirovics of Latvia's Way, Aivars Jerumanis of the Christian Democratic Union, and Guntis Ulmanis of the Latvian Farmers Union. Ulmanis succeeded in gaining the necessary majority vote on the third ballot and was inaugurated as president on July 8, 1993. He appointed Valdis Birkavs, a leader of Latvia's Way, as prime minister and asked him to form a government. The Cabinet of Ministers approved by the Saeima on July 20, 1993, was a coalition of members of Latvia's Way, the Latvian Farmers Union, and the Christian Democratic Union.

In July 1994, as a result of a dispute regarding tariffs on agricultural imports, the Latvian Farmers Union withdrew from the ruling coalition, and the Birkavs government resigned. Andrejs Krastins, deputy chairman of the Saeima and chairman of the Latvian National Independence Movement, failed to form a new government. Then Maris Gailis of Latvia's Way engineered a coalition with two groups that emerged from a split in the Harmony for Latvia movement—the National Union of Economists, which advocates an expanded economic role for the state and greater concessions on citizenship rights for the Russians and other ethnic minorities, and Harmony for the People. In September the Gailis government, including Birkavs as foreign minister, was confirmed.

One of the most important issues facing the Saeima was citizenship. Proposals concerning a citizenship bill ranged from retaining the citizenship criteria used for the purposes of the 1993 general elections to granting automatic citizenship to all residents of Latvia. A citizenship bill was passed in June 1994, despite its controversial quota restricting naturalization to fewer than 2,000 people per year. Under heavy domestic and international pressure, however, the Saeima relented, and another citizenship bill, without the quota provision, was passed in July and signed into law by President Ulmanis in August. It requires that applicants have a minimum of five years of continuous residence (in contrast to a December 1991 draft law's sixteen-year residency requirement); a rudimentary knowledge of the Latvian language, history, and constitution; and a legal source of income. Applicants must also take an oath of loyalty to Latvia and renounce any other citizenship.

Mass Media

Beginning in 1985, Gorbachev's policy of *glasnost* gave newspaper and magazine editors in Latvia and other republics of the Soviet Union unprecedented opportunities to publish information on a wide range of formerly proscribed subjects, including crime, illegal drugs, occupational injuries, and environmental issues. Thus, an article published in October 1986 in the Latvian literary journal *Literatura un Maksla*, discussing the environmental impact of a new hydroelectric station that was to be built on the Daugava River, helped to arouse so much public opposition that a decision was made by the Soviet government in 1987 to abandon the project (see Natural Resources, this ch.). Subsequently, after the pivotal June 1988 plenum of the Latvian Writers Union, the speeches delivered at this plenum, denouncing the Soviet Latvian status quo and demanding greater autonomy for the Latvian republic, received nationwide attention when they were published in four successive issues of *Literatura un Maksla* (see The Pursuit of Independence, 1987–91, this ch.).

In the early 1990s, as the transition to a market-oriented economy began and competition intensified, both the circulation and the content of newspapers and magazines changed. Rising production costs caused subscription rates and newsstand prices to increase, and sales declined steadily. Nevertheless, in 1995 Latvia had a daily newspaper circulation rate of 1,377 per 1,000 population, compared with 524 per 1,000 population in Finland, 402 per 1,000 population in Germany, and 250 per 1,000 population in the United States. More than 200 newspapers and 180 magazines were in circulation.

Foreign Relations

Establishing Foreign Relations

Prior to the declaration of renewal of Latvia's independence on May 4, 1990, several individuals were responsible for foreign affairs. Their presence in this field was wholly symbolic, however, because all decisions on foreign policy were made by government administrators and party officials in Moscow. After the May 4 declaration, a new Ministry of Foreign Affairs was established, headed by Janis Jurkans, chairman of the Foreign Affairs Committee of the Popular Front of Latvia. Initially, the entire ministry, composed of a few dozen workers, was squeezed into a single house in the medieval center of Riga and had antiquated amenities and limited space.

The ministry had to start from the very beginning. Some of its personnel were sent abroad to learn the essentials of diplomatic protocol. Even the most prosaic of office equipment had to be scavenged. Initially, Jurkans was forced to deal with some holdover personnel with links to the KGB, but several of them were eased out of their jobs for incompetence and other overt transgressions. On June 19, 1990, the KGB created a furor in the republic when it arrested and expelled from Latvia (presumably with Moscow's blessing) a young Latvian-American volunteer who had provided English-language translations and other services for the ministry in dealing with foreign countries.

During this period of transition, Latvia received much help from the Latvian embassy in Washington. This embassy had been maintained as an independent outpost representing free Latvia throughout the years of Soviet occupation. It had been financed from the investments and gold deposited in the United States by the government of independent Latvia before World War II. Similar offices throughout the world offered advice and contacts with local governments. Indeed, the embassy in Washington was able to provide Minister Jurkans with about US$60,000 to further the cause of Latvia's independence, which was then the main thrust of Latvian foreign policy.

Until August 21, 1991, and the end of the Moscow putsch, Latvia was not able to convince any Western country to locate an embassy in the republic. The countries feared offending the Soviet Union and could not answer the logistical question of how to settle in Riga when all border guards at the airports and seaports were still under Soviet command. Most Western countries had not abrogated the de jure status of independent Latvia; the issue concerned purely de facto recognition. Several countries, such as Denmark, opened cultural offices in Riga, and, more important, many countries invited Minister Jurkans and Prime Minister Ivars Godmanis abroad to meet their heads of state and government and to present their arguments for

Latvia's independence. Several meetings with President George H.W. Bush and other world dignitaries received wide media coverage.

An invaluable diplomat during this period of transition was the highly respected Latvian poet Janis Peters, who had been sent to Moscow to represent Latvia's interests. Peters also had many contacts and was highly regarded by the Russian intelligentsia. He was based in the prewar Latvian embassy, which had already been returned to Latvia several years earlier. A modern hotel, the Talava, had been built within its compound by Latvian communist dignitaries seeking trouble-free accommodations on their various sojourns in Moscow. The embassy building and the hotel became convenient locations for a multitude of contacts by economic, cultural, and political emissaries from Latvia.

Before August 21, 1991, Latvia's attempts to join international organizations were unsuccessful in spite of efforts by France and other countries to allow it to participate as an observer. Only at the regional level was some success achieved with the signing by Latvia, Estonia, and Lithuania of the Baltic Agreement on Economic Cooperation in April 1990 and the renewal in May 1990 of the 1934 Baltic Treaty on Unity and Cooperation. At the bilateral level, Latvia and Russia under Boris N. Yeltsin signed a treaty of mutual recognition in January 1991, but this treaty was not ratified by the Russian Supreme Soviet.

After the failed Moscow putsch, Latvian independence was recognized by the Soviet Union and most countries of the world, and Latvia became a member of the UN. These events were exhilarating for Latvians, who had been under Moscow's domination for almost half a century. However, new responsibilities of representation entailed a totally new set of problems. Setting up new embassies and consulates in major Western countries required the choosing of suitable personnel from among people without previous diplomatic experience. A considerable number of ambassadors were selected from diaspora Latvians in the United States, Britain, Denmark, France, and Germany.

Financing was another major constraint. Initiatives were taken to reclaim the embassy buildings that had once belonged to independent Latvia but had been appropriated by the Soviet Union or by host governments. In some instances, cash settlements and building exchanges became the only solution.

155

Problems were also experienced in the opposite direction. Foreign countries wanting to establish embassies in Riga often had to scramble for suitable sites at a time when ownership and jurisdictional questions over property presented an interminable maze of inconsistent decrees and agreements. At times the Latvian cabinet had to step in to provide locations. Some of the major Western countries were able to settle into their prewar buildings. Others found new quarters or set up their offices in temporary shelters in hotels and other buildings. A great controversy erupted over the restitution of the prewar Russian embassy building, which for decades had been used for Latvian cultural and educational purposes.

Minister Jurkans spent much time traveling abroad. His distinctly liberal ideology ingratiated him with his Western hosts. In the process of representing Latvia, however, many Latvians began to feel that he was becoming too independent and did not reflect Latvia's real demands. After Jurkans's resignation in the spring of 1993, his replacement as interim minister was Georgs Andrejevs, a surgeon of Russian descent. Andrejevs joined the Latvia's Way movement and was reappointed minister of foreign affairs after the June 1993 elections. According to polling data, Andrejevs became one of the most popular politicians among ethnic Latvians, but ironically he did not find much resonance among non-Latvians living in the republic.

In June 1993, the Latvian Ministry of Foreign Affairs employed 160 people, a relatively low number, reflecting the limitations of government financing. Prewar Latvia had had 700 employees in the same ministry, and countries comparable in size to Latvia employ about 1,000 people on average.

Foreign Policy Directions

Latvian foreign policy has of necessity been preoccupied with its eastern neighbor, Russia. The lack of stability and the seemingly contradictory signals coming from Russia created strains in this relationship. A primary point of contention in the early 1990s concerned the evacuation of the armed forces, which were formerly Soviet but now Russian. Another major issue involved citizenship limitations on Russian-speaking settlers whose ties with Latvia began only after June 1940 and the occupation by the Red Army.

In late August 1993, the Russian armed forces were withdrawn from neighboring Lithuania, which has a relatively small native Russian population. In Latvia the timetable for the departure of the remaining 16,000 to 18,000 troops took longer to negotiate. Russia tried to connect the withdrawal to the issue of citizenship rights for Latvia's large Russian minority, but it failed to receive international support for such linkage. Another issue was the status of a radar base at Skrunda, which Russia considers an integral part of its antimissile early warning system.

Nervous about Russia's intentions, the Latvians could not forget that in 1940 a pretext for the takeover and annexation of Latvia was to protect Soviet bases established there in 1939. On January 18, 1994, Russian foreign minister Andrey Kozyrev explicitly claimed Russia's right to maintain troops in the Baltic states to avoid a security vacuum and to preempt the establishment of forces hostile to Russia. Similar statements had been enunciated earlier by the Russian defense minister and other officials.

Russia's continued military presence became a major bargaining chip for Russian internal politics and foreign policy. Along with Russia's claims about the strategic importance of the radar base at Skrunda, the Russian government said there was no room in which to lodge incoming officers from Latvia. Some Russian generals and governmental officials broached the possibility of tying their troop withdrawals to North Atlantic Treaty Organization (NATO) troop reductions. Others asked for large grants to build living quarters back in Russia. Yeltsin declared that the troop withdrawals were tied to the human rights question in Latvia, especially as it pertained to residents of Russian origin. Many Latvians attributed the delay to the hope of some Russian military and political leaders that political changes might occur in Moscow and the status quo ante reestablished.

Under such circumstances, the Latvian leadership concluded that the best hope for security would be membership in NATO rather than neutrality. NATO, however, demonstrated a willingness to assist Latvia and the other Baltic states only in an advisory capacity. Much to their disappointment, Latvian leaders determined that joining NATO was an elusive goal.

Ultimately, in exchange for the withdrawal of the Russian troops, Latvia consented to lease the Skrunda facility to Russia for five years. The accord, signed in Moscow in April 1994, stipulates that the radar base must cease operation by August 31, 1998, and be dismantled by February 29, 2000. Agreements were also signed on social security and welfare for active and retired Russian military personnel and their families in Latvia. With the exception of several hundred military specialists at Skrunda, all active-duty Russian troops were withdrawn from Latvia by August 31, 1994, leaving behind a hodge-podge of toxic chemicals and buried, undetonated ordnance.

Latvia and Estonia received much help from Scandinavia, the United States, and other Western countries in pressuring Russia to remove its troops. To counter the argument that these troops would have no accommodations in Russia, several countries, including Norway and the United States, provided funding to construct new housing for Russian officers.

Other issues between Latvia and Russia included Russia's annexation of the northeastern border district of Abrene in 1944. Latvia's transitional parliament, the Supreme Council, reaffirmed the validity of the pre-Soviet borders in its Decree on the Nonrecognition of the Annexation of the Town of Abrene and the District of Abrene, adopted in January 1992. Although the withdrawal of Russian troops figured much more prominently than the border issue in Latvian-Russian negotiations in the early 1990s, it could resurface in the context of wider negotiations of claims and reparations.

The ongoing pressures from Russia have given impetus for Latvia to strengthen its ties with international institutions. As a member of the UN, Latvia was able to refute Russian charges on the abuse of human rights in Latvia. Latvia also has joined many of the subsidiary bodies of the UN, such as the World Health Organization (WHO) and the United Nations Educational, Scientific and Cultural Organization (UNESCO). Latvia has also joined NATO's Partnership for Peace, a program of cooperation with the newly independent states.

Although Estonia and Lithuania were accepted as members of the Council of Europe (see Glossary) in early 1993, in spite of strong Russian objections, Latvia had only the status of an observer. Full membership for Latvia, precluded earlier by the unresolved issue of citizenship rights, was granted in early 1995.

In the early 1990s, the Council of the Baltic Sea States (CBSS) became a particularly useful forum for foreign policy contacts. This council was proposed on October 22, 1991, during a meeting of the German and Danish foreign ministers, Hans-Dietrich Genscher and Elleman Jensen, respectively. Its first directions were set by the ten countries bordering the Baltic Sea, including Russia, when representatives met on March

5–6, 1992. Concrete proposals for Latvia have included the coordination of an international highway project, Via Baltica, from Tallinn to Warsaw.

The Scandinavian countries and Germany are among Latvia's most active international supporters. Mutually friendly bilateral relations are maintained with members of the Visegrád Group (consisting of Poland, the Czech Republic, Slovakia, and Hungary). Latvia also has been able to develop advantageous relations with Belarus and Ukraine. A generally good and cooperative relationship exists with neighboring Estonia and Lithuania. At the economic level, these states have signed free-trade agreements. They are also cooperating at the military level. Military cooperation among the Baltic states included an agreement in October 1994 to form, with Western assistance, a Baltic peacekeeping battalion, headquartered in Latvia.

Together with the other Baltic countries, Latvia has many more adjustments to make in its evolution from "cause to country," as noted by Paul Goble in Tallinn's *Baltic Independent*, May 21–27, 1993: "The peoples and governments of the Baltics must cope with the difficult challenge of being taken seriously as countries . . . The Balts must find their way in the world as three relatively small countries on the edge of Europe—and for many people, on the edge of consciousness—rather than figure as central players in a titanic struggle between East and West."

National Security

Defense

One of the important debates after independence stemmed from the issue of whether Latvia requires its own armed forces. According to one argument against a national armed forces, the most likely aggressor is Russia, and if this state wants to violate Latvia's sovereignty by force, even the best equipped and most dedicated Latvian army could slow down such an assault only for a brief period of time. Those supporting a national armed forces pointed to their possible contribution in establishing law and order within the republic, in coping with emergencies, in controlling borders, and in providing a symbol of statehood and a source of pride. Those with a knowledge of Latvian history explained that in June 1940 when the Soviet Union presented Latvia with an ultimatum, the lack of any military resistance helped to dupe many in the world into accepting the myth of Latvia's voluntarily joining the Soviet Union. Any new ultimatum from Russia would very likely include a serious consideration of armed resistance by the Latvian forces, even if only to prove a point to the rest of the world. Former Minister of Defense Talavs Jundzis provided exactly such a rationale: "Sometimes I am asked: 'How can you with your 9,000-man defense forces stand up against a 300,000 or up to 3 million-man aggressor force?' The answer is simple. Our resistance by itself will generate an international reaction. It will be clear to everyone as to what is happening and even if we are again occupied, international public opinion will not accept such a regime and it would not last long." Jundzis provided another reason for Latvia's armed forces, which is based on Latvian historical experience: "Aggressive announcements from the Organization of Russian Army Officers about their disobedience to their commanders and their readiness to use weapons to defend themselves remind us of our struggle for independence in 1919, when after the end of World War I, the abandoned soldiers from Russian and German armies united under the leadership of the adventurer Bermont to attack and occupy the newly born state of Latvia."

Latvia was able to create a Ministry of Defense only after September 1991, when Latvia was formally recognized as an independent state by the Soviet Union. Before independence, the Soviet armed forces were in charge of defense and with increasing difficulty attempted to force the young men of Latvia to register for the draft. In November 1991, after the creation of the new Latvian ministry, Jundzis, a Popular Front of Latvia deputy and chairman of the Latvian Supreme Council's Committee on Defense and Internal Affairs, became the first minister of defense in Latvia since June 1940.

The Latvian Ministry of Defense, unlike that of Ukraine and other former Soviet republics, did not receive or appropriate any of the armaments existing on its territory. All armaments were for sale, but only at world market prices. The Latvian armed forces, however, were successful in obtaining their headquarters and several other abandoned buildings.

Latvia's defense concept is based on the Swedish-Finnish rapid response force model. In 1994 the armed forces totaled 6,600, including 1,650 in the army, 630 in the navy, 180 in the air force, and 4,140 in the border guard. Plans call for 9,000 active members in the armed forces. Latvia also has the security

Barricade erected in Riga's old town in January 1991 to defend strategic buildings from attack by Soviet troops
Courtesy Linda Sudmalis

service of the Ministry of Interior and the reserve Home Guard (Zemessardze). In addition to serving as a national guard, the Home Guard, with an estimated 17,000 members, assists the border guard and the police. When they reach the age of nineteen, men serve a mandatory one-year period of active military duty, but men and women at least eighteen years of age may volunteer for military service. Alternative service for conscientious objectors is available.

The armed forces are poorly equipped. In the early 1990s, donations of jeeps and field kitchens came from Germany, patrol boats from Germany and Sweden, and uniforms from Norway. The army's equipment includes two BRDM–2 reconnaissance vehicles and thirteen M–43 armored personnel carriers. The navy has about six coast guard vessels, three patrol craft, two minesweepers, one special-purpose vessel, and one tugboat. The air force's equipment includes two Soviet An–2 and two Czechoslovak L–410 aircraft and several Soviet Mi–2 and Mi–8 helicopters.

Many officers are ethnic Latvians from the former Soviet armed forces, who, according to critics, are set in their ways and are difficult to retrain. Such reformers as former Minister of Defense Valdis Pavlovskis, a retired United States Marine Corps officer and instructor, attempted to remedy this situation through the establishment of local military institutes, including the Latvian Military Academy, and through enrollment in programs at Western military institutes. Ongoing correspondence and part-time training programs also were introduced.

The Ministry of Defense provides extremely low remuneration because it is short of funds. The 1993 state budget allotted only 2.9 percent of its expenditures for national security, which includes the Ministry of Defense, the security service of the Ministy of Interior, and the Home Guard. This sum is claimed to be only one-tenth of what would be required for normal functioning of the forces. In the second half of 1992, only 40.5 million Latvian rubles were allotted for food, 42 million rubles for clothing, and 79.8 million rubles for equipment purchases, but 59.3 million rubles were allotted for capital construction. In 1993 about US$48 million was allocated to defense.

Crime and Law Enforcement

Crime was a serious problem in Latvia in the early 1990s, as it was in the other Baltic states and elsewhere in the former Soviet Union. The total number of reported crimes increased from 34,686 in 1990 to 61,871 in 1992 and then dropped to 52,835 in 1993. The number of convictions rose from 7,159 in 1990 to 11,280 in 1993. Theft accounted for more than three-quarters of all crimes, although the number of reported cases declined from 51,639 in 1992 to 41,211 in 1993. The incidence of murder or attempted murder was 2.6 times higher in 1993 than in 1990. Drug-related offenses more than tripled in this period. Drugs as well as alcohol, weapons, scrap metals, and consumer products were often smuggled into the country.

Subjected to the spread of organized crime from Russia, Latvia cooperated with neighboring Estonia and Lithuania and other countries via the International Criminal Police Organiza-

Liberty Monument in Riga
Courtesy Chester Pavlovski

tion (Interpol). The Latvian authorities were gradually replacing the Soviet-trained police, although allegations of corruption in the law enforcement community persisted. Political corruption and white-collar crime also posed significant problems. The lack of funding for remuneration, equipment, and even gasoline for police vehicles hampered law enforcement operations. The Home Guard assisted in police patrols but had no power to make arrests.

Latvia's penal code includes the death penalty. One person, sentenced to death in July 1992 for premeditated murder under aggravated circumstances, was executed in 1993. Two death sentences were commuted, leaving no prisoners on death row at the end of 1993. There were no known instances of political or other extrajudicial killings, of political abductions, of torture, of arbitrary arrest or exile, or of denial of a fair public trial. The government welcomed visits by human rights organizations and received delegations from the Organization for Security and Cooperation in Europe, the Council of Europe, and the UN, among others.

Outlook

Latvia was the first Baltic republic to begin the process of public empowerment and disentanglement from the legacy of a half-century of Soviet rule, initiating the 1987 "calendar" demonstrations, which commemorated long-suppressed critical turning points in Latvian history. Thereafter, Estonia and then Lithuania picked up the torch in a unique historical relay race whose end point was independence.

With independence, however, Latvia had to adjust to totally new circumstances. New rules of the game had to be introduced and accepted. Democratic structures and practices had to be formed or revived. The initial rigors of a market economy and of privatization had to be endured. A new orientation to the rule of law and to the public clash of many voices had to be sanctioned and supported.

Much progress has been made in all these areas; much still remains to be done. The pressure of nationality relations, citizenship issues, economic strategies and priorities, and political confrontations between radical and moderate factions will no doubt remain for some time. These internal problems, however, do not surpass the coping capacity of Latvian political and social structures. The major threat lies in the potential actions of neighboring Russia, where forces of imperial irredentism are finding many political allies.

Ideally, Latvia's future would be best assured by a stable and peaceful Russia. This is a goal supported by most Latvian politicians. If such a goal becomes unattainable, however, Latvia would be compelled to rely on external protection provided by its Western neighbors. It remains to be seen if Latvia will be granted the same protective status as that enjoyed by Denmark, Belgium, the Netherlands, and other European countries under the NATO umbrella.

*   *   *

Among the best works on Latvian history are Arnolds Spekke's *History of Latvia: An Outline* and Alfreds Bilmanis's *A History of Latvia.* The interwar period is described well in Georg Von Rauch's *The Baltic States: The Years of Independence, 1917–1940* and the Soviet period in Romuald J. Misiunas and Rein Taagepera's *The Baltic States: Years of Dependence, 1940–1990.* The period of national awakening is analyzed and described by Juris Dreifelds in "Latvian National Rebirth," *Problems of Communism,* July–August 1989, and by Anatol Lieven in *The Baltic Revolution.* An unsurpassed classic on Latvian geography is *Latvia: Country and People* by J. Rutkis. The *National Report of Latvia to UNCED, 1992,* prepared for the Rio de Janeiro World Conference by the Environmental Protection Committee of Latvia, is a very good summary of post-Soviet Latvia and its environmental problems. A good source of statistical data is *Latvija Skaitlos* (*Latvia in Figures*), the annual report of Latvia's State Committee for Statistics (Valsts Statistikas Komiteja). Invaluable and current information on Latvia's economy is provided by the monthly *Baltic Business Report.* Very good analytical articles on various aspects of government and politics in Latvia can be found in the *RFE/RL Research Report.* A most useful compendium of articles on foreign policy has been published in *New Actors on the International Arena: The Foreign Policies of the Baltic Countries,* edited by Pertti Joenniemi and Peeter Vares, and on national security in *Comprehensive Security for the Baltics: An Environmental Approach,* edited by Arthur H. Westing. (For further information and complete citations, see Bibliography.)

Chapter 3. Lithuania

Wayside wooden sculpture near Druskininkai

Country Profile

Country

Formal Name: Republic of Lithuania (Lietuvos Respublika).

Short Form: Lithuania (Lietuva).

Term for Citizen(s): Lithuanian(s).

Capital: Vilnius.

Date of Independence: On March 11, 1990, newly elected Lithuanian Supreme Soviet proclaimed independence; Soviet Union granted recognition September 6, 1991. February 16, Independence Day, national holiday; on this day in 1918, independent Republic of Lithuania proclaimed.

Geography

Size: 65,200 square kilometers, approximately size of West Virginia.

Topography: Alternating lowlands and highlands; many lakes, particularly in east, and rivers. Fertile soil. Forest and woodlands 28 percent; mainly pine, spruce, and birch. Arable land 49 percent; meadows and pastureland 22 percent. Highest elevation 297 meters.

Climate: Maritime position moderates otherwise continental climate. Average January temperature 1.6°C on coast and 2.1°C in Vilnius; average July temperature 17.8°C on coast and 18.1°C in Vilnius. Average annual precipitation 717 millimeters on coast and 490 millimeters in east.

Society

Population: 3,717,000 (1995 estimate). Population declined in early 1990s because of low natural growth rates and net out-migration. In 1994 birth rate 12.0 per 1,000 population; death

169

rate 12.8 per 1,000 population. Total fertility rate 2.1 children per woman in 1991. Population density 57.0 persons per square kilometer. Life expectancy 69.1 years in 1993 (63.3 years for males and 75.0 years for females).

Ethnic Groups: According to 1994 official estimate, Lithuanians 81.1 percent, Russians 8.5 percent, Poles 7.0 percent, Belarusians 1.5 percent, Ukrainians 1.0 percent, and others (including Latvians, Tatars, Gypsies, Germans, Estonians, and Jews) 0.9 percent.

Languages: Official language Lithuanian; Russian, Polish, Belarusian, Ukrainian, and other languages also used.

Religion: Predominantly Roman Catholic. Other denominations include Evangelical Reformed, Evangelical Lutheran, Russian Orthodox, Uniate, and Jewish.

Education: According to 1992 constitution, education compulsory from age six to sixteen and free at all levels. In 1993–94 some 510,500 students in 2,317 primary and secondary schools, 45,200 students in 108 secondary specialized institutions, and 53,000 students in fifteen higher education institutions (including universities). Optional religious instruction introduced in schools in 1991. Literacy rate 99 percent in 1994.

Health and Welfare: Sufficient facilities to guarantee free medical care. In 1990 forty-six physicians and dentists, 127 paramedical personnel, and 124 hospital beds per 10,000 inhabitants. Private health care practice legalized in late 1980s, but health care system remains mostly state owned and state run. Medical care does not meet Western standards; hindered by shortages of medical equipment, supplies, and drugs. National social security system provides cradle-to-grave social insurance and social benefits.

Labor Force: 1.9 million (1994 estimate); industry 32 percent; construction 12 percent; agriculture 18 percent; science, education, and culture 14 percent; health care 7 percent; transportation and communications 7 percent; and trade and government 10 percent.

Economy

Gross National Product (GNP): Estimated at US$4.9 billion in 1993; per capita income US$1,310. Gross domestic product (GDP) estimated at 20 billion litai in 1994; real GDP fell by 13.4 percent in 1991, by 35.0 percent in 1992, and by 16.5 percent in 1993, but grew by 2.0 percent in 1994. Inflation rate in 1994 estimated at 45 percent.

Agriculture: 24.0 percent of GDP in 1992. Significant reforms introduced in 1990s; 83 percent of agricultural privatization program completed by mid-1993. Large farms broken up into small holdings, often too small to be economically viable. Agricultural output fell by 50 percent from 1989 to 1994. Principal crops wheat, feed grains, flax, rye, barley, sugar beets, legumes, potatoes, and vegetables.

Industry: 33.9 percent of GDP in 1992. Industry provided 33 percent of employment in 1994. Industrial production declined by more than 50 percent in 1993.

Energy: Receives most of its electricity from Ignalina nuclear power plant, but highly dependent on fuels imported from Russia.

Exports: US$1 billion (1994 estimate). Major commodities machinery, electronics, textiles, light industrial products, and food products.

Imports: US$1.3 billion (1994 estimate). Major commodities natural gas, oil, coal, machinery, chemicals, and light industrial products.

Major Trading Partners: Russia, Germany, Ukraine, Belarus, Latvia, Poland, France, Italy, and United States.

Currency and Exchange Rate: Litas (pl., litai) introduced June 1993 and became sole legal tender August 1993. 1 litas = 100 centas. In October 1992, Russian ruble replaced by provisional coupon currency, the talonas (pl., talonai), pegged at parity with ruble; talonas had been circulating parallel with ruble since May 1992. In March 1996, 4.0 litai = US$1.

Fiscal year: Calendar year.

Transportation and Telecommunications

Roads: In 1994 about 55,603 kilometers total, of which 42,209 kilometers asphalted.

Railroads: In 1994 about 2,000 kilometers of railroads (1,524-millimeter gauge), of which 122 kilometers electrified. Train service available to Daugavpils in Latvia and to Poland and Belarus.

Civil Aviation: International airports at Vilnius and Siauliai. State-owned Lithuanian Airlines operates flights to Amsterdam, London, Paris, Copenhagen, Berlin, Frankfurt, and forty-three cities in former Soviet Union. Service also provided by Aeroflot, Austrian Airlines, Drakk Air Lines, Hamburg Airlines, LOT (Polish Airlines), Lufthansa, Malév, SAS (Scandinavian Airlines), and Swissair.

Shipping: 600 kilometers of inland waterways navigable year round. Inland port Kaunas; maritime port Klaipeda. During Soviet period, 90 percent of Klaipeda's traffic went to other Soviet republics.

Telecommunications: 900,000 telephone subscriber circuits, or 240 per 1,000 persons, among most advanced of former Soviet republics. In 1993 an estimated 1.4 million television sets and more than 1.4 million radios in use, or one per 2.7 persons.

Government and Politics

Government: Independent democratic republic. President, elected for term of five years and a maximum of two consecutive terms, is head of state. Seimas, a unicameral legislative body, holds supreme legislative authority. Its 141 members are elected for four-year terms. It initiates and approves legislation sponsored by prime minister. Cabinet, known as Council of Ministers, is headed by prime minister, who is appointed by president with approval of Seimas.

Judicial System: Based on civil law system, with no judicial review of legislative acts. Independent of authority of legislative and executive branches of government, but subject to their influence. Judicial power held by Supreme Court; Seimas appoints and dismisses its judges on recommendation of head of state. Other courts include Constitutional Court, Court of Appeals, and district, local, and special courts.

Politics: Two main political organizations: Lithuanian Democratic Labor Party (LDLP; successor to Communist Party of Lithuania), which won more than half of seats in Seimas elected October 1992; and Fatherland Union, main opposition grouping and successor to Sajudis independence movement. Numerous overlapping factions, coalitions, and smaller parties.

Administrative Divisions: Forty-four regions (*rajonai*; sing. *rajonas*—rural districts) and eleven municipalities, divided into twenty-two urban districts and ninety-two towns.

Foreign Relations: Member of United Nations and its specialized agencies, World Bank, and International Monetary Fund, and a number of European economic and security organizations. Since independence, cornerstone of Lithuanian foreign policy has been integration with European security institutions: Organization for Security and Cooperation in Europe (OSCE), Council of Europe (COE), European Union (EU), North Atlantic Cooperation Council (NACC), World Trade Organization (WTO), and, ultimately, North Atlantic Treaty Organization (NATO). Member of OSCE, COE, and NACC, and associate member of EU. Concluded Baltic Agreement on Economic Cooperation April 12, 1990, with Latvia and Estonia. Member of Council of the Baltic Sea States. Agreements on economic cooperation signed with Russia in November 1993; with Ukraine, February 1994; and with Poland, April 1994. On July 18, 1994, free-trade agreement signed with European Union effective January 1, 1995, to eliminate tariff barriers during six-year transition period.

National Security

Armed Forces: In 1994 armed forces totaled 8,900, including army (4,300), navy (350), air force (250), and border guard

(4,000). Mandatory draft period of one year in active-duty status; alternative service for conscientious objectors available. Also, 12,000-member Home Guard force. In February 1993, some 14,000 Russian troops remained in Lithuania; last Russian troops withdrawn August 1993.

Military Budget: About 1 percent of government expenditures allocated for defense in 1993.

Figure 11. Lithuania, 1995

LYING BETWEEN EAST AND WEST, through six centuries Lithuania has endured and been devastated by the clash of interests between the Swedes, the French, and the Germans on the one side and the Russians on the other. Many generations of Lithuanians have had to rebuild after the destruction brought upon them as a result of East-West conflicts or domestic insurrections against Russia. Lithuanians also have been forced to take sides, although they have tried to assert their own will, especially in modern times.

Lithuania became independent in 1918, but in 1940 it was occupied and annexed by the Soviet Union. Soviet hegemony, which wreaked further devastation, lasted until 1991, when Lithuania once again achieved recognition as an independent state. The circumstances of the Soviet takeover and the refusal of the United States and other nations to recognize de jure Lithuania's forcible incorporation into the Soviet Union have distinguished Lithuania, as well as the neighboring states of Estonia and Latvia, from the other former Soviet republics in international law and politics throughout the postwar era.

Historical Setting

Early History

Lithuanians belong to the Baltic group of nations. Their ancestors moved to the Baltic region about 3000 B.C. from beyond the Volga region of central Russia. In Roman times, they traded amber with Rome and around A.D. 900–1000 split into different language groups, namely, Lithuanians, Prussians, Latvians, Semigallians, and others. The Prussians were conquered by the Teutonic Knights, and, ironically, the name "Prussia" was taken over by the conquerors, who destroyed or assimilated Prussia's original inhabitants. Other groups also died out or were assimilated by their neighbors. Only the Lithuanians and the Latvians survived the ravages of history.

Traditions of Lithuanian statehood date from the early Middle Ages. As a nation, Lithuania emerged about 1230 under the leadership of Duke Mindaugas. He united Lithuanian tribes to defend themselves against attacks by the Teutonic Knights, who had conquered the kindred tribes of Prussia and also parts of present-day Latvia. In 1251 Mindaugas accepted Latin Christianity, and in 1253 he became king. But his nobles disagreed with his policy of coexistence with the Teutonic Knights and with his search for access to western Europe. Mindaugas was killed, the monarchy was discontinued, and the country reverted to paganism. His successors looked for expansion toward the Slavic East. At that early stage of development, Lithuania had to face the historically recurring question dictated by its geopolitical position—whether to join western or eastern Europe.

At the end of the fourteenth century, Lithuania was already a large empire extending from the Baltic Sea to the shores of the Black Sea. Grand Duke Jogaila (r. 1377–81 and 1382–92) of the Gediminas Dynasty faced a problem similar to that faced by Mindaugas 150 years earlier: whether to look to the East or the West for political and cultural influences. Under pressure from the Teutonic Knights, Lithuania, a kingdom of Lithuanians and Slavs, pagans and Orthodox Christians, could no longer stand alone. Jogaila chose to open links to western Europe and to defeat the Teutonic Knights, who claimed that their mission was not to conquer the Lithuanians but to Christianize them. He was offered the crown of Poland, which he accepted in 1386. In return for the crown, Jogaila promised to Christianize Lithuania. He and his cousin Vytautas, who became Lithuania's grand duke, converted Lithuania to Christianity beginning in 1387. Lithuania was the last pagan country in Europe to become Christian. The cousins then defeated the Teutonic Knights in the Battle of Tannenberg in 1410, stopping Germanic expansion to the east.

Attempts by Vytautas to separate Lithuania from Poland (and to secure his own crown) failed because of the strength of the Polish nobility. Lithuania continued in a political union with Poland. In 1569 Lithuania and Poland united into a single state, the Polish-Lithuanian Commonwealth, whose capital was Kraków, and for the next 226 years Lithuania shared the fate of Poland. During this period, Lithuania's political elite was dominated by the Polish nobility and church, resulting in neglect of the Lithuanian language and introduction of Polish social and political institutions. It also opened the doors to Western models in education and culture.

In 1795 an alliance between the Germanic states—Prussia and Austria—and the Russian Empire ended Poland's independent existence. Lithuania became a Russian province. Two insurrections, initiated by the Poles in 1831 and again in 1863, failed to liberate the country. The Russian Empire eliminated Polish influence on Lithuanians and introduced Russian social and political institutions. Under tsarist rule, Lithuanian schools were forbidden, Lithuanian publications in the Latin script were outlawed, and the Roman Catholic Church was severely suppressed. However, the restrictive policies failed to extinguish indigenous cultural institutions and language.

A national awakening in the 1880s, led by the secular and clerical intelligentsia, produced demands for self-government. In 1905 Lithuania was the first of the Russian provinces to demand autonomy. Independence was not granted because the tsar firmly reestablished his rule after the Revolution of 1905. But the demand, articulated by the elected Grand Diet of Vilnius, was not abandoned. World War I led to the collapse of the two empires—the Russian and the German—making it possible for Lithuania to assert its statehood. Germany's attempt to persuade Lithuania to become a German protectorate was unsuccessful. On February 16, 1918, Lithuania declared its full independence, and the country still celebrates that day as its Independence Day.

Independence, 1918–40

During 1918–20 Lithuania successfully fought a war with newly independent Poland to defend its independence. At the end of 1920, however, Poland annexed Lithuania's capital city and province of Vilnius, which it held until World War II. Lithuania refused to have diplomatic relations with Poland until 1938 on the grounds that Poland illegally held the Vilnius region. After declaring independence, Lithuania also fought against the Bermondt-Avalov army, a German-sponsored group of military adventurers that sought to preserve German influence in the Baltic region, and against Russia. In November 1918, the Red Army invaded the country but ultimately was repulsed by the forces of the young Lithuanian government. On July 9, 1920, Soviet leader Vladimir I. Lenin signed a peace treaty with Lithuania, "forever" denouncing Russia's claims to the territory and recognizing the Lithuanian state.

In the early 1920s, Lithuania had a border dispute with Germany. The city and region of Klaipeda (Memel in German) had been under German rule for 700 years. Originally inhabited by Lithuanians, it was detached from Germany in 1919 by the Treaty of Versailles and placed under French administration. In 1923 Lithuanians organized an insurrection and took over the Klaipeda region.

These conflicts burdened Lithuania's international diplomacy. Domestically, however, they fed the development of national identity and cultural awareness, displacing German and Polish influence.

Lithuania's early disorganization caused a delay in its recognition by Western powers; the last to do so was the United States in 1922. Washington recognized Lithuania's independence only after it had become clear that Western intervention in Russia could not restore the Russian Empire and that the communists were firmly entrenched in Moscow.

Independent Lithuania, led by political leaders mostly in their thirties or early forties, became a democratic republic with a strong legislature, a weak executive, a multiparty system, and a proportional system of representation. Christian Democratic coalitions dominated the democratic period. However, almost a third of the country was illiterate, and farmers—87 percent of the population—were conservative and unfamiliar with democratic processes. In 1926 the Socialist-Populist coalition government was removed by a military coup. Antanas Smetona, a former acting president, was elected to the presidency by a rump parliament. Within three years, he established an authoritarian regime. Political parties were outlawed and the press censored, but Smetona did not completely suppress civil rights. Smetona established Tautininkai, a nationalist political party, which reappeared in the parliament in 1991 after Lithuania regained independence from the Soviet Union.

From 1920 to 1940, independent Lithuania made great strides in nation building and development. A progressive land reform program was introduced in 1922, a cooperative movement was organized, and a strong currency and conservative fiscal management were maintained. Schools and universities were established (there had been no institutions of higher education and very few secondary schools under Russian rule), and illiteracy was substantially reduced. Artists and writers of the period produced works that have become classics.

The Soviet Republic

On August 23, 1939, Joseph V. Stalin and Adolf Hitler concluded the notorious Nazi-Soviet Nonaggression Pact (also known as the Molotov-Ribbentrop Pact). The agreement had a secret protocol that divided Poland, much of Central Europe, and the Baltic states between Germany and the Soviet Union. Lithuania, at first assigned to the German sphere of influence, in September was transferred to the Soviet Union. In October 1939, the Soviet Union forced on Lithuania a nonaggression pact that allowed Moscow to garrison 20,000 troops in the country. In return, the city of Vilnius, now occupied by Soviet troops, was granted to Lithuania. On June 15, 1940, Lithuania was overrun by the Red Army. At first a procommunist, so-called people's government was installed, and elections to a new parliament were organized. The elections were noncompetitive; a single approved list of candidates was presented to the voters. The parliament met on July 21, declared Soviet rule, and "joined" the Soviet Union as the Lithuanian Soviet Socialist Republic on August 6, 1940. The United States and many other countries refused to recognize the Soviet occupation.

Soviet rule brought about radical political and economic changes and Stalinist terror, which culminated in deportations to Siberia of more than 30,000 people on the night of June 14–15, 1941. Germany interrupted the Stalinist terror by attacking the Soviet Union on June 22, 1941. The next day, the Lithuanian Activist Front, an organization of anti-Soviet resistance groups, revolted against the Soviet occupiers. Partisans took over the largest cities—Kaunas and Vilnius—and declared restoration of Lithuanian independence. The Germans replaced the provisional government with a Lithuanian Vertrauensrat (Council of Trustees), which was headed by an ethnic Lithuanian, General Petras Kubiliunas, and was given some autonomy in local affairs.

The Lithuanian leadership went underground. An anti-Nazi resistance movement developed, publishing underground newspapers, organizing economic boycotts, and gathering arms. The resistance hoped that after victory the Western allies would insist on the restoration of Lithuanian statehood.

A Soviet-sponsored underground also existed in Lithuania beginning in 1942. It staged military raids against German transportation, administrative, and economic enterprises. The Soviet forces were aided by the remnants of the Communist Party of Lithuania, now barely surviving in the underground.

The nationalist Lithuanian resistance was supported by many Lithuanian political parties and resistance groups, including the Social Democrats and a coalition known as the Supreme Committee for the Liberation of Lithuania, which continued its activities many years after Lithuania was retaken by the Red Army. In 1943 this resistance frustrated German efforts at organizing a Lithuanian Schutz-Staffel (SS) legion. The Nazis responded by arresting Lithuanian nationalists and by closing universities. Moreover, occupation authorities succeeded, in the period 1941–44, in recruiting or capturing tens of thousands of people to work in Germany or to serve in the German military. Many perished in prisons or concentration camps. The main victims, however, were members of Lithuania's Jewish community. About 185,000 Jews, or 85 percent of the community's population, were massacred by Nazi squads, which were helped by Lithuanian collaborators in a number of localities.

Soviet armies recaptured Lithuania in the summer of 1944, although Klaipeda did not fall until January 1945. Antanas Snieckus, the Communist Party of Lithuania leader, returned from Moscow with the other officials who had fled before the advancing German armies. Lithuania's full Sovietization, however, was obstructed from 1944 to 1952 by an armed partisan resistance movement, which cost an estimated 20,000 to 30,000 partisan casualties.

Soviet rule in Lithuania displayed well-known features of communist rule. The party had a monopoly on power, and the management of the economy was centralized. The regime collectivized agriculture from 1947 to 1951. Secret police terrorized the society and attempted to transfer Lithuanian nationalist loyalties to the communists. Deportations to Siberia were resumed. Religion was brutally suppressed. One Roman Catholic bishop was shot, one perished in prison, two died shortly after release, and two were banished for more than thirty years, leaving only one in office. Almost one-third of the clergy was deported, although survivors were allowed to return after Stalin's death in 1953. Eventually, the training of new priests was essentially stopped.

Institutions of power—the party, the secret police, and the government—at first were mainly in Russian hands. In the postwar period, ethnic Lithuanians constituted only 18.4 percent of the republic's communist party members. Beginning in the 1950s, college graduates and those who wanted to make careers in economic, cultural, or political life realized that the Soviet system was not transitory, so they joined the communist party. The party swelled to a membership of 205,000 by 1989, but most of these members were opportunists, very different from the few revolutionary fanatics who had administered

Hill of Crosses, near Siauliai, symbolizes defiance of Soviet rule.
Courtesy Jonas Tamulaitis

Lithuania in the immediate postwar period. Still others joined the party in the expectation that they would be of better use to the preservation of Lithuanian traditions, language, and culture in the ranks of the ruling group. There developed a stratum of communists who wanted to promote not only Moscow's but also Lithuania's advantage.

Underground resistance never disappeared, although the armed underground was destroyed. As a movement, resistance was first sparked by efforts to defend the Roman Catholic Church. After the Soviet invasion of Czechoslovakia in 1968, which led to increased repression in the Soviet Union, the dissident movement spread. In the 1970s, Lithuania had numerous underground publications. The most significant and regularly published among them was *The Chronicle of the Catholic Church of Lithuania*. It was never uncovered by the Soviet secret police, the Committee for State Security (Komitet gosudarstvennoy bezopasnosti—KGB), and was published for twenty years. In 1972 a young student, Romas Kalanta, immolated himself in protest against Soviet rule. Army units had to be sent in to quell a street rebellion by students that followed the self-immolation. The Committee for the Defense of Religious Rights and the Helsinki Watch Committee were established in the underground. Dissident work brought arrests and imprisonment. At the same time, the Lithuanian intelligentsia, especially writers and artists, demanded greater freedom of creative expression and protection of the Lithuanian language, traditions, and cultural values from the pressure to Russify that intensified during the administration of Leonid I. Brezhnev (1964–82).

The Move Toward Independence, 1987–91

The situation did not change until Mikhail S. Gorbachev came to power in 1985. Even then, Lithuania's communist party leadership hesitated to embrace Gorbachev's program of limited economic reforms under his policy of *perestroika* (see Glossary). The death of Petras Griskevicius, first secretary of the Communist Party of Lithuania, in 1987 did little to improve the atmosphere for reform. The new first secretary, Ringaudas Songaila, was a conservative functionary. But encouraged by new winds from Moscow, Baltic dissidents began in 1987 to hold public demonstrations in Riga, Tallinn, and Vilnius. In 1988, against the wishes of Songaila's regime, Lithuanian, engaged in widespread celebration of the February 16 Independence Day. Lithuanian intellectuals were pushed into taking more forceful action as well. Meeting at the Academy of Sciences on June 3, 1988, communist and noncommunist intellectuals formed "an initiative group" to organize a movement to support Gorbachev's program of *glasnost* (see Glossary), democratization, and *perestroika*. A council composed equally of communist party members and nonparty members was chosen to organize the Lithuanian Reconstruction Movement, which became known subsequently simply as Sajudis (Movement). The Communist Party of Lithuania leadership did not like this independent action but, knowing Gorbachev's limited acceptance of "informal" societies, did not interfere with the effort.

The movement supported Gorbachev's policies, but at the same time it promoted Lithuanian national issues such as restoration of the Lithuanian language as the "official" language. Its demands included revelations of the truth about the Stalinist years, protection of the environment, cessation of construction on a third nuclear reactor at the Ignalina nuclear power plant, and disclosure of secret protocols of the Nazi-Soviet Nonaggression Pact. Sajudis used mass meetings to advance its goals. At first, party leaders shunned these meetings, but by mid-1988 their participation became a political necessity. Thus, a Sajudis rally on June 24, 1988, was attended by Algirdas Brazauskas, then party secretary for industrial affairs.

In October 1988, Brazauskas was appointed first secretary of the party to replace Songaila, and Sajudis held its founding conference in Vilnius. It subsequently elected as its chairman Vytautas Landsbergis, a professor of musicology who was not a member of the communist party. In the elections to Moscow's newly authorized Congress of People's Deputies (see Glossary) in March-May 1989, Sajudis was victorious. From the communist party, the voters elected only Brazauskas and Vladimiras Beriozovas, his associate, whom Sajudis did not oppose. From that time, Brazauskas cooperated fully with Sajudis. Lithuanian sovereignty—as distinguished from Lithuanian independence, which had been declared on February 16, 1918—was proclaimed in May 1989, and Lithuania's incorporation into the Soviet Union was declared illegal. In August a human chain from Tallinn to Vilnius commemorated the fiftieth anniversary of the Nazi-Soviet Nonaggression Pact. In December Brazauskas forced the Communist Party of Lithuania to secede from the Communist Party of the Soviet Union and to give up its monopoly on power.

But even the separation of the Communist Party of Lithuania from Moscow did not save it in the electoral contest for the Supreme Soviet of the republic in March 1990. In the election, the Communist Party of Lithuania won only twenty-three of the 141 seats. On March 11, the newly elected parliament voted unanimously for independence. Brazauskas lost the election for chairman of the presidium of the Supreme Soviet to Landsbergis.

Moscow did not accept the legality of the independence vote, however; in April 1990, it imposed an economic blockade that lasted for three months, until the Lithuanian legislature, now known as the Supreme Council, agreed to a six-month moratorium on its independence declaration. Later, Moscow obstructed Lithuanian efforts to gain Western recognition, and on January 13, 1991, attempted to use force to remove the Lithuanian government in Vilnius and to reestablish Soviet rule. Although this attempted coup ended in a massacre of civilians—thirteen died, and hundreds were wounded—by the Soviet army, Lithuania's determination did not change. Finally, the failure of the August 1991 coup in Moscow permitted Lithuania to regain self-determination and prompted the international community to recognize it as an independent state. The United States extended recognition on September 2, and the Soviet Union did so on September 6. Lithuania was admitted to the United Nations on September 16, 1991.

Physical Environment

Lithuania is situated on the eastern shore of the Baltic Sea. Lithuania's boundaries have changed several times since 1918, but they have been stable since 1945 (see fig. 2). Currently, Lithuania covers an area of about 65,200 square kilometers. About the size of West Virginia, it is larger than Belgium, Denmark, the Netherlands, or Switzerland.

Lithuania's northern neighbor is Latvia. The two countries share a border that extends 453 kilometers. Lithuania's eastern border with Belarus is longer, stretching 502 kilometers. The border with Poland on the south is relatively short, only ninety-one kilometers, but is very busy because of international traffic. Lithuania also has a 227-kilometer border with Russia. Russian territory adjacent to Lithuania is Kaliningrad Oblast, which is the northern part of the former German East Prussia, including the city of Kaliningrad. Finally, Lithuania has 108 kilometers of Baltic seashore with an ice-free harbor at Klaipeda. The Baltic coast offers sandy beaches and pine forests and attracts thousands of vacationers.

Topography, Drainage, and Climate

Lithuania lies at the edge of the East European Plain. Its landscape was shaped by the glaciers of the last Ice Age. Lithuania's terrain is an alternation of moderate lowlands and highlands.The highest elevation is 297 meters above sea level, found in the eastern part of the republic and separated from the uplands of the western region of Zemaiciai by the very fertile plains of the southwestern and central regions. The landscape is punctuated by 2,833 lakes larger than one hectare and an additional 1,600 ponds smaller than one hectare. The majority of the lakes are found in the eastern part of the country. Lithuania also has 758 rivers longer than ten kilometers. The largest river is the Nemunas (total length 917 kilometers),

*Memorial in Vilnius to Lithuanians killed during the Soviet assault
on the city's television-radio station in January 1991
Courtesy Maya Laurinaitis*

which originates in Belarus. The other larger waterways are the
Neris (510 kilometers), Venta (346 kilometers), and Sesupe
(298 kilometers) rivers. However, only 600 kilometers of
Lithuania's rivers are navigable.

The country's climate, which ranges between maritime and
continental, is relatively mild. Average temperatures on the
coast are 1.6°C in January and 17.8°C in July. In Vilnius the
average temperatures are 2.1°C in January and 18.1°C in July.
Average annual precipitation is 717 millimeters on the coast
and 490 millimeters in the eastern part of the country. The
growing season lasts 202 days in the western part of the country
and 169 days in the eastern part.

Once a heavily forested land, Lithuania's territory today consists of only 28 percent woodlands—mainly pine, spruce, and
birch forests. Ash and oak are very scarce. The forests are rich
in mushrooms and berries.

The Environment

Concerned with environmental deterioration, Lithuanian
governments have created several national parks and reserva-

tions. The country's flora and fauna have suffered, however, from an almost fanatical drainage of land for agricultural use. Environmental problems of a different nature were created by the development of environmentally unsafe industries, including the Ignalina nuclear power plant, which still operates two reactors similar to those at Chornobyl' (Chernobyl' in Russian), and the chemical and other industries that pollute the air and empty wastes into rivers and lakes. According to calculations by experts, about one-third of Lithuanian territory is covered by polluted air at any given time. Problems exist mainly in the cities, such as Vilnius, Kaunas, Jonava, Mazeikiai, Elektrenai, and Naujoji Akmene—the sites of fertilizer and other chemical plants, an oil refinery, power station, and a cement factory. Water quality also is poor. The city of Kaunas, with a population of more than 400,000, still has no water purification plant. Only one-quarter of sewage-contaminated water in the republic is processed because cleaning facilities are not yet available. River and lake pollution also is a legacy of Soviet carelessness with the environment. The Kursiu Marios (Courland Lagoon), for example, separated from the Baltic Sea by a strip of high dunes and pine forests, is about 85 percent contaminated. Beaches in the Baltic resorts, such as the well-known vacation area of Palanga, are frequently closed for swimming because of contamination. Forests affected by acid rain are found in the vicinity of Jonava, Mazeikiai, and Elektrenai, which are the chemical, oil, and power-generation centers.

As a Soviet republic, Lithuania was among the first to introduce environmental regulations. However, because of Moscow's emphasis on increasing production and because of numerous local violations, technological backwardness, and political apathy, serious environmental problems now exist.

Natural Resources

Lithuania's landscape is pleasing to the eye but modest in natural resources. The republic has an abundance of limestone, clay, quartz sand, gypsum sand, and dolomite, which are suitable for making high-quality cement, glass, and ceramics. There also is an ample supply of mineral water, but energy sources and industrial materials are all in short supply. Oil was discovered in Lithuania in the 1950s, but only a few wells operate, and all that do are located in the western part of the country. It is estimated that the Baltic Sea shelf and the western region of Lithuania hold commercially viable amounts of oil, but when exploited this oil will satisfy only about 20 percent of Lithuania's annual need for petroleum products for the next twenty years. Lithuania has a large amount of thermal energy along the Baltic Sea coast, however, which could be used to heat hundreds of thousands of homes, as is done in Iceland. In addition, iron ore deposits have been found in the southern region of Lithuania. But commercial exploitation of these deposits probably would require strip mining, which is environmentally unsound. Moreover, exploitation of these resources will depend on Lithuania's ability to attract capital and technology from abroad.

Society

Population

In 1995 Lithuania had an estimated population of 3,717,000, which was 44,000 fewer people than in 1992. Of the total, females were in the majority, as in most Central European countries and in Russia. The population group that has increased most quickly in Lithuania, as in many other relatively developed countries, consists of senior citizens and pensioners (those over age sixty) (see fig. 12). For example, pensioners grew in number from 546,000 to 906,000 between 1970 and 1991. This group grew from 17.3 percent of the population in 1980 to 19.5 percent in 1992. The zero-to-fifteen-year-old age-group, by comparison, diminished slightly from 25.2 percent in 1980 to 23.9 in 1992, not as a result of increased mortality but as a result of a continuing decline in the birth rate. The group of working-age people (aged sixteen to fifty-nine for men and fifteen to fifty-four for women) also decreased, from 57.5 percent to 56.6 percent. The birth rate decreased from 17.6 per 1,000 population in 1970 to 12.5 per 1,000 population in 1993 and 12.0 per 1,000 population in 1994. Mortality increased from 10.5 per 1,000 population in 1980 to 10.9 in 1991 and 12.8 in 1994. Life expectancy in 1993 was 63.3 years for males and 75.0 years for females, or an average of 69.1 years. This, too, was on the decline from the peak years of 1986–87, when the average was 72.5 years (67.9 years for males and 76.6 years for females). The decrease coincides with the worsening economic situation and the decline in the quality of health services during the postindependence economic transition.

The average Lithuanian family is still somewhat larger than families in the neighboring Baltic states, but it has been declin-

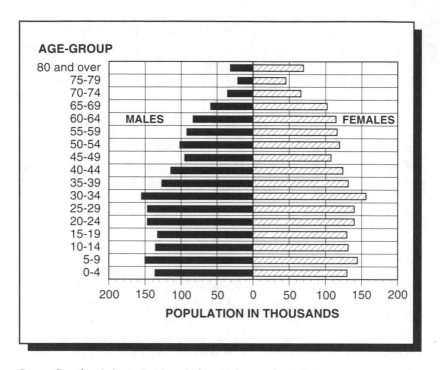

Source: Based on information from Lithuania, Lietuvos statistikos departamentas, *Social and Economic Development in Lithuania, January–March 1994*, Vilnius, 1994, 8.

Figure 12. Population of Lithuania by Age and Gender, 1994

ing. The average family size shrank to 3.2 by 1989. People marry young, but their marriages are often quickly dissolved. The divorce rate has been increasing. In 1989, of 9.3 marriages per 1,000 population, there were 3.3 divorces. The highest divorce rate is among ethnic Russians and in ethnically mixed families. These statistics indicate the existence of social problems with which society has been ill equipped to deal. Churches are not allowed to intervene to address these problems, and the profession of social work is still virtually nonexistent. The postcommunist government must face the formidable task of developing a social work sector.

Under Soviet rule, especially in the last decade, one-half or more of the annual population increase resulted from immigration, primarily from Russia. But this situation has changed. More people emigrate to former Soviet republics than arrive from them, and more people leave for the West than come from there. In 1990 Lithuania's net migration loss to former

Soviet republics was 6,345. Loss to the West includes Jewish emigration. Gains from the West include returning Americans and Canadians of Lithuanian descent.

Soviet industrialization brought about fast and sustained urban development. Annually, almost 1 percent of the rural population has moved to cities since the early 1950s. In 1939 only 23 percent of the population lived in cities; in 1992 the urban percentage was 69. Lithuania has five cities with a population of more than 100,000. The largest is the capital, Vilnius, established in 1321 (1994 population 584,000); Kaunas, the capital between the two world wars, founded in 1361 (1994 population 424,000); the port city of Klaipeda, established in 1252 (1994 population 205,000); the center of the electronics industry, Siauliai, founded in 1236 (1994 population 147,000); and the city of chemical and automobile parts industries, Panevezys, founded in 1548 (1994 population 132,000).

In 1994, according to official estimates, 81.1 percent of Lithuania's population consisted of ethnic Lithuanians. The remaining 18.9 percent was divided among Russians (8.5 percent), Poles (7.0 percent), Belarusians (1.5 percent), Ukrainians (1.0 percent), and others, including Jews, Latvians, Tatars, Gypsies, Germans, and Estonians (0.9 percent). Altogether, people of more than 100 nationalities live in Lithuania.

The proportion of the ethnic Lithuanian population—more than 90 percent of whom speak Lithuanian—stayed at 80 percent or a fraction higher until 1989, when it dropped slightly below 80 percent. The decrease resulted in fears that a pattern of decline would develop as a result of increasing Russian immigration, which might endanger the survival of Lithuania's culture and national identity as it did in Estonia and Latvia.

The Russian minority consists of old and new immigrants. Many Russians settled in Lithuania in the nineteenth century or in the early twentieth century, shortly after the Bolsheviks came to power in Moscow. Two-thirds of the Russian minority, however, are immigrants—or their descendants—of the Soviet era, many of whom regard Lithuania as their homeland. They usually live in larger cities. In Vilnius 20.2 percent of the population was Russian in 1989. The same year, in Klaipeda, 28.2 percent of the inhabitants were Russians; in Siauliai, 10.5 percent. Ignalina, where the nuclear power plant is located, had a Russian majority of 64.2 percent. Less than 10 percent of the population in Kaunas and the resort towns of Druskininkai, Palanga, or Neringa was Russian, however. These percentages most likely will decline slightly in the 1990s because some Russians, finding it difficult to accept that they live in a "foreign" country, are leaving Lithuania. The majority of Russians, however, have shown little inclination to leave; 88 percent of those polled in the fall of 1993 described relations between their group and the ethnic Lithuanian population as good, and more than 60 percent felt that economic conditions for people like themselves would be worse in Russia than in Lithuania.

Poles live primarily in the city of Vilnius (18.8 percent of Vilnius's population in 1989) and in three adjacent rural districts. In 1989 the ethnic Polish population in the Salcininkai district constituted 79.6 percent; in the rural district of Vilnius, it was 63.5 percent; and in the district of Trakai, it was 23.8 percent. Small Polish groups also live in a number of other localities. Since the late 1940s, the Polish presence in Lithuania has declined considerably. About 200,000 Poles left Lithuania for Poland in 1946, under an agreement signed between Warsaw and Vilnius. Afterward, the Polish percentage of Lithuania's population declined from 8.5 percent in 1959 to 7.0 percent in 1989, primarily as a result of the influx of Russians. The Polish population of eastern Lithuania is composed of inhabitants whose families settled there centuries ago, of immigrants who came from Poland in the nineteenth and early twentieth centuries when the region was part of Poland, and of many assimilated Lithuanians and Belarusians.

Jews began settling in Lithuania in the fourteenth century. In time, Vilnius and some other cities became centers of Jewish learning, and Vilnius was internationally known as the Jerusalem of the North. Between the two world wars, Jews developed an active educational and cultural life. The Jewish community, which did not experience large-scale persecution until World War II, was almost entirely liquidated during the Nazi occupation. In 1989 only 12,400 Jews were left in Lithuania, and emigration after independence had cut their number to an estimated 6,500 by 1994.

For centuries, Vilnius has been an ethnically diverse city. Historically, the city has served as a cultural center for Lithuanians, Poles, Jews, and Belorussians. In the sixteenth and early seventeenth centuries, it also was a center of Ukrainian religious and cultural life. At the turn of the century, the largest minority ethnic group was Jewish. After World War II, the largest minority ethnic group was Polish. The population of Vilnius

Main pedestrian thoroughfare in downtown Kaunas
Courtesy Judith Gefter
Kalvariju Market in Vilnius
Courtesy Jonas Tamulaitis

in 1989 was 50.5 percent Lithuanian, 20.2 percent Russian, 18.8 percent Polish, and 5.3 percent Belorussian.

Health and Welfare

The Lithuanian constitution of 1992 provides guarantees of social rights that were earlier provided by the Soviet regime. The constitution puts special emphasis on the maintenance and care of the family. It expresses in detail, for example, the guarantee for working mothers to receive paid leave before and after childbirth (Article 39). The constitution provides for free public education in all state schools, including schools of higher education (Article 41). The constitution forbids forced labor (Article 48); legalizes labor unions and the right to strike (Articles 50 and 51); guarantees annual paid vacations (Article 49); and guarantees old-age and disability pensions, unemployment and sick leave compensation, and support for widows and families that have lost their head of household, as well as for others in situations as defined by law (Article 52). Finally, the constitution guarantees free medical care (Article 53).

All political groups support these guarantees—considered more or less inviolable—although it is not clear to what extent the government will be able to fund the promised services during the continuing economic transition. The amounts of support and the quality of services have declined from the modest, but always predictable, level first established in the Soviet period.

The national system of social security consists of programs of social insurance and social benefits designed to continue the benefits provided by the Soviet system. Social insurance includes old-age retirement; survivor and disability pensions; unemployment compensation; pregnancy, childbirth, and child supplements; certain welfare support; and free medical care. It is cradle-to-grave insurance. According to a 1990 law, payments cannot be lower than necessary for a "minimal" living standard. In 1990 old-age and disability pensions in Lithuania were slightly more generous than in Estonia and Latvia. The budget for the program is separate from the national and local budgets. Only military pensions and some other special pensions are paid from the national budget.

Social insurance is financed, according to a law passed in 1991, from required payments by workers and employers, from income generated by the management of state social insurance activities, and from budgetary supplements by the state if the program threatens to run a deficit. To be eligible for an old-age pension, a male worker must be at least sixty years of age and have at least a twenty-five-year record of employment. A woman must be fifty-five and have a record of twenty years of employment. This category of recipients includes not only factory and government workers but also farmers and farm workers.

A program of social benefits is financed by local governments. It includes support payments for women during pregnancy and childbirth and for expenses after the child's birth. The program features single payments for each newly born child, as well as child support for single parents or families. These latter payments continue up to age limits established by law. The state also maintains a number of orphanages, sanatoriums, and old-age homes.

In the medical field, Lithuania has sufficient facilities to fulfill the guarantee of free medical care. In 1990 the country had more than 14,700 physicians and 2,300 dentists; its ratio of forty-six physicians and dentists combined per 10,000 inhabitants compared favorably with that of most advanced countries. In addition, in 1990 Lithuania had more than 47,000 paramedical personnel, or 127 per 10,000 population and 46,200 hospital beds, or 124 beds per 10,000 population. In the medical profession, Lithuania's cardiologists are among the most advanced in the former Soviet Union. In 1987 the first heart transplant operation was performed at the cardiac surgery clinic of Vilnius University. Hundreds of kidney transplants have been performed as well. One reasonably reliable and generally used indicator of the quality of a country's health services system is infant mortality. In 1990 Lithuania's infant mortality rate of 10.3 per 1,000 population was among the lowest of the Soviet republics but higher than that of many West European countries.

Special features of Lithuania's health status are high alcoholism (191 cases per 100,000 persons), low drug abuse (3.1 cases per 100,000), and few cases of human immunodeficiency virus (HIV) infection. Reported cases of HIV in 1992 were under 100. The main causes of death are cardiovascular diseases, cancer, accidents, and respiratory diseases. In addition to alcoholism, important risk factors for disease are smoking, a diet high in saturated fat, hypertension, and environmental pollution.

Notwithstanding efficient ambulance service and emergency care, medical services and facilities in Lithuania suffer from a lack of equipment, supplies, and drugs, as well as from inertia in the operation and administration of health services. The system is mainly state owned and state run. Private medical practice, begun only in the late 1980s, has not progressed appreciably because of the economic crisis. Since 1989 the government has encouraged church groups and others to enter the field of welfare services and medicine. The best-known such group is the Roman Catholic charitable organization Caritas.

Health care expenditures increased from 3.3 percent of the gross national product (GNP—see Glossary) in 1960 to 4.9 percent of GNP in 1990, but this figure is still low by world standards. Lithuania is unable to afford investments to improve its health care infrastructure at this time. Lithuania needs humanitarian assistance from the world community in importing the most critically needed drugs and vaccines. Disease prevention needs to be emphasized, especially with regard to prenatal, pediatric, and dental care. To reduce the occurrence of prevalent risk factors, the government needs to make fundamental improvements in public education and health programs.

Lithuania's standard of living in the early 1990s was slightly below Estonia's and Latvia's but higher than in the rest of the former Soviet Union. At the end of 1992, the standard of living had declined substantially, however. Energy shortages caused severe limitations in heating apartments and providing hot water and electricity. Before the post-Soviet economic transition, Lithuanians had abundant food supplies and consumed 3,400 calories a day per capita, compared with 2,805 calories for Finns and 3,454 calories for Swedes. But an average Lithuanian had only 19.1 square meters of apartment living space (less in the cities, more in rural areas), which was much less than the 30.5 square meters Finns had in the late 1980s. Housing, moreover, had fewer amenities than in the Scandinavian countries; 75 percent of Lithuanian urban housing had running water in 1989, 62 percent had hot water, 74 percent had central heating, 70 percent had flush toilets, and 64 percent had bathing facilities. Formerly low utility rates skyrocketed in the 1990s. Rents also increased, although by the end of 1992 almost 90 percent of all state-owned housing (there was some privately owned housing under Soviet rule) had been privatized—bought from the state, mostly by those who lived there. In 1989 families were well equipped with radios and televisions (109 and 107 sets, respectively, per 100 families). Most had refrigerators (ninety-one per 100 families), and many had

Elderly woman on the outskirts of Druskininkai
Courtesy Maya Laurinaitis

washing machines (seventy), bicycles (eighty-four), vacuum cleaners (sixty), sewing machines (forty-eight), and tape recorders (forty-four). Every third family had a private automobile (thirty-six automobiles per 100 families). Detracting from the quality of life, however, was the increasing rate of violent crime, especially in the larger cities (see Crime and Law Enforcement, this ch.).

Religion

Traditionally, Lithuania has been a Roman Catholic country. Although severely affected by Soviet repression, the Roman Catholic Church remains the dominant and the most influential denomination. However, Lithuania in the past has had two small but active Protestant denominations, the Evangelical Reformed (Calvinist) and the Evangelical Lutheran. In addition, Orthodox Christianity as well as Judaism have roots at least as old as those of Roman Catholicism. In 1991 a Western poll found that 69 percent of respondents in Lithuania identified themselves as Roman Catholics (in 1939 the percentage was 85), 4 percent identified themselves as Orthodox, and 1 percent professed Evangelical Christian beliefs. New in this self-identification was a large category—25 percent—who did not profess any religion. Lithuanian journalists have also noted

Skyline view of Kaunas
Courtesy Maya Laurinaitis

that twenty-one out of the 141 new members of parliament elected in 1992 left out "so help me God" from the oath when sworn in as deputies.

In 1992 Lithuania's Roman Catholic Church consisted of two archdioceses (Vilnius and Kaunas) and four dioceses (Kaisiadorys, Panevezys, Vilkaviskis, and Telsiai). The church is presided over by Cardinal Vincentas Sladkevicius in Kaunas. For thirty years, Sladkevicius, then a bishop, was held by Soviet authorities in internal exile. The church has 688 parishes, two theological seminaries (one reestablished in 1990), and several convents and monasteries. There is also one Uniate, or Eastern-Rite Catholic, congregation.

The archeparchy (archdiocese) of the Russian Orthodox Church has forty-five parishes and two monasteries. Archbishop Chrisostom and his archeparchy are under the jurisdiction of the Patriarch of Moscow. The Old Believers (see Glossary) have fifty-one congregations. The Lithuanian Evangelical Lutheran Church under Bishop Jonas Kalvanas has thirty-three congregations, and the Evangelical Reformed Church (Calvinist) has eight. Other Christian denominations include Baptists, Seventh-Day Adventists, and Pentecostals. The non-Christian religious groups include Jews (two communities), Muslims (four communities), Krishna followers (two communities), and one Karaite (see Glossary) group.

Traditionally, most Roman Catholics in Lithuania were either Lithuanians or Poles, and the Orthodox and Old Believer adherents were predominantly Russians. This division has not changed, although currently it is no longer possible to assume religious affiliation on the basis of ethnic identity. The Calvinist and Evangelical Lutheran groups are very small—an estimated 15,000 Calvinists and 35,000 Lutherans. The younger Protestant denominations are even smaller but are intensely active. Generally, Lithuanian society in the 1990s is secularized, although, as in many postcommunist countries, younger people are searching for some sort of spiritual fulfillment.

The Roman Catholic Church is the oldest continuously surviving Lithuanian institution. As such, it has played a dominant role in the development of Lithuanian society, especially crucial during those long stretches of time when Lithuanians had no state of their own. At first highly influenced by the Polish community, the church under Bishop Motiejus Valancius in the nineteenth century promoted Lithuanian language and publications, which prepared the country for the national awakening of the 1880s. Because Russian imperial authorities had forbidden the publication of Lithuanian books in the Latin alphabet, Valancius had them printed in German-ruled, Protestant East Prussia and then smuggled into Lithuania. The bishop also organized a network of secret Lithuanian schools. In 1918 the church supported the establishment of Lithuania as an independent and democratic republic. Years later, it endorsed land reform, and in the 1930s the bishops opposed and restrained Smetona's authoritarian rule. Under Soviet rule, the church served as a focal point of resistance and dissident activities. Its theological outlook, however, has been conservative.

Protestants also have contributed significantly to Lithuania's cultural development. The first book printed in Lithuanian was a Lutheran catechism, published by Martynas Mazvydas in East Prussia in 1547. Protestant Lithuanians from this region published the literature of national awakening. Later, Protestants—both Lutheran and Calvinist—supplied political leadership out of proportion to their numbers in the population.

In Lithuania between the two world wars, the Roman Catholic Church and other denominations had a constitutionally guaranteed monopoly over registration of marriages, births, and deaths. Religious education in public schools was compulsory. Although there was no established religion, all denominations received some state support in rough proportion to their size. The Soviet authorities totally separated churches not only from the state but also from individual support. On June 12, 1990, Lithuania's newly elected independent parliament adopted an act of restitution of the Roman Catholic Church's condition status quo ante but promised compensation for the losses suffered under Soviet rule and pledged cooperation on a parity basis. The constitution of 1992 guarantees "freedom of thought, religion, and conscience" to all and "recognizes traditional churches and religious organizations of Lithuania." Other religious organizations have to pass a test to ensure that their teachings do not "contradict the law and morality." All recognized churches are guaranteed the rights of legal persons and can govern themselves without state interference. Religious teaching in public schools is allowed if parents desire it. Religious marriage registration also is legally valid, as in the United States. The government maintains an office of counselor on religious affairs.

Language and Culture

Like Latvian and Old Prussian, the Lithuanian language belongs to the Baltic branch of the Indo-European language family. The size of the territory in which Lithuanian was spoken shrank considerably through the ages. Today it is roughly coterminous with the boundaries of Lithuania except for some areas of Lithuanian speakers in Poland and Belarus, and except for the diaspora living in the United States, Canada, Western Europe, Latin America, Australia, and even Siberia.

The medieval Lithuanian rulers did not develop a written form of the Lithuanian language. The literary Lithuanian language, based on a southwestern Lithuanian dialect, came into use during the last quarter of the nineteenth century, replacing the use of the Samogitian, or western Lithuanian, dialect. At the beginning of the twentieth century, the use of Lithuanian was confined mainly to the peasantry, but the language was revived subsequently. In 1988 it was declared the official language of Lithuania, as it had been during 1918–40 and the early years of Soviet rule.

Unlike Estonia and Latvia, Lithuania's cultural development was affected by Poland rather than Germany. The imperial Russian regime had an enormous impact on Lithuania from 1795 to 1915, and the Soviet Union had similar influence from 1940 to 1991. Direct contacts with western Europe also made significant contributions beginning in the sixteenth century. Lithuanian nobility in the sixteenth to eighteenth centuries and Lithuanian intellectuals since the turn of the twentieth century brought back ideas and experiences from Italy, Germany, and France. Also, between the two world wars independent Lithuania's direct communication with western Europe affected the development of educational and religious institutions, the arts and literature, architecture, and social thought. Lithuania's historical heritage and the imprint of the Western outlook acquired in the twentieth century were strong enough to make Soviet citizens feel that by going to Lithuania they were going abroad, to the West.

Lithuanian folk art, especially woodcarving and weaving, contributed to the growth of Lithuanian artistic development. Traditionally, Lithuanian folk artists carved mostly crosses, wayside chapels, and figures of a sorrowful Christ—very symbolic and characteristic of Lithuanian crossroads. Under Soviet rule, which outlawed religious subjects, woodcarvings became sec-

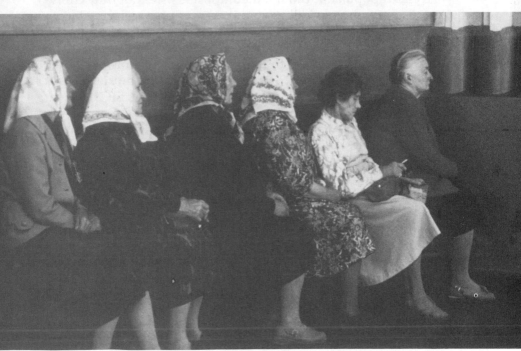

*Religious ceremonies, such as this christening in Kaunas, became
common as the communist regime disintegrated.
Courtesy Jonas Tamulaitis
Women at Roman Catholic mass in Druskininkai
Courtesy Maya Laurinaitis*

ular. Today, Lithuania's roads and gardens are dotted with wooden crosses, poles, and other carvings.

Among Lithuanian artists, probably the best known is Mikalojus Ciurlionis (1875–1911), an originator of abstract painting and a composer whose music became the main subject of study by Professor Vytautas Landsbergis, Lithuania's de facto president 1990–92 and a leader of the independence movement. During the Soviet period, Lithuanian art was best known for graphic arts and for stained glass windows, but the most prominent art forms included abstract painting, sculpture, commercial art, and amber jewelry.

Lithuanian music is as ancient as its art. Folk music has had great influence on its development, and choral singing—periodically demonstrated in huge singing festivals—remains extremely popular. Lithuanian composers write not only choral but also symphonic, ballet, chamber, and opera music. A conservatory, established in 1933, has contributed much to the development of musical culture. In addition to the conservatory, Lithuania supports four higher music schools, three art schools, two pedagogical music schools, eighty music schools for children, five symphony orchestras, ensembles for medieval and contemporary music, and an internationally known string quartet. Many instrumentalists and soloists are winners of international prizes. Folk music ensembles also abound.

Opera and ballet are important elements of Lithuania's national culture. Dancers are trained at the Vilnius School of Choreography and the Kaunas School of Music, as well as in Russia.

All of these activities were state supported under the Soviet system. Membership in artistic associations usually assured work in the profession. All of this now has to be reorganized on a private basis, and both the state and the artists are struggling to find satisfactory working arrangements. Many supporters of the arts believe that art should be state-supported but not state controlled.

The movie industry was established in the late 1940s. Lithuanian filmmakers released four full-length films in 1989 and five in 1990; they also released twenty-eight short films, twenty-four newsreels, and four documentaries. Artistic photography has roots that are older than the Soviet regime in Lithuania.

Sports are also a prevalent national pastime. Lithuania's most popular game is basketball, and a few Lithuanians play professionally in the United States and in European countries.

Lithuania's individual athletes have won Olympic medals and routinely compete in European events.

Education

The population of Lithuania is highly educated. Virtually all those in the age-group fifteen to thirty-nine have completed basic schooling. The average level of education, however, gradually drops for those older than forty. Large numbers of students attend special schools and schools of higher education. In 1993 Lithuania had 67.3 students per 1,000 population in universities and other institutions of higher education, and 46.4 in vocational schools. These numbers compared with 25.9 and 49.0, respectively, for Estonian and Latvian university students and 18.6 and 36.1 for vocational school students. Lithuania had 106 university graduates per 1,000 population. Enrollment rates compared favorably with those in Western Europe. Lithuania had a literacy rate of 99 percent in 1994.

Schools using Lithuanian as the language of instruction are a product of the twentieth century. The system of education—primary, secondary, and higher—was developed between the two world wars. Soviet officials further expanded it, added adult education, and severely ideologized and politicized the philosophy of education and the teaching process. Independent Lithuania has replaced a "Soviet school" with a "national school" philosophy, although the system still maintains some Soviet organizational features. Primary and secondary education together last twelve years. Three types of schools exist: schools that include grades one to four, those that include grades one to nine, and those that include grades one to twelve. Schooling begins at age six. Since 1978 secondary education has been compulsory. In 1993–94 there were 2,317 primary and secondary schools, 108 secondary specialized institutions, and fifteen higher education institutions in the country. Separate schools exist with Russian or Polish as the language of instruction.

Lithuania's "flagship" institution of higher learning is Vilnius University. Others include Vytautas Magnus University in Kaunas, founded by the Lithuanian diaspora of the United States and based on the American model, and the new university in Klaipeda. Unlike the Soviet universities, Lithuanian universities are self-governing and have their autonomy guaranteed by law. The entire system of education is administered by the Ministry of Education and Culture.

Following Soviet practice, research and teaching functions in Lithuania are institutionally separated. Research is mainly conducted by the seventeen institutes of the Academy of Sciences. Altogether, in 1990 forty-six research institutes employed 15,400 scientists. Research is relatively weak in the humanities and the social sciences. Probably the most internationally distinguished activity in these fields is the study of Baltic linguistics under the aegis of the center for such studies in Vilnius. Studies in probability theory by the faculty of Vilnius University are internationally known, and important advances have been made in semiconductor physics and chemistry, biochemistry and genetics, studies related to various aspects of environmental protection, and other fields of the natural sciences and technology. Distinguished advanced research has been carried out in the fields of medicine (especially in cardiovascular disease) and agriculture. Internationally, the best recognized Lithuanian contribution is in biotechnology.

Economy

In the early and mid-1990s, Lithuania's economy went through a dynamic transition from the centralized economy prevalent during Soviet control of Lithuania to a market-driven economy dominated by private enterprise and oriented toward trade with Western Europe and North America. This transition began in 1991, and the volatile first stage—structural adjustment—was largely complete as of 1994. During this period, the economy declined precipitously while the Lithuanian government implemented fundamental economic reforms, including price reform, privatization, government reform, introduction of the litas (pl., litai) as the national currency (for value of the litas—see Glossary), and trade adjustment. Dependence on Russian energy hampered Lithuania's economy at a crucial time of transformation from the centralized state-run economy to a free-market system. Industrial production in Lithuania dropped by 36 percent from December 1992 through June 1994.

Despite these grim statistics, Prime Minister Adolfas Slezevicius was determined to adhere strictly to International Monetary Fund (IMF—see Glossary) recommendations for a speedy transition to a market economy. Slezevicius maintained that former socialist countries that did not rapidly reform fared far worse than those that did. The IMF noted that substantial progress had been achieved in Lithuania between 1992 and

Statue of Polish-Lithuanian poet Adam Mickiewicz (Adomas Mickevicius) in Vilnius
Courtesy Chester Pavlovski

1994 and that, after successfully reducing inflation, the country was ready to turn its attention to reforming its tax, privatization, social security, and finance policies.

Economic recovery began at minimal levels in mid-1993 and continued subsequently as a result of an increase in foreign assistance, loans and investment, trade, and private-sector employment. Most foreign investment came from the United States, Russia, Germany, Britain, Austria, and Poland.

Economic Reforms

During the early 1990s, the government launched a comprehensive program of market-oriented reforms, which included the privatization of state-owned enterprises, the lifting of price controls, land reform, and reform of the banking sector. Also, a new national currency, the litas, was introduced in June 1993.

Privatization

Privatization occurred at a rapid rate in the 1992–94 period (especially with respect to farmland, housing, and small enterprises), and about half of the large and medium-size enterprises scheduled for privatization were sold through public share offerings. The Law on Initial Privatization of State Property of the Republic of Lithuania, passed in early 1991 and amended several times in 1993 (primarily with regard to land reform and restitution), served as the principal basis for undertaking privatization. To start the process, the law authorized the issuance of investment vouchers to residents of Lithuania, to be used for the purchase of housing or other property. Most housing property eligible for privatization had been privatized by the end of 1993. Large enterprises also were to be privatized, with priority given to purchases of shares by employees of those enterprises. The number of shares that employees had the right to purchase in companies being privatized was increased in 1993 from 30 percent of total shares to 50 percent. By November 1994, more than 5,000 enterprises, or 80 percent of the assets earmarked for privatization, had been sold off.

Lithuania sought to regulate privatization of agriculture and to liquidate collective farms. The 1991 privatization law initiated agricultural land reform based on the proposition that nationalized land must be returned while unclaimed land could be sold to prospective private farms on long-term installment plans. Agricultural privatization proceeded rapidly; by the middle of 1993, some 83 percent of the agricultural privatization program had been completed.

Corruption and violence occasionally marred the privatization process. There were difficulties with auction sales of enterprises because speculators and organized crime conspired in bidding, bribed officials, or scared away competition with physical threats. Nevertheless, by the middle of 1994 the government had privatized state property worth a total of 489 million litai (35 million litai in cash and 454 million litai in vouchers and other forms of compensation), allocating the cash received to national and local privatization funds.

Land Reform

The greatest difficulties in implementing Lithuania's privatization program were experienced in agriculture because rapid privatization caused fear and confusion in that sector. The laws provided for the dismemberment of collective farms but did not definitively ensure their replacement by at least equally productive private farms or corporations. The many small private farms that appeared on the landscape were inefficient. Conflicts frequently arose over title to land. Many new owners did not intend to cultivate the regained land or to actively engage in farming, and as a result tens of thousands of hectares

One of many newly privatized farms in Lithuania
Courtesy Maya Laurinaitis
Early morning milk pickup from farm in Panoviai
Courtesy Victor Visockis

were left fallow. Collective farm managers and their friends stole or cheaply acquired tractors, cattle, and other property.

Price Reform

Inflation resulted from the lifting of price controls and from the shortages that resulted from trade disruption around the time of the collapse of the Soviet Union. Inflation, which was 225 percent in 1991, increased to 1,100 percent in 1992, fell to 409 percent in 1993, and dropped further to about 45 percent in 1994. Wages remained stable in 1991 but declined 30 percent in real terms in 1992. Prices increased several times more than wage and pension raises.

Prime Minister Slezevicius coped with the high rate of inflation by avoiding the temptation to promise compensation to pensioners and others whose savings were wiped out by inflation. He also avoided giving in to demands for increased subsidies and support for utilities and public transportation, which traditionally had been provided by the central government. The opposition, led by former Prime Minister Gediminas Vagnorius, was pressing for compensation to savers and investors, but the public voted not to support the measure in an August 1994 referendum. By adhering to Lithuania's structural adjustment program, which had been worked out in cooperation with the IMF, Slezevicius demonstrated his confidence in the reform process.

Monetary and Fiscal Policy

The litas was introduced as the new national currency on June 25, 1993. It became the sole legal tender in August 1993. The litas has been stable since then, maintaining a value of 4.0 litai = US$1 since its introduction.

Lithuania has made progress in reducing government expenditures to match government revenues. In March 1990, Lithuania began the difficult process of eliminating subsidies, introducing new taxes, and administering a new tax collection system. Personal income taxes, corporate profit taxes, and a value-added tax (VAT—see Glossary) were introduced. The personal income tax rate ranges from 18 to 33 percent. The corporate profit tax rate is 29 percent, with a discounted rate of 24 percent on retained earnings and 10 percent on the earnings of agricultural enterprises. The VAT is 18 percent, and there are excise taxes on alcohol, tobacco, petroleum, furniture, jewelry, land, and other items and transactions. Lithuania has been reluctant to reduce its high tax burden for fear of fiscal instability, but high taxes have led to an environment that encourages underreporting and corruption, stimulating the underground economy.

The budget of the central government ran a deficit throughout the late 1980s. The amount of the deficit at that time was relatively small—about 3 percent of the gross domestic product (GDP—see Glossary). The central government ran a budget surplus of 3 percent of GDP in 1991. The budget had a surplus in 1993 but a slight deficit—1 percent of GDP—in 1994.

After independence in 1991, the government began to restructure its expenditures. Subsidies were reduced from 37 percent of government expenditures in 1985 to 6 percent in 1992, while expenditures for the social safety net (social security, welfare, housing, and communal activities) increased from 15 percent to 32 percent of expenditures over the same period. These shifts in expenditures are a result of the central government's assumption of responsibility for the social safety net from enterprises that had been responsible for them during the Soviet period. Projected government expenditures in 1995 equaled 26 percent of GDP.

Reform of the Banking Sector

Prime Minister Slezevicius acknowledged that weakness in the banking sector was one of the most important challenges for his government and, if not properly supervised, could limit long-term economic growth. Lithuania needs to do more to live up to this commitment. Despite several bank failures, the number of banks increased from twenty to twenty-six from 1992 to 1994.

Significant factors guiding the reform of the banking sector are the technical advice and assistance of the IMF, which in October 1994 granted Lithuania a three-year US$201 million credit, and the reforms required for membership in the European Union (EU—see Glossary). The IMF has blamed the Bank of Lithuania's loose monetary policy in part for rising inflation. Some Western observers cite the central bank's institutional weakness and lack of autonomy as the main reasons for its ineffectiveness. The EU requirements are set forth in a white paper that describes the sectoral conditions that each prospective member of the EU must satisfy prior to joining. These requirements touch on every sector of the economy. Membership in the EU is a primary goal of Lithuania's domestic and national security policies. The white paper requires an efficient and open financial market and a banking system that encourages market-directed capital flows. Member states are required to pass and implement legislation concerning the soundness of banking institutions.

Lithuania's 1994 reform program included a review of the bank licensing system, privatization of the three state banks (Savings Bank, Agricultural Bank, and State Commercial Bank), a review of capital requirements to ensure compliance with international standards, and the introduction of new plans for accounts at the Bank of Lithuania and for commercial banks. The program also called on the government to pass stronger bankruptcy legislation and to ensure its enforcement.

Structure of the Economy

After the Soviet Union took control of Lithuania's economy, it developed both light industry and heavy industry to tie Lithuania into the Soviet system. As a workshop for Moscow's military-industrial complex, Lithuania reaped significant rewards. Its people enjoyed one of the highest standards of living in the Soviet Union, similar to those of Estonia and Latvia. Especially on farms, goods became visibly more abundant and life grew more comfortable during the early 1970s. The reason was simple: Brezhnev's regime in Moscow reversed policies of farm exploitation and began subsidizing farmers instead. But a chronic shortage of necessities, the poor quality of goods, and the absence of many services kept the standard of living only at East European levels—not at those of the West.

During their control of Lithuania, Soviet officials introduced a mixed industrial-agricultural economy. In 1991 industry produced about half of GDP; agriculture and trade each supplied about one-quarter.

Industry

Lithuania's industrial sector produced 51.3 percent of GNP in 1991, but industrial production has subsequently experienced declines—by a reported 50 percent in 1993, for example. The sector employed 38 percent of the labor force in 1992.

Under Soviet rule, most economic activity was centrally managed from Moscow; Lithuania managed only 10 percent of its industrial capacity. Many industrial firms worked for the military. According to President Algirdas Brazauskas, who for many years had managed Lithuania's industries as the communist party's secretary for industry, Lithuania had a leading position as a maker of electronics for military and civilian use, and it had been a major supplier of specialized military and industrial technology to the Soviet Union.

In 1985, the year Gorbachev came to power, Lithuania accounted for just 0.3 percent of the Soviet Union's territory and 1.3 percent of its population, but it turned out a significant amount of the Soviet Union's industrial and agricultural products: 22 percent of its electric welding apparatus, 11.1 percent of its metal-cutting lathes, 2.3 percent of its mineral fertilizers, 4.8 percent of its alternating current electric motors, 2.0 percent of its paper, 2.4 percent of its furniture, 5.2 percent of its socks, 3.5 percent of underwear and knitwear, 1.4 percent of leather footwear, 5.3 percent of household refrigerators, 6.5 percent of television sets, 3.7 percent of meat, 4.7 percent of butter, 1.8 percent of canned products, and 1.9 percent of sugar.

Lithuania's key industrial sectors include energy (especially electric power generation), chemicals, machine building, metal working, electronics, forestry products, construction materials and cement, food processing, and textiles (see table 27, Appendix). The country also has a ship-building capacity, with drydocks in Klaipeda for construction and repair of ocean-going fishing vessels. It has a large cement works and an oil-refining plant with an annual capacity of refining 11 million tons of oil. In the past, both facilities produced largely for export. Lithuania's electric energy comes from hydroelectric and thermal power plants fueled by coal and oil in Kaunas, Elektrenai, Mazeikiai, and Vilnius, as well as a nuclear power plant at Ignalina (see fig. 13).

Agriculture

The agricultural sector contributed 24.0 percent of GDP in 1992 and employed 19.0 percent of the labor force. Lithuania's agriculture, efficient by Soviet standards, produced a huge surplus that could not be consumed domestically. Traditionally, Lithuania grew grain (wheat, rye, barley, and feed grains), potatoes, flax, and sugar beets, and it developed dairy farming, meat production, and food processing. About 48 percent of the arable land was used for grain, 41 percent for forage crops, 5 percent for potatoes, and 3 percent for flax and sugar beets. Crops accounted for one-third and livestock for two-thirds of the total value of agricultural output. Lithuanian agriculture,

Figure 13. Economic Activity in Lithuania, 1995

which was collectivized during the early years of Soviet rule, became relatively efficient in the late 1950s when Moscow granted the communist leadership in Vilnius greater control of agricultural policy. Lithuanian farm workers were 50 percent more productive than the Soviet average but much less productive than their Western counterparts. Similarly, Lithuanian crop yields and milk production per cow, although very high by Soviet standards, ran either equal to or much below the yields obtained by Western farms. But even in Lithuania, one-third of agricultural production came from private plots of land and not from collective or state farms. Nevertheless, Lithuanian agricultural production was high enough to allow the export of about 50 percent of total output.

Significant reforms were introduced in the early 1990s, particularly after the restoration of independence, to reestablish private ownership and management in the agricultural sector. Although Lithuania succeeded in privatizing more agricultural land than Estonia or Latvia, agricultural production decreased by more than 50 percent from 1989 to 1994. One problem is that farms were broken up into smallholdings, averaging 8.8 hectares in size, often not large enough to be economically viable. A serious drought in 1994 further reduced agricultural output and cost farmers an estimated 790 million litai in production.

Energy and Minerals

Lithuania receives more than 87 percent of its electricity from the Ignalina nuclear power plant. But Lithuania is highly dependent on fuels imported from Russia, and this energy dependence plagues Lithuania's industries. The trading relationship is unstable because political factors determine whether or not the supply will be interrupted. Energy use in Lithuania is inefficient by world standards, given Lithuania's level of economic development. In 1991 about one-half of the electricity produced at the 5,680-megawatt Ignalina nuclear power plant was exported to Belarus, Latvia, and Kaliningrad Oblast in Russia. But, partly because of reduced demand in the former Soviet republics and partly for political reasons, Lithuania's electricity exports declined substantially from 1991 to 1994.

Lithuania has large processing facilities for oil, which can be exported to the West through Ventspils (Latvia) or the new Lithuanian transport and storage facility at Butinge. Butinge is equipped with modern technology and was constructed by Western firms with funding provided by international financial institutions. This facility may allow more intensive utilization of the oil-processing facility at Mazeikiai, which has an annual capacity of 12 million tons, one of the largest in the Baltic region. Mazeikiai needs upgrading to operate profitably.

With the exception of forests and agricultural land, Lithuania is poorly endowed with natural resources. It exports some chemical and petroleum products, but its only significant industrial raw materials are construction materials, such as clay, limestone, gravel, and sand. Its peat reserves total about 4 billion cubic meters. There are moderate oil and gas deposits offshore and on the coast. In 1993 recoverable oil reserves were estimated at 40 million tons on the coast and 38 million tons offshore.

Tourism

Lithuania may develop an important tourism industry if investments are made in its infrastructure to bring facilities up to Western standards. The resort town of Neringa was famous during the Soviet period for its excellent seaside climate. But Neringa fears the effects of too much foreign influence and wants special protection from an expected onslaught of foreign investors, most of whom come from Germany. In Vilnius and other cities, there is a shortage of quality hotels. State-owned hotels, of which there are still many, tend to provide inferior accommodations and service.

Labor Force

Lithuania had an estimated labor force of 1.9 million in 1994. Thirty-two percent of workers were employed in industry, 12 percent in construction, and 18 percent in the agricultural sector. Most of the remainder worked in a variety of activities in the services sector—14 percent in science, education, and culture; 10 percent in trade and government; and 7 percent each in health care and in transportation and communications.

Trade-union activities are specifically provided for in the constitution and are protected by legislation. The Joint Representation of Lithuanian Independent Trade Unions is an organization of twenty-three of the twenty-five trade unions and was founded October 22, 1992. Teachers and other government workers not involved in law enforcement or security work are permitted to join unions. Strikes and other confrontations between labor and management have occurred but are limited by the nascent free-enterprise system and the perception that employment alternatives are limited. Public employees organized strikes in 1992. Some Lithuanian trade unions are affiliated with international trade organizations, and organizational assistance has been provided by Western countries, especially the Nordic countries. Safe employment practices, regulation of workplace safety, and protection from reprisal by employers against employees who complain about illegal working conditions are provided for in the constitution. A minimum wage must be paid, and child labor is prohibited.

Transportation and Telecommunications

Lithuania's transportation system has great potential, and transit traffic by rail, road, and ship represents an important part of Lithuania's future development (see fig. 14). There were about 2,000 kilometers of railroads (1,524-millimeter gauge) in 1994, of which 122 kilometers were electrified.

There were 55,603 kilometers of roads in 1994, of which 42,209 kilometers were asphalted. The road system is good. The country is crossed by a route from Klaipeda to Minsk via Kaunas and Vilnius. A new international highway, Via Baltica, will stretch from Tallinn to Warsaw via Riga and Kaunas.

Lithuania has struggled, however, to develop its national airline, Lithuanian Airlines. Although an agreement has been reached with American Airlines, it may not be possible to restructure the company into a profitable operation because there is excess capacity in the region. Lithuanian Airlines had one B–737 and sixty-three Soviet-made aircraft in 1993. The main international airport is in Vilnius. A second international airport was opened at Siauliai in 1993. In addition to Lithuanian Airlines, service is provided by Aeroflot, Austrian Airlines, Drakk Air Lines, Hamburg Airlines, LOT (Polish Airlines), Lufthansa, Malév, SAS (Scandinavian Airlines), and Swissair. Destinations include Amsterdam, London, Paris, Copenhagen, Berlin, Frankfurt, and forty-three cities throughout the former Soviet Union.

Klaipeda is the major coastal point, and Kaunas is the major inland port. Some 600 kilometers of inland waterways are navigable year round. Lithuania's merchant fleet consists of forty-four ships, totaling about 323,505 deadweight tons, including twenty-nine cargo vessel, three railcar carrier vessels, one roll-on/roll-off vessel, and eleven combination vessels.

Lithuania has begun to modernize its telecommunications industry. A law deregulating certain aspects of telecommunications went into effect in January 1992. Private investors now have the right to offer long-distance service to the public, but

Figure 14. Transportation System of Lithuania, 1995

restrictions on the participation of foreign capital have slowed this type of activity. Both telecommunications and transportation will require large investments to modernize the infrastructure and to reform the enterprises. This sector is plagued with inefficiencies. Nevertheless, Lithuania's telephone service is among the most advanced in the former Soviet republics. There were 240 telephone lines serving 1,000 persons in the early 1990s. International connections exist via satellite from Vilnius through Oslo or from Kaunas through Copenhagen.

Lithuania has two television companies and five radio companies. In 1993 some 1.4 million television sets and more than

1.4 million radios were in use, or one per 2.7 persons. Two national radio programs are broadcast by the state-owned Leituvos Radijas ir Televizija. Radio Vilnius broadcasts in Lithuanian and English. There are national, regional, and minority language television programs.

Foreign Economic Relations

Foreign Trade

Because of its small domestic market, Lithuania is dependent on trade to ensure its prosperity. It has made impressive progress since the late 1980s. Imports declined from 61 percent of GDP in 1980 to 23 percent in 1991. Most significant, trade was shifted to Western Europe from the former Soviet Union. In 1993 three-quarters of Lithuanian exports went to the other Baltic states and the other former Soviet republics. But this percentage is projected to drop dramatically so that most exports will be to the rest of the world by 1996. In the first half of 1994, the countries of the former Soviet Union accounted for about 53 percent of Lithuania's trade, and West European markets made up about 47 percent of Lithuania's trade (see table 28, Appendix). In previous years, trade with Western markets had made up only about 10 percent of trade.

According to 1994 estimates, exports totaled approximately US$1 billion, up from US$805,014 in 1992, and imports amounted to nearly US$1.3 billion, up from US$805,776 (see table 29; table 30, Appendix). Lithuania had an overall negative trade balance of US$267 million in 1994, according to IMF estimates. An estimated surplus of US$63 million in the services account and a deficit of US$192 million in the current account resulted in a negative balance of payments overall.

When the Soviet Union imposed an economic blockade on Lithuania in April 1990, many enterprises nimbly shifted production away from goods required under central planning (for example, computers for the defense industry) to consumer goods. These transformations demonstrated the flexibility of many enterprises under difficult circumstances and set the stage for economic growth and prosperity.

Tariffs are imposed on a wide range of imported goods, but they are scheduled to be reduced gradually until 2001, when Lithuania's free-trade regime will be fully implemented. The lowest tariff schedule applies to countries with which Lithuania has most-favored-nation status. These countries, about twenty in number, include the United States, Canada, Russia, Belarus, Ukraine, and Australia. A slightly higher tariff schedule applies to goods imported from about twenty countries with which Lithuania has a free-trade agreement, such as Estonia, Latvia and the members of the EU. These tariffs are scheduled to be reduced during the six years following 1995 and will be abolished for industrial products at the end of that time. The tariffs on food products imported from the EU are scheduled to be substantially reduced except for sugar, butter, and oil and for a limited number of other items.

Imports consist primarily of natural gas, oil, coal, machinery, chemicals, and light industrial products. Oil and natural gas are imported from Russia, natural gas is imported from Ukraine, and cotton and wool are imported from the Central Asian republics of the former Soviet Union. Lithuania exports primarily machinery, light industrial products, electronics, food products, and textiles.

On July 18, 1994, Lithuania signed a free-trade agreement with the EU that went into effect at the beginning of 1995. It calls for a six-year transition period during which trade barriers will be dismantled. The agreement grants Lithuania tariff exemptions on industrial goods, textiles, and agricultural products. Full membership in the EU is a primary goal of Lithuanian economic policy.

Foreign Debt

Lithuania did not acknowledge responsibility for any debts of the Soviet Union. The international community supported its contention that it should not be responsible for debts incurred while it was "occupied." International financial institutions, especially the IMF and the World Bank (see Glossary), issued credits to Lithuania after independence. Lithuania's total debt, which was about US$38 million at the beginning of 1993, mushroomed to US$500 million by the end of 1994. Increases in the debt to US$918 million by the end of 1996 are projected. As a percentage of GDP, the debt will rise from 3.6 percent to 10.6 percent by 1997. However, repayment terms are manageable, and the proceeds of these credits fund needed and productive investments. The large inflow of foreign credits and investments is responsible for maintaining living standards at an acceptable level in the wake of a steep decline in production in 1992 and 1993 and negative trade balances.

Dock facilities at harbor of Klaipeda
Courtesy Jonas Tamulaitis
Department store in pedestrian mall in Siauliai
Courtesy Victor Visockis

Foreign Investment

The largest foreign investor is the United States tobacco and food services company Philip Morris, which purchased the state tobacco company in Klaipeda for US$25 million in 1993. Foreign investment was critical in maintaining public support for economic reform during the first years after independence and resulted in an influx of hard currency (from foreign assistance, loans, and investment) and increased activity by the private sector. Most foreign investment came from Britain, Germany, the United States, Russia, Poland, and Austria (see table 31, Appendix). Total foreign capital invested in the country was estimated to be 551 million litai in November 1994. About three-quarters of the foreign investors were involved in joint ventures.

Lithuania's Law on Foreign Investments, introduced in 1990 and amended in 1992, guarantees the unrestricted repatriation of all after-tax profits and reinvested capital. A new draft of this law places restrictions only on foreign investment in sensitive industries, such as defense and energy. Foreign investors receive generous profit tax rebates of up to 70 percent. A draft amendment to the constitution would lift the prohibition on landownership by foreigners. Nevertheless, in part because of the growth of organized crime, Lithuania's ability to attract more foreign investment has been impaired. Neste, the Finnish oil company that operates twelve gas stations in Lithuania, halted future investment after an attack, presumably carried out by organized crime, on a company representative in Klaipeda in October 1994.

Lithuania in 1994 received a number of foreign loans, including ECU10 million (for value of the European currency unit—see Glossary) over fifteen years from the European Investment Bank (EIB) for reconstruction of the airport in Vilnius and an ECU14 million loan from the EIB for reconstruction of the port of Klaipeda. Other foreign loans included a US$25 million agricultural sector loan from the World Bank, and loans of ECU22 million and ECU9 million from the European Bank for Reconstruction and Development (EBRD) and Japan's Export-Import Bank, respectively, for the modernization of the country's telecommunications system. The EBRD also disbursed US$6 million in 1993 as part of an ECU36 million energy infrastructure loan. By February 1994, the World Bank had disbursed US$45 million of a US$60 million import rehabilitation loan approved in 1992. Lithuania obtained an

ECU33 million loan in 1994 from the EBRD to improve safety at the Ignalina nuclear power plant and a seventeen-year US$26.4 million loan to refurbish its coal- and oil-fired power plant.

Reform Yields Results

Lithuania experienced initial difficulties with economic reform, especially with reform of agriculture, because of the government's insistence that social welfare levels be retained and that privatization of enterprises would be subject to regulations forbidding the elimination of jobs and employee services. Mistakes in fiscal policies, especially those committed by the Bank of Lithuania, and the increase in energy and other prices by Russia, as well as difficulties with payments for goods exported from Lithuania, also fueled inflation, promoted a black market, and emptied the stores. Production decreased. In 1993 industrial production dropped more than 50 percent compared with 1991. Agricultural production declined by 39 percent. Unemployment, including partial unemployment, rose from 9,000 to more than 200,000. By the end of 1992, the lack of heat and shortages of hot water in wintertime were conspicuous evidence of a deep economic crisis in the land.

Nevertheless, the economic decline was considered to be of a temporary nature, caused by the difficulties of the transition—common to former Soviet states—to a free-market economy. The IMF and the World Bank were satisfied with privatization and reform efforts, and the latter provided a development loan of US$82 million. On a scale of zero to ten, Germany's Deutsche Bank in 1991 ranked Lithuania's potential for agricultural production as ten and for industrialization as approximately eight. Promising sectors for future profitable investment include building materials, electricity, transportation, and tourism.

Government and Politics

Lithuania is an independent democratic republic. Its new constitution is that of a presidential democracy with separation of powers and a system of checks and balances. In some ways, the institutional structure of the government is similar to that of the United States; however, it is closer to the system former French president Charles de Gaulle gave to the Fifth Republic of France—a strong presidency leading a parliament divided into many factions.

The Constitutional System

On the same day that Lithuania declared independence on March 11, 1990, its parliament adopted a provisional constitution, called the "provisional basic law," which established a framework for the new state's government. The constitution comprehensively listed guarantees of democratic rights and rules of democratic process, but basic elements of the Soviet-style government were maintained. Thus, legislative and executive functions were combined under the leadership of parliament, and the court system was kept totally dependent on legislative definitions and appointments. The legislature's name—Supreme Soviet—also was maintained. Its presidium became the foremost leadership body, and the chairman of the presidium became the chief of parliament, of state, and, in effect, of the executive. The provisional basic law, too, was made relatively easy to change.

Despite its democratization, the Soviet model quickly proved that it was not suitable for a new, substantively democratic system of government. It took two years of conflict and frustration, however, before contending parties agreed to a compromise between a parliamentary system of legislative superiority with a figurehead president and a very strong presidential system in which the legislature would be at best coequal with the president.

The constitution was approved by the voters in a referendum on October 25, 1992. Seventy-five percent of those voting favored the document. Thus, it was adopted by a solid majority, although the percentage of voters participating in the referendum was smaller (57 percent) than had been the case in most elections until then.

The constitution of 1992 reflects the institutions and experiences of the United States, France, and Germany as integrated into Lithuanian tradition. It also incorporates guarantees of a social safety network inherited from the Soviet Union. In its introductory provisions, the document not only places a high value on democracy but also asserts the right of defense against attempts by force to encroach upon or overthrow "state independence, territorial integrity, or the constitutional system" (Article 3). It also disallows division of Lithuanian territory into any "statelike structures"—an obvious reference to territorial autonomy as a solution to ethnic minority problems in the country. Furthermore, the status of Lithuania as an "independent democratic republic" can be changed only by a referendum and only if three-fourths of Lithuanian citizens approve it. Similarly, the first seventeen articles (which define the characteristics of the state, citizenship, state language, and symbols) and Articles 147, 148, and 149 (which determine the methods for constitutional changes or amendments) can be altered only by a referendum. Article 150 of the constitution forbids Lithuania from joining the Commonwealth of Independent States (CIS—see Glossary). Finally, the constitution incorporates the declaration of independence of March 11, 1990.

Fundamental human rights and democratic values, including freedom of "thought, faith, and conscience," are enshrined in the constitution, which also guarantees the status of legal person to religious denominations and allows religious teaching in public schools. In addition to personal, political, and religious rights, the constitution secures social rights. As already noted, these include free medical care, old-age pensions, unemployment compensation, and support for families and children.

The power to govern is divided between the legislative and executive branches, with an independent judiciary acting as interpreter of the constitution and of the branches' jurisdictions, as well as arbiter of conflicts between them. The constitution clearly acknowledges the danger of concentration of power in a single person or institution. The legislature has regained its old name, Seimas, which was used in the interwar years. The executive consists of a president and a prime minister with a cabinet, known as the Council of Ministers. The judiciary is composed of the Supreme Court and subordinate courts (the Court of Appeals, district courts, and local courts), as well as the Constitutional Court, which decides on the constitutionality of acts of the Seimas, the president, and the government.The Office of the Procurator General is an autonomous institution of the judiciary. Creation of special courts, such as administrative or family courts, is allowed, although establishing courts with "special powers" is forbidden in peacetime.

The parliament consists of 141 members, seventy elected from party lists on the basis of proportional representation and seventy-one from single-member districts. To be seated in the Seimas on the basis of proportional representation, a party must receive at least 4 percent of the votes cast. An exception is made for ethnic minority groups, however, which do not need to pass the 4 percent threshold. The legislature is elected for four years. Candidates for the legislature must be at least twenty-five years old. Members of the Seimas may serve as prime minister or cabinet member, but they may not hold any other position in either central or local government or in private enterprises or organizations. The parliament must approve the prime minister, as well as his or her government and program. It also may force the government's resignation by rejecting twice in sequence its program or by expressing no confidence by a majority of legislators in secret ballot.

The powers of the legislature are checked by a number of devices: first, by certain constitutional limitations; second, by the president as defined under the constitution; and third, by the Constitutional Court. Articles 64, 131, and 132 of the constitution circumscribe the ability of the Seimas to control the government, especially the budget. Article 64 specifies the times of parliamentary sessions. Although extension is possible, ordinarily the legislature cannot sit longer than seven months and three days, divided into two sessions. The budget submitted by the government can be increased by the legislature only if the latter indicates the sources of financing for additional expenditures. If the budget is not approved before the start of the budget year, proposed expenditures cannot be higher than those of the previous year. Finally, the legislature is not entrusted with making decisions concerning the basic characteristics of Lithuanian statehood and democracy. These are left to the citizens by means of referendum. Similarly, the initiative for making laws is not limited to the legislature but also belongs to the citizens, who can force the legislature to consider a law by submitting a petition with 50,000 signatures.

The powers of the legislature are further checked by those of the president, who may veto legislation, both ordinary and constitutional, passed by the legislature. Normally, laws are not promulgated without the signature of the president. A presidential veto can be overridden, but only by an absolute majority of the Seimas membership. The president can also dissolve the parliament if it refuses to approve the government's budget within sixty days or if it directly votes no confidence in the government. However, the next elected parliament may retaliate by calling for an earlier presidential election.

The president is elected directly by the people for a term of five years and a maximum of two consecutive terms. The president is not, strictly speaking, the chief of the executive branch or the chief administrator. The Lithuanians borrowed the French model of the presidency, then adapted it to their needs. Candidates must be at least forty years old. To be elected in the first round, 50 percent of the voters must participate and a candidate must receive more than half of the total votes cast. If 50 percent of the voters do not participate, a plurality wins the presidency unless it constitutes less than one-third of the total vote. If the first round does not produce a president, a second round is held within two weeks between the two top candidates. A plurality vote is sufficient to win.

The president is the head of state. The president also selects the prime minister (with the approval of the Seimas), approves ministerial candidates, and appoints the commander in chief of the armed forces—with legislative confirmation. The president resolves basic foreign policy issues and can confer military and diplomatic ranks, appoint diplomats without legislative approval, and issue decrees subject to the legislature's right to later overturn a decree by legislative action.

Finally, the president has considerable powers to influence the judicial branch. The president has the right to nominate (and the Seimas to approve the nomination of) three justices to the Constitutional Court and all justices to the Supreme Court. The president also appoints, with legislative approval, judges of the Court of Appeals. However, legislative confirmation is not required for the appointment or transfer of judges in local, district, and special courts.

The Constitutional Court checks both the legislative and the executive branches of government by ruling on whether their legislation and/or actions are constitutional. The court consists of nine justices appointed by the legislature, three each from the nominees of the president, the parliamentary chairman, and the chief justice of the Supreme Court. The president nominates the chief justice of the Constitutional Court. Cases for consideration by the Constitutional Court, however, may be brought only by one-fifth of the membership of the Seimas, the ordinary courts, or the president of the republic.

Politics

The new system of government became operative with the election of President Algirdas Brazauskas in February 1993.

Brazauskas came from the Lithuanian Democratic Labor Party (LDLP), successor to the Communist Party of Lithuania. The Brazauskas government surprised many of its critics during 1994 by its continued commitment to rapid economic reform and to Lithuania's independence. Rural interests, which formed the bedrock of support for the LDLP, were unhappy with the failure to roll back implementation of the free market in agriculture and with the breakup of centralized state farms and cooperatives.

Since the declaration of independence, Lithuanian politics have been stormy, especially the struggle between the former Communist Party of Lithuania and the movement for independence, Sajudis. On its own, the Communist Party of Lithuania had won only twenty-three seats out of the 141 seats in the March 1990 parliamentary elections. Sajudis and other political parties that supported independence had won a majority. In addition, the Lithuanian Social Democratic Party (LSDP) won nine seats; the Christian Democratic Party of Lithuania (CDPL), two; the Lithuanian Democratic Party (LDP), two; and the Lithuanian Green Party, four. Noncommunist parties were in their infancy—small and weak. Seventy members of parliament did not belong formally to any party, although virtually all of them were ideologically close to Sajudis.

Parliamentary organization was complicated by the numerous parliamentary factions, unrelated to party strength or differentiation in society. Parliamentary factions had no fixed constituencies to which they were accountable. In 1992 there were nine parliamentary factions and a nonfaction group consisting of twenty independent deputies. The largest was the Center faction (eighteen members), followed by the Moderates (sixteen), the LDLP (twelve), the Liberals (ten), the Poles (eight), and the Nationalists (nine). The United Sajudis faction had sixteen members, and the Santara faction of Sajudis had ten.

The weakness of the LDLP was deceptive. This group had lost adherents in the parliament, but in April 1990, while still known as the Communist Party of Lithuania, it won approximately 40 percent of the votes—and offices—in local elections. It was strong in small towns and rural areas. Later in 1990, these reformist communists adopted a new name and an essentially social democratic program, gaining a new lease on political life.

Sajudis headquarters in winter, Vilnius
Courtesy Stanley Bach

In this political landscape, the position of chairman of the presidium of the Supreme Soviet (de facto president) was won in May 1990 by Vytautas Landsbergis, the president of Sajudis and a professor of musicology who had never been a member of the Communist Party of Lithuania. Landsbergis defeated the former leader, Brazauskas, by two-thirds of the vote. Brazauskas refused to accept the position of deputy chairman. Kazimiera Prunskiene, an economist, was chosen as prime minister, whereupon she immediately quit the Communist Party of Lithuania. Brazauskas agreed to serve as one of the deputy prime ministers. The other deputy prime minister was Romualdas Ozolas, a philosopher and former communist who eventually joined the Center faction in the parliament.

Soon, however, a conflict developed between Landsbergis and Prunskiene, primarily over Lithuania's response to the 1990 Soviet blockade. Landsbergis stood firm and defiant.

Prunskiene, after visiting Western leaders, pursued compromise with the Soviet Union, as suggested by these leaders. In early 1991, Prunskiene took the first radical steps in economic reform, but the Sajudis forces used that action to unseat her. A fellow economist, Albertas Simenas, was chosen as her successor, but he temporarily disappeared during the turmoil created by the Soviet army, which staged a putsch against the Lithuanian government and on January 13, 1991, massacred unarmed civilians. Landsbergis summoned the people to defend the parliament. His heroic determination and leadership won him further domestic recognition as a national leader and a favorable international reputation abroad. For a moment, all political groups united against Soviet aggression. Lithuanians refused to participate in Gorbachev's referendum on the continuation of a federal union and instead held their own "national poll," which confirmed overwhelming support for independence. However, unity did not last long.

In Simenas's absence, Gediminas Vagnorius became prime minister. He initiated economic reforms and continued the political struggle against Brazauskas's party that Landsbergis had begun in the spring of 1990. Vagnorius's efforts frequently were frustrated by the parliament, and the LDLP formally declared opposition to the government in the fall of 1991. Reform measures, especially in agriculture, were not successful. His struggle with the leadership of the Bank of Lithuania over the introduction of a Lithuanian currency, the litas, was unsuccessful because neither the bank nor a majority in parliament supported his program.

In the meantime, the strength of the Sajudis group and of the coalition in parliament that supported Vagnorius was withering. The leadership of the independence movement, furthermore, was gradually shifting to more conservative nationalist positions after the third conference of the movement in December 1991. Anticommunist activities were facilitated by access to KGB archives, and past collaboration with the KGB was made a political issue. The atmosphere was not improved by the ultimately unsuccessful attempts by Sajudis to pass a law that would temporarily bar from public office certain categories of former officeholders in the communist party power structure. The attempt sharpened confrontation between the nationalist and former communist party forces. Landsbergis sought to strengthen the powers of the executive branch and his own position by establishing an executive presidency. But on May 23, 1992, his proposal failed in a referendum.

After several attempts in parliament to remove the unpopular prime minister in the summer of 1992, Vagnorius had to resign in July, and new parliamentary elections were agreed upon for October. Aleksandras Abisala, another Sajudis leader, took over from Vagnorius with the acquiescence of the opposition. However, neither his attempts to correct the economic situation nor his conciliatory politics improved Sajudis's chances in the upcoming elections of October 25, 1992.

Seventeen groups or coalitions ran candidates for the 141 seats of the new parliament, the Seimas, but some did not muster enough votes for the 4 percent threshold. Against everyone's expectations—and even to Brazauskas's own surprise—the LDLP and its satellites won an absolute majority of seventy-three seats (51 percent). Landsbergis's forces still hoped for a strong showing of their coalition, but the Sajudis-Santara coalition succeeded in winning only sixteen seats, including three contested ones. The Social Democratic representation decreased to eight seats, the Christian Democrats increased to ten, and the Center barely squeaked through with two victories in single-member districts but did not meet the 4 percent threshold for seats elected by party lists. Three new groups entered the parliament—the Citizens Charter with ten seats; Political Prisoners and Exiles with twelve; and the Christian Democratic Association, a splinter of the Christian Democratic Party with one. One seat was won by an independent. The Polish minority, however, was able to win four seats because it was not required to reach the 4 percent threshold.

The significance of the parliamentary elections result was threefold: the nationalist forces of Landsbergis were crushed, the postcommunist politicians led by Brazauskas made an amazing comeback, and the political center in the parliament was destroyed. Neither the Center nor the Liberal faction met the 4 percent threshold for seats elected by party lists. Political polarization of the country was confirmed: there was a strong and well-organized left, and there was a weak, shattered, and splintered right.

The polarization was even more conspicuously demonstrated in the direct presidential election of February 14, 1993. The Lithuanian ambassador to the United States, Stasys Lozoraitis, lost to Brazauskas, who won majorities everywhere except in the urban district of Kaunas. The final vote was 61.1 percent for Brazauskas and 38.2 percent for Lozoraitis. Brazauskas was catapulted to office by the rural population. His majority was increased by the vote from urban districts with Polish or Russian majorities. Brazauskas won for the same reasons his party earlier captured the majority in the parliament: economic crisis, disappointment with Sajudis, dislike of the once very popular Landsbergis, and, most of all, the electorate's trust in Brazauskas as a well-known and popular candidate whose campaign succeeded in portraying the ambassador as a "foreigner" ignorant of Lithuania's concerns.

The Western press saw the election as a victory for former communist party members who would stop reform and return Lithuania to some sort of association with the former Soviet Union. However, the LDLP was no longer communist, and, although sympathetic to Russia, it was committed to Lithuania's independence. The new president stated repeatedly that he would preserve Lithuania's independence, although Landsbergis, now in the role of opposition leader, continued to warn of threats to Lithuania's status as an independent state. Brazauskas resigned as leader of the LDLP, as required by the constitution.

Shortly after the election, President Brazauskas appointed Raimundas Rajeckas, a distinguished economist with an academic background, as his special counsel. Rajeckas had been associated with Harvard and other Western universities and had served as Brazauskas's campaign manager. He functioned as a "deputy president." Brazauskas also accepted the resignation of Prime Minister Bronislovas Lubys and chose as his successor an economist, Adolfas Slezevicius, president of a private joint Lithuanian-Norwegian company and former deputy minister of agriculture for dairy and meat production. Slezevicius continued to implement Lithuania's political and economic reforms while pursuing an improved relationship with Russia.

Mass Media

The collapse of the communist system brought about the privatization of most publishing. Although the government still plays a role in book publishing, all newspapers and journals are privately owned, usually by limited stock companies or by private individuals. The number of periodicals has increased dramatically, and competition is intense. There are several main dailies. *Lietuvos aidas* was first published by the Landsbergis government but is now private, although editorially it supports

Landsbergis and Sajudis. *Lietuvos rytas,* an independent daily, leans slightly to the left and is very conscious of the power and responsibility of the press. It is edited by the former editor of *Komjaunimo tiesa,* the largest daily in Lithuania, and has a circulation of more than 100,000. *Tiesa* now is the voice of the Democratic Labor Party after previously being published by the Communist Party of Lithuania. *Respublika,* founded and owned by a prize-winning journalist and former member of the Soviet Union's Congress of People's Deputies, specializes in "investigative journalism" and leans to the left.

In 1990 Lithuanian newspaper circulation and book publishing suffered a decline because of a shortage of paper, a result of the Soviet economic blockade. In 1989 Lithuanian newspaper circulation per 1,000 inhabitants was 1,223—higher than in Latvia (1,032) but lower than in Estonia (1,620). Annual circulation of magazines and other periodicals was eleven copies per inhabitant (compared with twenty-eight in Latvia and twenty-six in Estonia). Annual book and booklet publication was six copies per inhabitant (compared with six in Latvia and twelve in Estonia).

Library statistics indicate that newly published books and current periodicals are accessible to readers in remote rural areas. Lithuania had 1,885 libraries in the early 1990s, compared with 1,318 for Latvia and 629 for Estonia.

Foreign Relations

The course of Lithuania's foreign policy in the 1990s has been more stable than its domestic politics. This has been demonstrated by the fact that between March 1990 and November 1992 it had five prime ministers but only one minister of foreign affairs. Since independence the cornerstone of Lithuanian foreign policy has been integration with European security institutions: the Organization for Security and Cooperation in Europe (OSCE; until January 1995 known as the Conference on Security and Cooperation in Europe—see Glossary), the Council of Europe (COE), the European Union (EU), the North Atlantic Cooperation Council (NACC), the World Trade Organization (WTO), and ultimately, the North Atlantic Treaty Organization (NATO). Lithuania is a member of the OSCE, the COE, and the NACC and is an associate member of the EU. It hopes eventually to join the EU, the WTO, and NATO, and progress was made toward these goals in 1994.

In the beginning, Lithuania's aims were more fundamental. Lithuania's sole foreign policy concern in 1990 was to gain international recognition of the restored Lithuanian state. However, efforts directed at Gorbachev on the one hand and the Western powers on the other hand bore no fruit. Gorbachev could not afford the political cost of recognizing Lithuanian independence, nor did he believe in Lithuania's right to statehood. The West's attitude, according to Egon Bahr, a German foreign policy expert, was "We'll throw you a life preserver after you learn how to swim." Gorbachev informally agreed not to use force, and the West did not push him to permit Lithuanian independence.

However, after the Vilnius massacre of January 13, 1991, which revealed that Gorbachev had authorized attempts to overthrow Lithuania's government, Western states broke ranks. The first was Iceland, which declared that it recognized Lithuania's sovereignty. Iceland had extended recognition in 1922 and had never reneged on it. Next, Denmark expressed its commitment to early recognition. Paradoxically, the greatest appreciation of Lithuania's needs came from Russia. After learning about the Vilnius massacre, Russian president Boris N. Yeltsin met with Baltic leaders in Tallinn and expressed solidarity with Lithuania. This expression gained legal status on July 29, 1991. On that day, United States President George H.W. Bush signed the Strategic Arms Reduction Talks (START) treaty with Gorbachev in Moscow, and Yeltsin and Landsbergis signed a treaty "on the basis of relations" between the Republic of Lithuania and the Russian Soviet Federated Socialist Republic. The crucial item of the treaty was Article 1, which stated that "The High Contracting Parties recognize one another as full-fledged subjects of international law and as sovereign states according to their state status as established by the fundamental acts adopted by the Republic of Lithuania on 11 March 1990 and by the Russian Soviet Federated Socialist Republic on 12 June 1990." Lithuanians hastily ratified the treaty on August 19, 1991, the same day as a coup was carried out by conservative forces in Moscow against Gorbachev. It was not until January 17, 1992, however, that Russia ratified the agreement.

After the coup failed, the international community quickly recognized the independence of Lithuania and the other Baltic states. In September 1991, President Bush renewed the United States recognition of Lithuania of 1922 and announced that an ambassador would be sent to Vilnius. The Soviet Union recognized Lithuania's independence on September 6, 1991. On the recommendation of the United States and the Soviet Union, Lithuania was admitted to the United Nations (UN) on September 16. Then on December 21, the Soviet Union collapsed as a legal entity, and on December 24 Yeltsin informed UN secretary general Javier Pérez de Cuellar that the Russian Federation had assumed "all rights and obligations of the USSR." Thus, Russia still was, for all practical purposes, the Soviet Union, only under different leadership.

Once Lithuania joined the UN, Landsbergis indicated the next priorities of Lithuania's foreign policy: to join all accessible international organizations, and to legally strengthen the status of the new state while working toward the withdrawal of Russian troops, regarded by Lithuanians as an occupying force, from Lithuania. The Russian military strongly opposed this demand, claiming that the troops had no place to go. The commander of the Baltic Military District believed the troops would leave only after several years. Russian foreign minister Andrey Kozyrev suggested a "status of forces" agreement to legalize the Russian troop presence. In June 1992, the Baltic Council, a consultative body of Baltic leaders, appealed to the CSCE, the UN, and the Group of Seven (Canada, France, Germany, Italy, Japan, Britain, and the United States). The Group of Seven, the CSCE, and the UN, as well as NATO, counseled the Russians to set a definite withdrawal date. After protracted negotiations, Russia agreed to withdraw its troops from Lithuania. An agreement was signed in Moscow on September 8, 1992, setting the deadline for withdrawal at August 31, 1993, a year earlier than expected.

The withdrawal of Russian troops was completed on time, opening a new chapter between Russia and Lithuania and encouraging closer economic and other relations. When Lithuania first declared independence from the Soviet Union and tried to negotiate its status with the Gorbachev administration, it did not achieve its goals. But after the dissolution of the Soviet Union, Moscow and Vilnius tried to put the past behind them, even though the Soviet Union had imposed an economic blockade and had used violence to force Lithuania to renounce independence. Although diplomatic relations between the two countries were established in 1991, Russia did not send an ambassador to Lithuania until 1992, and Lithuania reciprocated only in March 1993. Relations between Vilnius and Moscow were often unsettled by press reports of violations of Lithuanian airspace throughout the first half of the 1990s. Despite a desire to control air traffic within its borders, Lithuania has been unable to come to an agreement with Russia to regulate air transit. The two countries did, however, sign an economic cooperation agreement in November 1993.

Preoccupied with Russia and with the West, Lithuanian policy makers had somewhat neglected Lithuania's other neighbors, especially Belarus and Ukraine. Nevertheless, trade with Belarus expanded, and a border agreement was reached. Ukrainian president Leonid Kuchma's administration was supportive of Lithuanian sovereignty, and the two countries signed an economic cooperation agreement in February 1994. Vilnius focused on a rapprochement with Poland, which resulted in a treaty of cooperation covering various fields, including defense, and providing even for joint maneuvers of their armed forces. The agreement was signed during a visit to Lithuania by Polish president Lech Walesa in April 1994 and was ratified by Lithuania in October 1994.

Lithuania seeks closer relations with Scandinavia. The Swedish king and the Danish queen have visited Lithuania. Close economic ties are being developed with Norway and Denmark. Denmark cooperates closely with Lithuania in military affairs and has agreed to train Lithuanian military units to serve as UN peacekeepers in the former Yugoslavia.

In relations with Western Europe and the United States, Lithuania has two main objectives. The first is economic cooperation and attracting Western capital to boost Lithuania's economy and to help with the transition to a free market and democracy. The second objective is to gain security guarantees so that Lithuania and the other Baltic states would not be left alone to face any threat from Russia. Vilnius has pursued these objectives by demonstrating its respect for Western values and by negotiating bilateral trade agreements, tax treaties, and consular and other agreements with West European countries and the United States.

National Security

If permanence of policy-making personnel is an indication of policy continuity, Lithuania's defense policy in the early 1990s has been even more consistent than its foreign policy. Audrius Butkevicius, a young physician, was appointed minister of defense in Prunskiene's government in 1990 and served several years under five prime ministers.

Lithuania's struggle for independence was a peaceful revolution in which violence was not used. Thus, Lithuania's government did not inherit guerrilla forces or special troops, only the regular law enforcement agencies that chose to support independence. Following the declaration of independence, however, the Sajudis governments paid attention to the development of some defensive capability, and budgetary appropriations increased until 1993 when they stabilized at 1 percent of the budget, or at least 1 percent less than appropriations for education and culture and 3 percent less than those for medical care and other health services.

Butkevicius maintained that Lithuanian defense policy has the goal of responding to three threats to Lithuania's national security. First, Lithuania is highly vulnerable to threats from beyond its borders because of its location. Second, Lithuania's internal security and the defense of its borders are also challenged by instability within the former Soviet Union and by authoritarianism and nationalism expressed by certain political parties and movements in Russia. Finally, Lithuania's domestic peace is threatened by the growing problem of organized crime, which destabilizes social institutions and is accompanied by smuggling—of drugs, weapons, and aliens—as well as by violent crime. These threats are countered in part by participating in the activities of the NACC, the OSCE, and the Western European Union (WEU). Moreover, Lithuania is developing good bilateral relations with the other Baltic states and with Poland and Belarus, and it is improving its relations with Russia. Another important forum in which threats to Lithuania's national security can be countered is the Nordic Council (see Glossary). Butkevicius has coordinated policies and enhanced ties with the Nordic countries, especially with Denmark.

Lithuania's main defense accomplishments so far have been the withdrawal of Russian military forces, the establishment of an army, and association with NATO. An agreement signed with Russia in September 1992 committed Russia to removing its troops by August 31, 1993. Withdrawal was completed on time. The Lithuanian army slowly began taking shape in the fall of 1991 but was not formally established until November 19, 1992.

Lithuania's contacts with NATO have been numerous. Most important, Lithuania joined NATO's Partnership for Peace program. Reciprocal visits by officials have been supplemented by NATO naval unit visits to Klaipeda, Lithuania's only major port. An American frigate was among the visitors in 1992. Together with Poland, Lithuania has participated in several NATO war exercises, the first of which was "Baltops 1993," held in June in the Baltic Sea. Baltops continued in subsequent summers.

Lithuania remains especially concerned about the Russian presence in the Baltic region, which will be permanently based in the exclave of Kaliningrad. Although Russia has said it will gradually reduce the numbers of its military forces there, there are currently tens of thousands of military personnel in Kaliningrad Oblast.

Armed Forces

The information available on Lithuania's defense establishment indicates that Lithuania's "security structure" includes armed forces run by the Ministry of Defense; a domestic police force subordinate to the Ministry of Interior; and a Parliamentary Defense Service that protects the parliament and the president of the republic. The chief of the Internal Security Agency insists that the agency—successor to some of the KGB's functions—has no security force, although he thinks that there ought to be a budget to establish a force to deal with criminal and subversive elements. Under Soviet rule, the KGB had its own army and also controlled the border guard.

The president of the republic chairs the State Defense Council, consisting of the prime minister, the speaker of the parliament, the minister of defense, and the chief of the armed forces. All of those people, except the speaker, are appointed by the president; therefore, the State Defense Council is likely to be dominated by the president. The council considers and coordinates the most important questions of national defense. The government, the minister of defense, and the chief of the armed forces are responsible to the Seimas for the management and leadership of the armed forces. The minister of defense must be a civilian or a retired military officer.

Total armed forces in 1994 numbered about 8,900, including a 4,300-member army, 350-member navy, 250-member air force, and 4,000-member border guard. A coast guard, which is modeled on the United States Coast Guard, is being established. There is also a 12,000-member Home Guard force. The army's equipment includes fifteen BTR–60 armored personnel carriers. The navy has two small Soviet Grisha-III frigates, one Swedish and two Soviet patrol craft, and four converted civilian vessels. The air force's equipment includes twenty-four Soviet An–2, two Czechoslovak L–410 and four L–39 aircraft, and three Soviet Mi–8 helicopters. Germany has donated jeeps and uniforms for Lithuania's armed forces.

The Home Guard is organized on the Scandinavian model and protects borders, strategic facilities, and natural resources. Lithuania's military structure also includes civil defense forces, which provide administrative control of hazardous facilities, transportation, and special rescue services. The national security service is part of the Ministry of Interior and is responsible for the fight against organized crime.

The constitution calls for one year of compulsory military training or alternative service (for conscientious objectors). Conscription for defense forces started in December 1991. However, of the 20,000 annually eligible and legally obligated young men, only 6,000 were inducted in 1992. This rate is expected to continue. Women are not called to duty, and there are no plans for them to serve in the military.

In the opinion of the commander of NATO forces in Northern Europe, Lithuanian troops are well trained by Western standards. In the past, Lithuanians trained in France's military antiterrorism school, and some Lithuanian officers and non-commissioned officers have attended military schools in the United States, France, and Denmark.

Crime and Law Enforcement

Crime increased dramatically in Lithuania in the 1990s. The number of reported crimes per 100,000 inhabitants in 1990 was 992. This number increased to 1,197 in 1991, to 1,507 in 1992, and to 1,612 in 1993. Both violent crimes and crimes against property increased substantially over this period. So far, law enforcement bodies, such as the Ministry of Interior, have been ineffective in combating this problem because information about their repressive activities during the Soviet period has discouraged public support. The law enforcement bodies have difficulty combining respect for the rule of law with aggressive intervention against crime, and criminals have expanded their activities.

The Ministry of Interior is responsible, along with local police forces, for fighting crime in Lithuania. Retraining, cooperation with foreign and international police forces, and a concentrated effort to rebuild public support have been emphasized to achieve a more effective police force. The Ministry of

Interior was expected to claim 20 percent of the state budget in 1995, according to a parliamentary deputy. In August 1994, the cabinet decried widespread corruption in the customs service. A commodity exchange president claimed later that year that 70 percent of imports into Lithuania were sold on the black market.

While violent crime continued to increase in 1994, property crime decreased. Overall crime dropped 19 percent in the first quarter of 1994 compared with the same period in 1993. Premeditated murder and attempted murder increased about 59 percent, and theft increased about 83 percent.

Organized crime is a serious problem in Lithuania. It en-.gages in violent crime as well as in smuggling aliens, drugs, radioactive materials, and weapons. The son of Georgi Deka-nidze, head of the notorious Vilnius Brigade, an organized crime ring, was to be executed in 1995 for the murder of a journalist who had been investigating organized crime. Dekanidze reportedly threatened in November 1994 to blow up the Ignalina nuclear power plant if his son were executed.

Penal Code and Prisons

The Office of the Procurator General is an independent institution responsible for enforcing the penal code and ensuring that detention of criminal suspects is based on reliable evidence of criminal activity. A magistrate must approve detention after seventy-two hours, and the right to counsel is guaranteed by law. Shortages of qualified attorneys limit this right in practice, however. Capital punishment is still legal but is rarely used.

Prison conditions in Lithuania are primitive, a legacy of the Soviet period, but have not been the subject of international concern or criticism to the same extent as in Russia and other former Soviet republics. Human rights organizations are active in the country, and their right to exist and operate is not challenged by the government. Lithuania, as part of its accession to the Council of Europe, submitted to an intensive investigation of its human rights practices and respect for democratic values. The UN High Commissioner for Human Rights, José Ayala Lasso, visited Lithuania in 1994 and stated that human rights and democratic values are respected in Lithuania. He suggested, however, that Vilnius needs to ratify conventions concerning racial discrimination, torture, and protocols on capital punishment, refugees, and persons without citizenship.

Outlook

Lithuania has started down the road of political and economic reform. If the government is able to hold its course, improved living standards and personal freedom will result. However, there will be significant obstacles on the road ahead. The most pressing challenge is to complete economic and political reforms in order to join the EU and reap the benefits of participating in the unified European market. These changes may upset ties between economic groups and political elites, particularly in the banking sector. Prime Minister Slezevicius has underscored the sweeping changes necessary in the banking sector as part of this process.

Lithuania's greatest security challenge arises from its often difficult relationship with Russia. Russia's large military presence in neighboring Kaliningrad is a source of tension because these military facilities are resupplied by rail routes that run through Lithuania. Russia and Lithuania currently regulate this transit through a "temporary" arrangement that was set up to expedite the transit of Russian forces withdrawing from Germany. All Russian military forces are now out of Germany, but the temporary arrangement continues until a satisfactory agreement can be negotiated. Russian military personnel have frequently violated Lithuanian regulations governing transit and have occasionally shown a lack of respect for Lithuania's status as a truly independent nation. It remains to be seen whether Lithuania will be able to balance the challenges posed by Russian military transit with its need to maintain good political and economic relations with Russia.

Economic relations with Russia over the near term will gradually diminish in importance as Lithuania reorients its goods and services toward the European market. But in the long run, if Russia respects Lithuania's sovereignty and if Russia continues its process of market reform and democratization, economic relations should begin to increase in importance. This can only occur if the two nations find stability in their bilateral relationship and mutual advantage in joint trade and investment.

*   *   *

Among the best sources of information concerning the emergence of the Lithuanian state and national identity are

Alfred E. Senn's *Lithuania Awakening* and *The Emergence of Modern Lithuania. Nations and Politics in the Soviet Successor States,* edited by Ian Bremmer and Ray Taras, includes an excellent essay on Lithuania by Richard Krickus. On Lithuania's transition to a market economy, the World Bank has published a comprehensive study, *Lithuania: The Transition to a Market Economy,* based on extensive field work and statistics from 1991. The Economist Intelligence Unit, which published a 1995 *Country Profile: Lithuania,* issues quarterly updates in its *Country Report: Baltic Republics: Estonia, Latvia, Lithuania.* The Lithuanian government also publishes quarterly statistics that give an in-depth look at the transition to a market economy. (For further information and complete citations, see Bibliography.)

Appendix

Table

Table 1. *Metric Conversion Coefficients and Factors*

When you know	Multiply by	To find
Millimeters........................	0.04	inches
Centimeters.......................	0.39	inches
Meters............................	3.3	feet
Kilometers........................	0.62	miles
Hectares	2.47	acres
Square kilometers.................	0.39	square miles
Cubic meters	35.3	cubic feet
Liters	0.26	gallons
Kilograms	2.2	pounds
Metric tons	0.98	long tons
....	1.1	short tons
....	2,204.0	pounds
Degrees Celsius (Centigrade)	1.8 and add 32	degrees Fahrenheit

Table 2. *Estonia: Total Population and Population by Nationality, Selected Years, 1922–89*
(in percentages)

Nationality	1922	1934	1959	1970	1979	1989
Estonian	87.7	88.2	74.6	68.2	64.7	61.5
Russian	8.2	8.2	20.1	24.7	27.9	30.3
German	1.7	1.5	0.1	0.6	0.3	0.2
Swedish.....	0.7	0.7	—[1]	—	—	—
Finnish	—	—	1.4	1.4	1.2	1.1
Ukrainian...	—	—	1.3	2.1	2.5	3.1
Belorussian..	—	—	0.9	1.4	1.6	1.7
Jewish	0.4	0.4	0.4	0.4	0.3	0.3
Other	1.3	1.0	1.2	1.2	1.5	1.8
TOTAL.....	100.0	100.0	100.0	100.0	100.0	100.0
Total population	1,107,059	1,126,413	1,196,791	1,356,000	1,464,476	1,565,662

[1] —means negligible.

Source: Based on information from Toivo V. Raun, *Estonia and the Estonians*, Stanford, California, 1991, 130; and Marje Jõeste, Ülo Kaevats, and Harry Õiglane, eds., *Eesti A & Õ*, Tallinn, 1993, 96.

Table 3. Estonia: Population of Largest Cities and Percentage Share of Estonians, 1934 and 1989

City	1934 Population	1934 Percentage of Estonians	1989 Population	1989 Percentage of Estonians
Tallinn............	137,792	85.6	478,974	47.4
Tartu	58,876	87.6	113,420	72.3
Narva.............	23,512	64.8	81,221	4.0
Pärnu.............	20,334	90.7	52,389	72.4
Viljandi	11,788	93.3	23,080	87.1
Valga..............	10,842	82.3	17,722	52.9
Rakvere	10,027	90.9	19,822	75.2
Võru..............	5,332	91.1	17,496	85.2
Haapsalu	4,649	88.3	14,617	66.4
Kuressaare.........	4,478	88.0	16,166	92.8
Tapa..............	3,751	93.7	10,439	37.0
Paide	3,285	93.5	10,849	86.7
Paldiski............	851	94.0	7,690	2.4
Kohtla-Järve[1].......	—[2]	—[2]	77,316	20.8

[1] Kohtla-Järve became a city after World War II.
[2] —not applicable.

Source: Based on information from Kulno Kala, "Eesti rahvuslikust koosseeisust pärast Teist Maailmasõda," *Akadeemia* [Tartu], 4, No. 3, 1992, 534.

Table 4. Estonia: Net In-Migration, 1956–90

Period	Net In-Migration
1956–60..	30,502
1961–65..	40,435
1966–70..	42,493
1971–75..	31,760
1976–80..	28,398
1981–85..	28,136
1986–90..	7,510

Source: Based on information from Estonia, Eesti Vabariigi Riiklik Statistikaamet, *Statistika Aastaraamat, 1991*, Tallinn, 1991, 26.

Table 5. Estonia: Natural Population Growth by Nationality, 1982–92[1]

Year	Estonians	Other Nationalities	Total	Percentage Share of Estonians
1982	638	4,608	5,246	12.4
1983	727	5,246	5,973	12.2
1984	157	5,004	5,161	3.0
1985	−152	4,439	4,287	−3.0
1986	1,171	4,949	6,120	19.1
1987	1,654	5,153	6,807	24.3
1988	1,949	4,579	6,528	29.9
1989	2,578	3,201	5,779	44.6
1990	1,079	1,718	2,797	38.6
1991	−355	−30	−385	−92.2
1992	−783	−1,333	−2,116	−37.0

[1] Natural population growth means number of births minus number of deaths.

Source: Based on information from Estonia, Eesti Vabariigi Riiklik Statistikaamet, *Statistika Aastaraamat, 1991*, Tallinn, 1991, 39.

Table 6. Estonia: Gross Domestic Product, 1989–93
(at constant prices and in percentage of real growth)

	1989	1990	1991	1992	1993
Value[1]	8,681	7,977	7,099	5,445	5,320
Percentage of real growth......	3.3	−8.1	−11.9	−23.3	−2.3

[1] In millions of 1990 Russian rubles.

Source: Based on information from Economist Intelligence Unit, *Country Report: Baltic Republics: Estonia, Latvia, Lithuania* [London], No. 1, 1994, 4.

Table 7. Estonia: Employment Distribution by Sector, 1990

Sector	Employees[1]	Percentage
Administration	17.1	2.1
Agriculture	94.5	11.9
Banking and insurance...................	4.0	0.5
Construction..........................	78.8	9.9
Data services	3.4	0.4
Education and culture	79.8	10.0
Forestry..............................	6.9	0.1
Health and sports.....................	49.0	6.2
Housing and services	35.4	4.5
Industry..............................	259.2	32.6
Science, research, and development........	18.0	2.3
Trade and catering	69.5	8.7
Transportation and communications	68.3	8.6
Other................................	11.6	1.5
TOTAL[2].............................	795.5	100.0

[1] In thousands.
[2] Figures may not add to totals because of rounding.

Source: Based on information from World Bank, *Estonia: The Transition to a Market Econ-omy*, Washington, 1993, 265–66.

Table 8. Estonia: Major Trading Partners, 1992 and 1993
(in percentages)

Country	Exports		Imports	
	1992	1993	1992	1993
Finland...............	21.1	20.7	22.6	27.9
Russia...............	20.8	22.6	28.4	17.2
Latvia...............	10.6	8.6	1.7	2.3
Sweden..............	7.7	9.5	5.9	8.9
Ukraine	6.9	3.6	3.2	n.a.[1]
Netherlands..........	5.0	4.1	1.8	3.6
Germany.............	3.9	8.0	8.3	10.7
Denmark	2.4	2.4	1.7	2.6
United States	1.9	1.9	2.4	2.7
Lithuania	1.5	3.7	3.6	3.3
Japan	n.a.	n.a.	2.7	4.2
Other	18.2	14.9	17.7	16.6

[1] n.a.—not available.

Source: Based on information from Estonia, Estonian State Statistics Board, *1993 Statistical Yearbook*, Tallinn, 1993, as reported by Baltic News Service, March 27, 1993; and Saulius Girnius, "The Economies of the Baltic States in 1993," *RFE/ RL Research Report* [Munich], 3, No. 20, May 20, 1994, 8–9.

Table 9. Estonia: Foreign Trade by Commodity Share, 1992

Commodity Share	Percentage
Exports	
Textiles and textile goods	14.0
Metals and metal products	11.3
Animals and animal products	11.2
Mineral products	10.9
Timber and timber products...................................	7.9
Imports	
Mineral products	27.2
Machinery and equipment	18.3
Textiles and textile goods	15.2
Automobiles and other vehicles	12.7

Source: Based on information from Estonia, Estonian State Statistics Board, *1993 Statistical Yearbook*, Tallinn, 1993, as reported by Baltic News Service, March 27, 1993.

Table 10. Estonia: Foreign Investment Capital in Estonia by Country of Origin, April 1993

Country	Total Investment[1]	Percentage
Sweden..................................	835.4	37.7
Finland.................................	663.7	30.0
Commonwealth of Independent States.........	235.7	10.6
United States............................	99.2	4.5
Netherlands.............................	76.5	3.5
Yugoslavia[2].............................	60.1	2.7
Germany	51.8	2.3
Other...................................	191.0	8.6
TOTAL[3]...............................	2,213.4	100.0

[1] In millions of kroons (for value of the kroon—see Glossary).
[2] Yugoslavia disintegrated in 1991. Two successor republics, Serbia and Montenegro, have asserted the formation of a joint independent state, which they call Yugoslavia, but the United States has not formally recognized this entity as a state.
[3] Figures may not add to totals because of rounding.

Source: Based on information from R. Ehrlich and L. Luup, eds., *Invest in the Future: The Future Is Estonia*, Tallinn, 1993, 36.

Table 11. Estonia: Foreign Loans and Credits to Estonia, 1992 (in thousands of United States dollars)

Source	Amount	Designated Use
European Union.................	45,000	Balance of payments support
Neste (Finland)..................	20,600	Purchase of fuel
Japan	20,000	Purchase of specific goods
Sweden........................	10,500	Balance of payments support
United States...................	10,000	Purchase of grain (export credit)
Finland Export Fund	8,500	Export credit
Switzerland	4,200	Balance of payments support
Norway........................	3,150	-do-
Finland........................	2,100	-do-
Austria	1,300	-do-
Statoil (Sweden)	750	Purchase of fuel
Iceland........................	25	EBRD membership[1]

[1] EBRD—European Bank for Reconstruction and Development.

Source: Based on information from Estonia, Ministry of Finance, as reported by Baltic News Service, November 24, 1993.

Table 12. Estonia: Structure of Industrial Production, 1990 and 1992
(in percentages)

Sector	1990	1992
Light industry	26.3	17.9
Food processing	24.5	30.4
Metals and machinery	17.0	8.5
Forestry, timber, pulp, and paper	9.2	9.0
Chemicals	7.7	9.1
Energy	7.1	14.0
Other	8.2	11.2
TOTAL[1]	100.0	100.0

[1] Figures may not add to totals because of rounding.

Source: Based on information from World Bank, *Estonia: The Transition to a Market Economy*, Washington, 1993, 314; and R. Ehrlich and L. Luup, eds., *Invest in the Future: The Future Is Estonia*, Tallinn, 1993, 18.

Table 13. Estonia: Livestock Products, 1990 and 1992

Product	1990	1992
Eggs (millions)	547.1	456.0
Meat (thousands of tons slaughter weight)		
Beef	79.9	58.7
Lamb	3.0	2.2
Pork	114.5	60.2
Poultry	21.6	10.2
Other	0.3	0.3
Total meat	219.3	131.6
Milk (thousands of tons)	1,208.0	919.3
Wool (tons)	205.0	311.0

Source: Based on information from Estonia, Estonian State Statistics Board, *1993 Statistical Yearbook*, Tallinn, 1993, 163–64.

Table 14. Estonia: Field Crop Production, 1990 and 1992

Crop	Area Sown[1]		Total Production[2]		Average Yield[3]	
	1990	1992	1990	1992	1990	1992
Cereals and legumes						
Winter crops						
Rye..............	65.9	59.2	177.9	153.4	27.0	25.9
Wheat	21.2	26.8	53.0	64.8	25.0	24.2
Total winter crops..........	87.1	86.0	230.9	218.2	26.5	25.4
Summer crops						
Barley	263.7	268.2	599.9	300.8	22.7	11.2
Legumes	0.1	0.4	0.2	0.4	13.7	9.2
Mixed grains.......	8.0	10.5	20.7	10.8	25.9	10.3
Oats..............	33.4	41.7	93.4	43.7	28.0	10.5
Wheat	4.8	16.7	12.4	24.6	25.8	14.7
Total summer crops..........	310.0	337.5	726.6	380.3	23.4	11.3
Total cereals and legumes......	397.1	423.5	957.5	598.5	24.1	14.1
Flax	2.0	0.9	0.4	0.2	2.0	2.0
Fodder roots	11.1	11.8	534.8	176.8	482.0	150.0
Potatoes.............	45.5	46.3	618.1	669.1	136.0	145.0
Vegetables	5.2	5.1	86.0	63.0	166.0	124.0

[1] In thousands of hectares.
[2] In thousands of tons.
[3] In quintals per hectare.

Source: Based on information from Estonia, Estonian State Statistics Board, *1993 Statistical Yearbook*, Tallinn, 1993, 159–61.

Table 15. Latvia: Population by Ethnic Origin, Selected Years, 1935–89
(in thousands)

Ethnic Origin	1935		1959		1970		1979		1989	
	Number	Percentage	Number	Percentage	Number	Percentage	Number	Percentage	Number	Percentage
Latvian...........	1,467.0	77.0	1,297.9	62.0	1,341.8	56.8	1,344.1	54.0	1,387.8	52.0
Russian...........	168.3	8.8	556.4	26.6	704.6	29.8	821.5	32.8	905.5	34.0
Jewish............	93.4	4.9	36.6	1.7	36.7	1.6	28.3	1.1	22.9	0.9
German...........	62.1	3.3	1.6	0.1	5.4	0.2	3.3	0.1	3.8	0.1
Polish............	48.6	2.6	59.8	2.9	63.0	2.7	62.7	2.5	60.4	2.3
Belorussian	26.8	1.4	61.6	2.9	94.7	4.0	111.5	4.5	119.7	4.5
Lithuanian	22.8	1.2	32.4	1.5	40.6	1.7	37.8	1.5	34.6	1.3
Estonian	6.9	0.4	4.6	0.2	4.3	0.2	3.7	0.1	3.3	0.1
Gypsy............	3.8	0.2	4.3	0.2	5.4	0.2	6.1	0.2	7.0	0.3
Ukrainian	1.8	—[1]	29.4	1.4	53.5	2.3	66.7	2.7	92.1	3.4
Tatar	—	0.0	1.8	0.1	2.7	0.1	3.8	0.2	4.8	0.2
TOTAL[2]	1,901.5	100.0	2,086.4	100.0	2,352.7	100.0	2,489.5	100.0	2,641.9	100.0

[1] —means negligible.
[2] Figures may not add to totals because of rounding.

Source: Based on information from Latvia, Valsts Statistikas Komiteja, *Latvija Sodien*, Riga, 1990, 13; *Cina* [Riga], June 23, 1971; and Latvia, *1989. Gada Vissavienibas Tautas Skaitisanas Rezultati Latvijas PSR*, Riga, 1990, 10.

Table 16. Latvia: Ethnic Composition of Largest Cities and Riga City Districts under Latvia's Jurisdiction, 1989 Census
(in percentages)

City or Riga City Section	Latvian	Russian	Belorussian	Ukrainian	Polish	Lithuanian	Other
Cities							
Jelgava	49.7	34.7	6.0	3.9	1.7	1.2	2.8
Jurmala	44.2	42.1	4.9	3.4	1.5	0.9	3.0
Ventspils	43.0	39.4	5.8	6.4	1.0	0.7	3.7
Liepaja	38.8	43.1	4.9	7.5	1.1	2.3	2.3
Rezekne	37.3	55.0	2.0	1.6	2.7	0.2	1.2
Riga	36.5	47.3	4.8	4.8	1.8	0.8	4.0
Riga city districts							
Kirova	47.8	38.7	2.6	2.9	1.7	0.6	5.7
Lenina	42.4	42.4	4.4	4.8	1.7	0.9	3.4
Proletariesu	39.9	44.6	4.2	4.5	1.7	0.7	4.4
Maskavas	33.4	50.0	5.0	4.4	2.1	0.9	4.2
Oktobra	32.0	49.1	6.4	6.4	1.8	0.7	3.6
Leningradas	31.9	51.6	5.2	5.3	1.7	0.7	3.6

Source: Based on information from Latvia, Valsts Statistikas Komiteja, *Latvijas Skaitlos, 1989 (Latvia in Figures, 1989)*, Riga, 1990; and *Latvia, 1989. Gada Vissavienibas Tautas Skaitisanas Rezultati Latvijas PSR*, Riga, 1990, 46.

Table 17. Latvia: Population Distribution by Ethnic Origin and Age-Group, 1989 Census

Age-Group	Latvian	Russian	Belorussian	Ukrainian	Polish	Lithuanian	Jewish	Other	Total
0–4.	114,179	75,050	5,064	5,527	2,294	1,412	933	3,210	207,669
5–9.	100,920	71,078	4,885	4,617	2,223	1,237	972	2,541	188,473
10–14.	94,778	64,026	4,661	4,702	2,279	1,390	951	2,156	174,943
15–19.	99,387	62,415	6,525	6,078	3,133	2,182	896	3,725	184,341
20–24.	91,970	62,260	9,193	9,176	3,611	2,426	824	4,777	184,237
25–29.	98,821	74,474	11,846	10,210	4,466	2,857	1,181	5,089	208,944
30–34.	89,396	76,755	11,526	9,753	4,095	2,657	1,564	4,522	200,268
35–39.	78,871	73,195	10,427	8,683	4,382	2,491	1,717	3,713	183,479
40–44.	76,125	55,149	7,879	6,359	4,663	2,417	1,948	2,442	156,982
45–49.	100,994	49,677	9,633	6,203	5,092	3,110	1,187	2,431	178,327
50–54.	89,899	55,652	10,171	6,183	4,553	2,948	1,727	2,326	173,459
55–59.	88,081	50,207	8,899	3,859	4,623	2,658	1,608	1,838	161,773
60–64.	76,548	51,311	7,007	4,236	3,708	2,103	2,063	1,696	148,672
65–69.	54,521	33,750	4,131	3,086	2,892	1,492	1,889	1,185	102,946
70 and over	133,034	50,465	7,753	4,055	8,374	3,249	3,437	1,972	212,339
Average age	35	32	37	33	42	39	44	32	n.a.[1]

[1] n.a.—not available.

Source: Based on information from unpublished 1989 Latvian census printouts. The totals by age category differ slightly from the final figures published in Latvia, *1989. Gada Vissavienibas Tautas Skaitisanas Rezultati Latvijas PSR*, Riga, 1990, 10. Thus, one has to assume the printout reflects preliminary data. The figures for the total population differ by only 31.

Table 18. Latvia: Births, Deaths, and Natural Increase by Ethnic Origin, Selected Years, 1980–91

Year	Latvian	Russian	Belorussian	Ukrainian	Polish	Lithuanian	Jewish	Other	Total
1980									
Births..............	17,918	11,839	2,225	1,197	850	662	213	630	35,534
Deaths..............	20,107	7,978	1,202	472	1,046	515	453	327	32,100
Natural increase.........	-2,189	3,861	1,023	725	-196	147	-240	303	3,434
1985									
Births..............	20,354	12,840	2,367	1,580	972	677	206	755	39,751
Deaths..............	20,537	9,023	1,451	618	1,057	569	461	450	34,166
Natural increase.........	-183	3,817	916	962	-85	108	-255	305	5,585
1986									
Births..............	21,613	13,317	2,419	1,799	990	748	222	852	41,960
Deaths..............	18,682	8,340	1,331	642	1,002	559	422	350	31,328
Natural increase.........	2,931	4,977	1,088	1,157	-12	189	-200	502	10,632
1987									
Births..............	21,617	13,396	2,471	1,808	1,002	745	189	907	42,135
Deaths..............	19,448	8,397	1,313	651	988	530	454	369	32,150
Natural increase.........	2,169	4,999	1,158	1,157	14	215	-265	538	9,985
1988									
Births..............	21,354	13,012	2,410	1,825	911	643	187	933	41,275
Deaths..............	18,962	9,018	1,412	683	1,042	544	385	375	32,421
Natural increase.........	2,392	3,994	998	1,142	-131	99	-198	558	8,854

Table 18. *Latvia: Births, Deaths, and Natural Increase by Ethnic Origin, Selected Years, 1980–91*

Year	Latvian	Russian	Belorussian	Ukrainian	Polish	Lithuanian	Jewish	Other	Total
1989									
Births.............	20,964	11,698	2,037	1,679	907	635	132	870	38,922
Deaths.............	18,784	9,239	1,425	760	1,008	554	454	360	32,584
Natural increase........	2,180	2,459	612	919	–101	81	–322	510	6,338
1990									
Births.............	21,438	10,910	1,840	1,443	827	601	108	751	37,918
Deaths.............	19,892	10,033	1,564	756	1,111	587	440	429	34,812
Natural increase........	1,546	877	276	687	–284	14	–332	322	3,106
1991									
Births.............	20,107	9,716	1,537	1,254	736	583	73	627	34,633
Deaths.............	19,797	10,261	1,583	762	971	567	404	404	34,749
Natural increase........	310	–545	–46	492	–235	16	–331	223	–116

Source: Based on information from Latvia, Statistikas Komiteja and Latvijas Zinatnu Akademijas Filozofijas un Sociologijas Instituts, *Etnosituaija Latvija*, Riga, 1992, 8.

Table 19. Latvia: Transborder Migration, 1961–89[1]
(in thousands)

Period	Came to Latvia		Left Latvia		Net Migration	
	Total	Average per Year	Total	Average per Year	Total	Average per Year
1961–65	238.1	47.6	159.1	31.8	79.0	15.8
1966–70	233.2	46.6	166.4	33.3	66.8	13.4
1971–75	292.3	58.5	232.0	46.4	60.3	12.1
1976–80	245.8	49.2	203.9	40.8	41.9	8.4
1981–85	255.6	51.1	213.5	42.7	42.1	8.4
1986–89	201.7	50.4	160.8	40.2	40.9	10.2
1986	54.5	n.a.[2]	43.3	n.a.	11.2	n.a.
1987	56.9	n.a.	40.7	n.a.	16.2	n.a.
1988	52.3	n.a.	41.1	n.a.	11.2	n.a.
1989	38.0	n.a.	35.7	n.a.	2.3	n.a.
1961–89	1,668.4		1,296.5		371.9	

[1] Between 1951 and 1955, the total net flow of migrants was only 16,900 (an average of 3,400 per year). Between 1956 and 1960, it increased to 58,000 (an average of 11,600 per year). The latter period, however, included thousands of returning deportees.
[2] n.a.—not available.

Source: Based on information from Latvia, Valsts Statistikas Komiteja, *Latvija Skaitlos, 1989 (Latvia in Figures, 1989)*, Riga, 1990, 35; and Latvia, Valsts Statistikas Komiteja, *Latvijas PSR Tautas Saimnieciba 1970*, Riga, 1971, 17–18.

Table 20. Latvia: Ethnic Minorities by Place of Birth, 1989
(in percentages)

Ethnic Minority	Latvia	Russia	Belorussia	Ukraine	Lithuania
Polish	65.8	3.1	22.3	—[1]	—
Jewish	53.3	12.3	9.9	19.7	—
Russian	54.8	36.2	2.2	2.4	—
Lithuanian	36.3	2.2	0.6	—	60.0
Belorussian	31.3	3.6	62.2	1.1	—
Ukrainian	19.4	8.5	1.6	65.7	—

[1] —means negligible.

Source: Based on information from Latvia, Valsts Statistikas Komiteja, Riga, May 24, 1991, unpublished document.

Table 21. Latvia: Religious Baptisms, Weddings, and Funerals by Religious Denomination, 1991

Religious Denomination	Baptisms		Weddings		Funerals	
	Number	Percentage	Number	Percentage	Number	Percentage
Evangelical Lutheran..	10,666	35.1	1,549	32.3	1,439	15.2
Roman Catholic....	10,661	35.0	2,651	55.3	4,995	52.8
Orthodox...	6,315	20.8	468	9.8	1,937	20.5
Old Believer...	1,273	4.2	33	0.7	730	7.7
Pentecostal..	662	2.2	37	0.8	25	0.3
Baptist......	462	1.5	20	0.4	130	1.4
Seventh-Day Adventist..	388	1.3	5	0.1	69	0.7
Jewish......	n.a.[1]	n.a	35	0.7	137	1.4
TOTAL[2]....	30,427	100.0	4,798	100.0	9,462	100.0

[1] n.a.—not applicable.
[2] Figures may not add to totals because of rounding.

Source: Based on information from *Kristus Dzive* [Riga], No. 5, 1992, 37.

Table 22. Latvia: Knowledge of Latvian Language among Persons of Russian Ethnic Origin by Age-Group, 1979 Census

Age-Group	Total in Age-Group	Latvian as First Language	Latvian as Second Language	Percentage Latvian Speakers
0–6	89,347	668	1,702	2.7
7–10	46,562	455	4,008	9.6
11–15	54,650	471	9,614	18.5
16–19	55,842	402	11,167	20.7
20–24	76,650	575	16,423	22.3
25–29	75,777	859	18,787	25.9
30–34	58,527	732	16,973	30.3
35–39	53,058	830	13,905	27.8
40–44	60,789	722	14,458	25.0
45–49	55,547	584	11,930	22.5
50–54	58,446	482	12,449	22.1
55–59	41,475	384	8,931	22.5
60–64	29,289	239	5,828	20.7
65–69	26,266	284	5,049	20.3
70 and over	39,128	300	5,504	14.8
Not known.............	111	2	15	n.a.[1]
TOTAL	821,464	7,989	156,743	20.1

[1] n.a.—not available.

Source: Based on information from ethnic Latvian data in Latvia, *Itogi vsesoyuznoy perepisi naseleniya 1979 goda po Latviyskoy SSR*, Riga, 1982, 90. Ethnic Russian data presented by Peteris Zvidrins at Association for the Advancement of Baltic Studies Conference in Seattle, June 1990.

Table 23. Latvia: Knowledge of Russian Language among Persons of
Latvian Ethnic Origin by Age-Group, 1979 Census

Age-Group	Total in Age-Group	Russian as First Language	Russian as Second Language	Percentage Russian Speakers
0–6	130,922	4,490	6,483	8.4
7–10	77,718	2,764	19,266	28.3
11–15	92,894	3,331	51,425	58.9
16–19	79,086	2,795	63,611	84.0
20–24	88,444	2,534	76,347	89.2
25–29	78,861	1,807	67,775	88.2
30–34	77,813	1,494	65,585	86.2
35–39	104,644	1,717	86,653	84.4
40–44	95,523	1,803	75,434	80.9
45–49	95,441	1,429	68,725	73.5
50–54	85,326	1,385	53,385	64.2
55–59	64,448	957	34,012	54.3
60 and over	272,773	2,414	114,830	43.0
Not known	212	2	76	n.a.[1]
TOTAL.	1,344,105	28,922	783,607	60.5

[1] n.a.—not available.

Source: Based on information from ethnic Latvian data in Latvia, *Itogi vsesoyuznoy
perepisi naseleniya 1979 goda po Latviyskoy SSR*, Riga, 1982, 90. Ethnic Russian
data presented by Peteris Zvidrins at Association for the Advancement of Baltic
Studies Conference in Seattle, June 1990.

Table 24. Latvia: Distribution of Labor Force by Sector, 1990
(in percentages)

Sector	Labor Force
Agriculture, forestry, and fishing	15.5
Industry	30.3
Transportation and communications	7.3
Construction	10.3
Trade	9.1
Credit and insurance.	0.5
Service and other branches[1]	27.0
TOTAL.	100.0

[1] Includes mainly housing and personal services, government, health and social security, education, and recreational and cultural services.

Source: Based on information from United States, National Technical Information Service, *Latvia: An Economic Profile*, Washington, August 1992, 5.

Table 25. Latvia: Agricultural Production on Private Farms, Selected Years, 1989–93

Product	1989	1991	1992	1993
Cattle[1]	15.1	62.5	141.2	144.5
Pigs[1]	7.0	43.0	85.4	97.4
Sheep[1]	6.4	27.6	52.9	41.3
Cereals and pulses[2]	10.8	89.7	206.3	432.7
Potatoes[2]	14.4	77.8	232.3	361.7
Milk[3]	9.5	73.5	177.9	282.2
Meat[3]	2.2	14.1	23.5	45.1

[1] In thousands.
[2] In thousands of tons.
[3] Live weight.

Source: Based on information from International Monetary Fund, *Economic Review: Latvia*, Washington, 1994, 73.

Table 26. Latvia: Growth of Private Farms, Selected Years, 1989–93

	1989	1991	1992	1993
Number of private farms	3,931	17,538	52,279	57,510
Total area[1]	65.6	186.2	872.9	1,108.4
Total sown area[1]	12.8	89.3	303.2	414.8

[1] In thousands of hectares.

Source: Based on information from International Monetary Fund, *Economic Review: Latvia*, Washington, 1994, 73.

Table 27. Lithuania: Production of Selected Industrial Products, 1989

Product	Quantity[1]
Energy	
Electric power (billions of kilowatt-hours)	29
Chemicals	
Mineral fertilizers (thousands of tons)	632
Sulfuric acid (thousands of tons)	512
Linoleum (thousands of square meters)	1,624
Machine building, metals, and electronics (thousands)	
Electric motors	7,659
Metal-cutting lathes	13
Electric meters	3,612
Television sets	615
Tape recorders	186
Refrigerators	350
Bicycles	423
Construction materials	
Bricks (millions)	1,121
Window glass (thousands of square meters)	4,172
Food processing	
Meat (industrial production) (thousands of tons)	447
Butter (thousands of tons)	78
Cheese (thousands of tons)	27
Confectionery goods (thousands of tons)	91
Fish and marine products (tons)	41
Textiles and soft goods	
Textiles (millions of square meters)	218
Shoes (millions of pairs)	12
Knitwear (millions of units)	18

[1] Estimated.

Source: Based on information from *The Baltic States: A Reference Book*, Tallinn, 1991.

Table 28.   *Lithuania: Foreign Trade by Country, January–June 1994*
(in percentages)

Country	Exports	Imports
Russia...	30	41
Germany..	10	14
Belarus..	7	3
Ukraine	7	6
Latvia...	7	2
Poland..	4	4

Source: Based on information from Lithuania, Ministry of Foreign Affairs, Department
   of Economic Relations, 1995.

Table 29.   *Lithuania: Exports by Selected Product and by Major*
Trading Partner, 1992 and 1993
(in thousands of United States dollars)

Product	Germany[1] 1992	Germany[1] 1993	France[1] 1992	France[1] 1993	Italy[1] 1992	Italy[1] 1993	Total[2] 1992
Food.........	11,764	26,930	648	1,478	1,733	1,169	164,025
Chemicals	16,418	22,002	7,335	12,836	301	640	74,711
Machinery....	1,615	11,440	356	278	909	511	197,006
Clothing......	8,804	35,528	1,243	4,350	133	214	55,804
Petroleum and petroleum products....	13,088	3,091	7,489	29,507	0	9	25,213
Other........	157,902	94,267	10,975	17,520	11,267	21,897	288,255
TOTAL	209,591	193,258	28,046	65,969	14,343	24,440	805,014

[1] Figures from partner countries' trade accounts.
[2] Figures from Lithuania's trade accounts.

Source: Based on information from Economist Intelligence Unit, *Country Report: Baltic
   Republics: Estonia, Latvia, Lithuania* [London], No. 1, 1995, 47.

*Table 30. Lithuania: Imports by Selected Product and by Major
Trading Partner, 1992 and 1993*
(in thousands of United States dollars)

Product	Germany[1] 1992	1993	United States[1] 1992	1993	France[1] 1992	1993	Total[2] 1992
Food	63,111	44,069	25,089	17,818	18,739	53,198	80,472
Chemicals. ...	12,387	22,684	98	424	3,274	3,418	70,842
Machinery ...	51,033	116,272	4,679	14,652	798	3,354	119,382
Clothing and footwear ...	4,481	12,263	1,599	252	321	993	9,486
Scientific instruments......	3,080	5,050	758	1,844	49	1,107	n.a.[3]
Other	33,173	102,213	11,887	21,501	2,383	7,932	525,594
TOTAL......	167,265	302,551	44,110	56,491	25,564	70,002	805,776

[1] Figures from partner countries' trade accounts.
[2] Figures from Lithuania's trade accounts.
[3] n.a.—not available.

Source: Based on information from Economist Intelligence Unit, *Country Report: Baltic
Republics: Estonia, Latvia, Lithuania* [London], No. 1, 1995, 47.

Table 31. Lithuania: Foreign Investment by Country, September 1994

Country	Percentage[1]
Britain	25
Germany..	16
United States	12
Russia	7
Poland	6
Austria	6
Other	28
TOTAL..	100

[1] Estimated.

Source: Based on information from Lithuania, Ministry of Foreign Affairs, Department
of Economic Relations, 1995.

Bibliography

Chapter 1

Ant, Jüri, et al., eds. *Ot dogovora o bazakh do anneksii: Dokumenty i materialy.* Tallinn: Perioodika, 1991.

Arjakas, Küllo, et al., eds. *Ot pakta Molotova-Ribbentropa do dogovora o bazakh: Dokumenty i materialy.* Tallinn: Perioodika, 1989.

Baltic States: A Reference Book. Tallinn: Estonian Encyclopedia, 1991.

Clemens, Walter C. *Baltic Independence and Russian Empire.* New York: St. Martin's Press, 1991.

Crowe, David. *The Baltic States and the Great Powers.* Boulder, Colorado: Westview Press, 1993.

Economist Intelligence Unit. *Country Report: Baltic Republics: Estonia, Latvia, Lithuania* [London], No. 1, 1994.

Economist Intelligence Unit. *Country Report: Baltic Republics: Estonia, Latvia, Lithuania* [London], No. 4, 1994.

Eesti NSV Loominguliste Liitude Juhatuste Ühispleenum, 1–2. aprillil 1988. Tallinn: Eesti Raamat, 1988.

Ehrlich, R., and L. Luup, eds. *Invest in the Future: The Future Is Estonia.* Tallinn: Informare, 1993.

Estonia. Eesti Vabariigi Riiklik Statistikaamet. *Statistika Aastaraamat, 1991.* Tallinn: 1991.

Estonia. Estonian State Statistics Board. *1993 Statistical Yearbook.* Tallinn: 1993.

The Europa World Year Book, 1994. London: Europa, 1994.

Fitzmaurice, John. *The Baltics: A Regional Future?* New York: St. Martin's Press, 1992.

Forgus, Silvia. "Soviet Subversive Activities in Independent Estonia (1918–1940)," *Journal of Baltic Studies,* 23, No. 1, Spring 1992, 29–46.

Frydman, Roman, Andrzej Rapaczynski, John S. Earle, et al., eds. *The Privatization Process in Russia, Ukraine, and the Baltic States.* New York: Central European University Press, 1993.

Girnius, Saulius. "The Economies of the Baltic States in 1993," *RFE/RL Research Report* [Munich], 3, No. 20, May 20, 1994, 1–14.

Hiden, John, and Patrick Salmon. *The Baltic Nations and Europe: Estonia, Latvia, and Lithuania in the Twentieth Century.* New York: Longman, 1991.

Høyer, Svennik, Epp Lauk, and Peeter Vihalemm, eds. *Towards a Civic Society: The Baltic Media's Long Road to Freedom; Perspectives on History, Ethnicity, and Journalism.* Tartu: Nota Baltic, 1993.

Invest in Estonia. Tallinn: Inorek Marketing, 1992.

Joenniemi, Pertti, and Peeter Vares, eds. *New Actors on the International Arena: The Foreign Policies of the Baltic Countries.* Tampere, Finland: Tampere Research Institute, 1993.

Jõeste, Marje, Ülo Kaevats, and Harry Õiglane, eds. *Eesti A & Õ.* Tallinn: Eesti Entsüklopeediakirjastus, 1993.

Kala, Kulno. "Eesti rahvuslikust koosseisust pärast Teist Maailmasõda," *Akadeemia* [Tartu], 4, No. 3, 1992, 508–35.

Kaplan, Cynthia. "Estonia: A Plural Society on the Way to Independence." Pages 206–21 in Ian Bremmer and Ray Taras, eds., *Nations and Politics in the Soviet Successor States.* New York: Cambridge University Press, 1993.

Karu, Ülo. *Kes on kes Eesti poliitikas, 1988–1992.* Tallinn: Eesti Entsüklopeediakirjastus, 1992.

Kasekamp, Andres. "The Estonian Veterans' League: A Fascist Movement?" *Journal of Baltic Studies*, 24, No. 3, Fall 1993, 263–68.

Kelder, Jaan, and Indrek Mustimets. *Keda me valisime?* Tartu: Tartumaa, 1993.

Kionka, Riina. "The Estonian Citizens' Committee: An Opposition Movement of a Different Complexion," *Report on the USSR* [Munich], 2, No. 6, 1990, 30–33.

Kirch, Aksel, Marika Kirch, and Tarmo Tuisk. "Russians in the Baltic States: To Be or Not to Be?" *Journal of Baltic Studies*, 24, No. 2, Summer 1993, 173–88.

Kiris, Advig, ed. *Restoration of the Independence of the Republic of Estonia: Selection of Legal Acts.* Tallinn: Estonian Institute for Information, 1991.

Kivirahk, Juhan, Rain Rosimannus, and Indrek Pajumaa. "The Premises for Democracy: A Study of Political Values in Post-Independent Estonia," *Journal of Baltic Studies*, 24, No. 2, Summer 1993, 149–60.

Kuddo, Arvo. "Rahva elujärjest," *Postimees* [Tartu], July 30–31, 1993.

Lieven, Anatol. *The Baltic Revolution: Estonia, Latvia, Lithuania and the Path to Independence.* New Haven: Yale University Press, 1993.

The Military Balance, 1994–1995. London: International Institute for Strategic Studies, 1994.

Misiunas, Romuald J., and Rein Taagepera. *The Baltic States: Years of Dependence, 1940–1991.* Berkeley: University of California Press, 1991.

Narodnyi Kongress: Sbornik materialov kongressa Norodnogo Fronta Estonii, 1–2 oktiabria 1988 g. Tallinn: Perioodika, 1989.

Õispuu, Silvia, et al. *Eesti ajalugu ärkamisajast tänapäevani.* Tallinn: Koolibri, 1992.

Parming, Tõnu. *The Collapse of Liberal Democracy and the Rise of Authoritarianism in Estonia.* London: Sage, 1975.

Pettai, Vello A. "Estonia: Old Maps and New Roads," *Journal of Democracy,* 4, No. 1, January 1993, 117–25.

Pillau, Endel, ed. *Eestimaa kuumsuvi 1988.* Tallinn: Olion, 1989.

Raidla, Peter. *Liidu kütkeis on raske vabaneda: Poliitikakuud aastail 1987–1991.* Tallinn: Rekrea, 1991.

Rauch, Georg von. *The Baltic States: The Years of Independence, 1917–1940.* Berkeley: University of California Press, 1974.

Raun, Toivo V. *Estonia and the Estonians.* 1st ed. Stanford, California: Hoover Institution Press, 1987.

Raun, Toivo V. *Estonia and the Estonians.* 2d ed. Stanford, California: Hoover Institution Press, 1991.

Raun, Toivo V. "The Re-establishment of Estonian Independence," *Journal of Baltic Studies,* 22, No. 3, Fall 1991, 251–58.

Read, Anthony, and David Fisher. *The Deadly Embrace.* New York: Norton, 1988.

Smith, Graham. *The Baltic States: The National Self-Determination of Estonia, Latvia, and Lithuania.* New York: St. Martin's Press, 1994.

Sootla, Georg, and Margus Maiste. *Tähtaasta 1988.* Tallinn: Eesti Raamat, 1989.

The Stateman's Year-Book, 1994–95. Ed., Brian Hunter. New York: St. Martin's Press, 1994.

Taagepera, Rein. *Estonia: Return to Independence.* Boulder, Colorado: Westview Press, 1993.

Taagepera, Rein. "Ethnic Relations in Estonia," *Journal of Baltic Studies*, 23, No. 2, Summer 1992, 121–32.

Titma, Mikk. *Chto u nas proiskhodit?* Tallinn: Perioodika, 1989.

United States. Central Intelligence Agency. *The World Factbook, 1994*. Washington: GPO, 1994.

World Bank. *Estonia: The Transition to a Market Economy*. Washington: 1993.

(Various issues of the following periodicals were also used in the preparation of this chapter: *Baltic Independent* [Tallinn]; *Päevaleht* [Tallinn]; *Postimees* [Tartu]; and *Rahva Hääl* [Tallinn], as well as reports of the Baltic News Service [Tallinn].)

Chapter 2

Andersons, Edgars, ed. *Crossroad Country Latvia*. Waverly, Iowa: Latvju Gramata, 1953.

Balabkins, Nicholas, and Arnolds Aizsilnieks. *Entrepreneur in a Small Country: A Case Study Against the Background of the Latvian Economy, 1919–1940*. Hicksville, New York: Exposition Press, 1975.

Baltic Review. *The Soviet Occupation and Incorporation of Latvia, June 17 to August 5, 1940*. New York: Vilis Stals, 1957.

The Baltic States: A Reference Book. Tallinn: Estonian, Latvian, Lithuanian Encyclopaedia, 1991.

Bilmanis, Alfreds. *A History of Latvia*. Princeton: Princeton University Press, 1951.

Bolz, Klaus, and Andreas Polkowski. "Trends, Economic Policies, and Systemic Changes in the Three Baltic States," *Intereconomics*, 29, May–June 1994, 147–56.

Bremmer, Ian, and Ray Taras, eds. *Nations and Politics in the Soviet Successor States*. New York: Cambridge University Press, 1993.

Bungs, Dzintra. "Local Election in Latvia: The Opposition Wins," *RFE/RL Research Report* [Munich], 3, No. 28, July 15, 1994, 1–5.

Bungs, Dzintra. "Russia Agrees to Withdraw Troops from Latvia," *RFE/RL Research Report* [Munich], 3, No. 22, June 3, 1994, 1–9.

Dreifelds, Juris. "Belorussia and the Baltics." Pages 323–85 in I.S. Koropeckyj and Gertrude E. Schroeder, eds., *Economics of Soviet Regions.* New York: Praeger, 1981.

Dreifelds, Juris. "Immigration and Ethnicity in Latvia," *Journal of Soviet Nationalities,* 1, No. 4, 1990–91, 41–81.

Dreifelds, Juris. "Latvian National Demands and Group Consciousness since 1959." Pages 136–61 in George W. Simmonds, ed., *Nationalism in the USSR and Eastern Europe in the Era of Brezhnev and Kosygin.* Detroit: University of Detroit Press, 1977.

Dreifelds, Juris. "Latvian National Rebirth," *Problems of Communism,* 38, No. 4, July–August 1989, 77–95.

Dreifelds, Juris. "Two Latvian Dams: Two Confrontations," *Baltic Forum,* 6, No. 1, Spring 1989, 11–24.

Economist Intelligence Unit. *Country Report: Baltic Republics: Estonia, Latvia, Lithuania* [London], Nos. 3–4, 1994.

Ezergailis, Andrew. *The Latvian Impact on the Bolshevik Revolution.* New York: Columbia University Press, 1983.

Freivalds, Osvalds. *Latviesu Politiskas Partijas 60 Gados.* Copenhagen: Imanta, 1961.

Germanis, Uldis. "The Rise and Fall of the Latvian Bolsheviks," *Baltic Forum,* 5, No. 1, Spring 1988, 1–25.

Grahm, Leif, and Lennart Konigson. *Baltic Industry: A Survey of Potentials and Constraints.* Stockholm: Swedish Development Consulting Partners, 1991.

Hough, William J.H., III. "The Annexation of the Baltic States and Its Effect on the Development of Law Prohibiting Forcible Seizure of Territory," *New York Law School Journal of International and Comparative Law,* 6, No. 2, Winter 1985, 301–33.

Huttenbach, Henry R. "The Sudeten Syndrome: The Emergence of a Post-Soviet Principle for Russian Expansionism," *Association for the Study of Nationalities Newsletter,* 4, No. 3, December 1992, 1–2.

International Monetary Fund. *Economic Review: Latvia.* Washington: 1992.

International Monetary Fund. *Economic Review: Latvia.* Washington: 1994.

International Monetary Fund. "Latvia: Review of the Stand-By Arrangement." (Unpublished manuscript.) Washington: November 1992.

Joenniemi, Pertti, and Peeter Vares, eds. *New Actors on the International Arena: The Foreign Policies of the Baltic Countries*. Tampere, Finland: Tampere Peace Research Institute, 1993.

Joint Baltic American National Committee. *A Legal and Political History of the Baltic Peace Treaties of 1920*. Washington:1990.

Katolu Kalendars. *Annual Yearbook of the Catholic Church in Latvia*. n. pl.: n.d.

Kavass, Igor I., and Adolfs Sprudzs, eds. *Baltic States: A Study of Their Origin and National Development; Their Seizure and Incorporation into the USSR*. Buffalo: William S. Hein, 1972.

Krumins, Juris. "Socio-Economic Differentiation of Infant and Adult Mortality: Experience of Soviet Registration System and Problems of Comparability." (Paper presented at Quetelet Seminar on the Collection and Comparability of Demographic and Social Data in Europe, September 17–20, 1991, Gemblaux, Belgium.) Gemblaux, Belgium: September 1991.

Latvia. *Itogi vsesoyuznoy perepisi naseleniya 1979 goda po Latviyskoy SSR*. Riga: 1982.

Latvia. *1989. Gada Vissavienibas Tautas Skaitisanas Rezultati Latvijas PSR*. Riga: 1990.

Latvia. Environmental Protection Committee. *National Report of Latvia to UNCED, 1992*. Helsinki: Government Printing Centre, 1992.

Latvia. Ministry of Welfare, Labor, and Health. *Health in Latvia*. 2d ed. Riga: Rotaprint, 1992.

Latvia. State Committee for Statistics. *National Economy of Latvia in 1990: Statistical Year-Book*. Riga: 1991.

Latvia. Statistikas Komiteja and Latvijas Zinatnu Akademijas Filozofijas un Sociologijas Instituts. *Etnosituacija Latvija: Fakti un Komentari*. Riga: 1992.

Latvia. Supreme Council of the Standing Commission on Human Rights and National Questions. *About the Republic of Latvia*. Riga: Rotaprint, 1992.

Latvia. Valsts Statistikas Komiteja. *Latvija Skaitlos, 1989* (*Latvia in Figures, 1989*). Riga: 1990.

Latvia. Valsts Statistikas Komiteja. *Latvija Skaitlos, 1993* (*Latvia in Figures, 1993*). Riga: 1994.

Latvia. Valsts Statistikas Komiteja. *Latvija Sodien*. Riga: 1990.

Latvia. Valsts Statistikas Komiteja. *Latvija Sodien*. Riga: 1992.

Latvia. Valsts Statistikas Komiteja. *Latvijas PSR Tautas Saim-nieciba 1970.* Riga: 1971.

Latvia. Valsts Statistikas Komiteja. *Latvijas Tautas Saimnieciba '90: Narodnoye Khozyaystvo Latvii '90.* Riga: Avots, 1991.

Latvia. Valsts Statistikas Komiteja. *Latvija un Pasaules Valstis: Statistiko Datu Krajums.* Riga: 1991.

Latvia. Valsts Statistikas Komiteja. *Zinojums Par Latvijas Republi-kas Tautas Saimniecibas Darba Rezultatiem.* Riga: 1992.

Latvia. Vides Aizsardzibas Komiteja. "Vides Aizsardziba Latvijas Republika 1990. Gada Parskats." (Unpublished manuscript.) Riga: 1991.

Lieven, Anatol. *The Baltic Revolution: Estonia, Latvia, Lithuania and the Path to Independence.* New Haven: Yale University Press, 1993.

Loeber, Dietrich André, V. Stanley Vardys, and Laurence P.A. Kitching, eds. *Regional Identity under Soviet Rule: The Case of the Baltic States.* Hackettstown, New Jersey: Association for the Advancement of Baltic Studies, 1990.

Marshall, Richard H., Jr., ed. *Aspects of Religion in the Soviet Union, 1917–1967.* Chicago: University of Chicago Press, 1971.

Marx, Stefan. "Russia's Withdrawal from the Baltics," *Jane's Intelligence Review* [London], 6, No. 12, December 1994, 565–66.

Mezs, Ilmars. *Latviesi Latvija: Etnodemografisks Apskats.* Kalama-zoo, Michigan: Latvian Studies Centre, 1992.

Michta, Andrew A. *The Government and Politics of Postcommunist Europe.* Westport, Connecticut: Praeger, 1994.

Misiunas, Romuald J., and Rein Taagepera. *The Baltic States: Years of Dependence, 1940–1990.* Berkeley: University of California Press, 1983.

Muiznieks, Nils. "Latvia: Origins, Evolution, and Triumph." Pages 182–205 in Ian Bremmer and Ray Taras, eds., *Nations and Politics in the Soviet Successor States.* New York: Cambridge University Press, 1993.

Nordic Investment Bank. *A Survey of Investment Plans and Needs in the Three Baltic Countries.* Copenhagen: Nordic Council of Ministers, 1991.

Nordic Project Fund. *Environmental Situation and Project Identifi-cation in Latvia.* Helsinki: 1991.

Petersen, Phillip. "Security Policy in the Post-Soviet Baltic States," *European Security,* 1, No. 1, Spring 1992, 13–49.

Plakans, Andrejs. *The Latvians: A Short History.* Stanford, California: Stanford University, 1995.

Rauch, Georg von. *The Baltic States: The Years of Independence, 1917–1940.* Berkeley: University of California Press, 1974.

Riekstins, Janis. "Genocids," *Latvijas Vesture* [Riga], No. 2, 1991, 34–39.

Rutkis, J. *Latvia: Country and People.* Stockholm: Latvian National Foundation, 1967.

Soviet Union. Gosudarstvennyy komitet po statistike. *Narodnoye khozyaystvo SSSR v 1989 g.* Moscow: Finansy i statistika, 1990.

Soviet Union. Gosudarstvennyy komitet po statistike. *Naseleniye SSSR 1988: Statisticheskiy yezhegodnik.* Moscow: Finansy i statistika, 1989.

Spekke, Arnolds. *History of Latvia: An Outline.* Stockholm: M. Goppers, 1957.

Trapans, Jan Arved, ed. *Toward Independence: The Baltic Popular Movements.* Boulder, Colorado: Westview Press, 1991.

United Kingdom. Royal Institute of International Affairs. Information Department. *The Baltic States: A Survey of the Political and Economic Structure and the Foreign Relations of Estonia, Latvia, and Lithuania.* London: Oxford University Press, 1938. Reprint. Westport, Connecticut: Greenwood Press, 1970.

United States. Commission on Security and Cooperation in Europe. *Elections in the Baltic States and Soviet Republics.* Washington: GPO, 1990.

United States. National Technical Information Service. *Latvia: An Economic Profile.* Washington: August 1992.

Valkonen, Tapani, Juris Krumins, and Peteris Zvidrins. "Mortality Trends in Finland and Latvia since the 1920s." In *Yearbook of Population Research in Finland,* 29. Helsinki: Population Research Institute, 1991.

Veinbergs, Alexander. "Lutheranism and Other Denominations in the Baltic Republics." Pages 405–19 in Richard H. Marshall, Jr., ed., *Aspects of Religion in the Soviet Union, 1917–1967.* Chicago: University of Chicago Press, 1971.

Westing, Arthur H., ed. *Comprehensive Security for the Baltics: An Environmental Approach.* London: Sage, 1989.

World Bank. *Latvia: The Transition to a Market Economy.* Washington: 1993.

WWF Project 4568. *Conservation Plan for Latvia Final Report.* (In Latvian.) Riga: Vide, 1992.

Zvidrins, Peteris. *Demografija.* 2d ed. Riga: Zvaigzne, 1989.

Zvidrins, Peteris, and I. Vanovska. *Latviesi: Statistiski Demografisks Portretejums.* Riga: Zinatne, 1992.

(Various issues of the following periodicals were also used in the preparation of this chapter: *Baltic Business Report; Baltic Independent* [Tallinn]; *Baltic Observer* [Riga]; *Cina* [Riga]; *Journal of Baltic Studies; Kalendars* [Riga]; *Kristus Dzive* [Riga]; and *This Week in the Baltic States* [Munich].)

Chapter 3

Adomonis, Tadas, and Klemensas Cerbulenas. *Lietuvos TSR dailes ir architekturos istorija* (History of the Art and Architecture of the Lithuanian SSR). Vilnius: Mokslas, 1987.

The Baltic States: A Reference Book. Tallin: Estonian, Latvian, Lithuanian Encyclopedia, 1991.

Beschloss, Michael R., and Strobe Talbott. *At the Highest Levels.* Boston: Little, Brown, 1993.

Bite, Vita. "Lithuania: Basic Facts," *CRS Report for Congress.* Washington: Library of Congress, Congressional Research Service, August 6, 1992.

Bremmer, Ian, and Ray Taras, eds. *Nations and Politics in the Soviet Successor States.* New York: Cambridge University Press, 1993.

Clark, Terry. "Coalition Realignment in the Supreme Council of the Lithuanian Republic and the Fall of the Vagnorius Government," *Journal of Baltic Studies,* Spring 1992, 57.

Dickman, Steven. "Lithuanian Biochemist Builds Enzyme Empire," *Science,* 257, September 11, 1992, 1473–74.

Economist Intelligence Unit. *Country Profile: Lithuania.* London: 1995.

Economist Intelligence Unit. *Country Report: Baltic Republics: Estonia, Latvia, Lithuania* [London], No. 4, 1994.

Economist Intelligence Unit. *Country Report: Baltic Republics: Estonia, Latvia, Lithuania* [London], No. 1, 1995.

Felstinskis, J., ed. *SSSR—Germaniya 1939–1941.* Vilnius: Mokslas, 1989.

Galaune, Paulis. *Lithuanian Folk Art.* Kaunas: Department of Humanities, Lithuanian University, 1930. Reprint. Vilnius: Mokslas, 1988.

Gimbutas, Marija. *The Balts.* New York: Praeger, 1963.

Girnius, Saulius. "The Economies of the Baltic States in 1993," *RFE/RL Research Report* [Munich], 3, No. 20, May 20, 1994, 1–14.

Hough, William J.H., III. "The Annexation of the Baltic States and Its Effect on the Development of Law Prohibiting Forcible Seizure of Territory," *New York Law School Journal of International and Comparative Law,* 6, No. 2, Winter 1985, 301–33.

International Monetary Fund. *IMF Economic Reviews, 6/1994: Lithuania.* Washington: 1994.

Jonikas, Petras. *Lietuviu kalba ir tauta amziu buvyje* (A History of the Lithuanian Language). Chicago: LIL, 1978.

Krickus, Richard. "Lithuania: Nationalism in the Modern Era." Pages 157–81 in Ian Bremmer and Ray Taras, eds., *Nations and Politics in the Soviet Successor States.* New York: Cambridge University Press, 1993.

Lietuviskoji tarybine enciklopedija (Soviet Lithuanian Encyclopedia). Vilnius: Mokslas, 1976–84.

Lietuviu enciklopedija (Lithuanian Encyclopedia). 37 vols. Boston: Lietuviu enciklopedijos leidykla, 1953–85.

Lithuania. *Lietuvos Respublikos Auksciausios Tarybos Reglamentas* (Rules of the Supreme Council of Lithuania). Vilnius: 1991.

Lithuania. Academy of Sciences. Institute of Geology and Geography, and Institute of Economics. *Lietuvos TSR ekonomine geografija* (Economic Geography of the Lithuanian SSR). Vilnius: PMLL, 1957.

Lithuania. Lietuvos Respublikos Auksciausios Tarybos ir Auksciausios Tarybos Presidiumo. *Dokumentu Rinkinys.* 3 vols. Vilnius: Lietuvos Respublikos Ausksciausioji Taryba, 1991.

Lithuania. Lietuvos Respublikos Auksciausios Tarybos, Lietuvos Respublikos Auksciausios Tarybos Presidiumo, Lietuvos Respublikos Vyriausybes. *Svarbiausiu Dokumentu Rinkinys.* Vilnius: Mintis, 1990.

Lithuania. Lietuvos Respublikos Auksciausios Tarybos pirmoji sesija. *Stenogramos.* 6 vols. Vilnius: Lietuvos Respublikos Auksciausioji Taryba, 1990–91.

Lithuania. Lietuvos statistikos departamentas. *Lietuva Skaiciais, 1991* (Lithuania in Figures, 1991). Vilnius: Information and Publishing Center, 1992.

Lithuania. Lietuvos statistikos departamentas. *Lietuva Skaiciais, 1993* (Lithuania in Figures, 1993). Vilnius: Information and Publishing Center, 1994.

Lithuania. Lietuvos statistikos departamentas. *Lietuvos statistiko metrastis 1989 metai.* Vilnius: Informacinis-leidybinis centras, 1990.

Lithuania. Lietuvos statistikos departamentas. *Main Economic Indicators of Lithuania, '94 May.* Vilnius: 1994.

Lithuania. Lietuvos statistikos departamentas. *Social and Economic Development in Lithuania, January–March 1994.* Vilnius: 1994.

Lithuania. Lietuvos TSR Mokslu Akademija. Istorijos Institutas. *Lietuvos pilys.* Vilnius: Mintis, 1971.

Lithuania. Lietuvos TSR Mokslu Akademija. Istorijos Institutas. *Lietuvos TSR rysiai su Rusijos Federacija.* Vilnius: Mokslas, 1987.

Lithuania. Lithuanian Information Institute. *Lithuania: Survey. A Businessman's Guide.* 3d ed. Vilnius: 1992.

Lithuania. Ministry of Foreign Affairs. Department of Nationalities. *National Minorities in Lithuania.* Vilnius: Centre of National Research of Lithuania, 1992.

Lithuania. Supreme Council. *Selected Anthology of Institutional, Economic, and Financial Legislation.* Vilnius: State Publishing Center, 1991.

Lithuania. Supreme Council. Office of Public Affairs. *Negotiations with the Russian Federation Concerning the Withdrawal of Russian Military Forces from the Territory of the Republic of Lithuania, July 29, 1991–September 8, 1992.* Vilnius: October 1992.

Loeber, Dietrich Andre, V. Stanley Vardys, and Laurence P.A. Kitching. *Regional Identity under Soviet Rule: The Case of the Baltic States.* Hackettstown, New Jersey: Institute for the Study of Law, Politics, and Society of Socialist States, University of Kiel, Germany, 1990.

Lorot, Pascal. *Le réveil balte.* Paris: Hackette, 1991.

Meissner, Boris, ed. *Die Baltischen Nationen.* 2d ed. Cologne: Markus Verlag, 1991.

The Military Balance, 1994–1995. London: International Institute for Strategic Studies, 1994.

Pakalnis, Romas. "The Future of Lithuanian Nature Is the Future of Lithuania," *Science, Arts, and Lithuania*, No. 1, 1991, 16–21.

Rose, Richard, and William Maley. "Conflict or Compromise in the Baltic States?" *RFE/RL Research Report* [Munich], 3, No. 28, July 15, 1994, 26–35.

Senn, Alfred E. *The Emergence of Modern Lithuania.* New York: University of Columbia Press, 1959.

Senn, Alfred E. *Lithuania Awakening.* Berkeley: University of California Press, 1991.

Soviet Union. Gosudarstvennyy komitet po statistike. *Narodnoye khozyaystvo SSSR v 1989 g.* Moscow: Finansy i statistika, 1990.

Soviet Union. Gosudarstvennyy komitet po statistike. *Narodnoye khozyaystvo SSSR v 1990 g.* Moscow: Finansy i statistika, 1991.

Tarulis, Albert. *American-Baltic Relations, 1918–1922.* Washington: Catholic University Press, 1965.

Tarulis, Albert. *Soviet Policy Toward the Baltic States, 1918–1940.* Notre Dame: University of Notre Dame Press, 1959.

Times-Mirror. *The Pulse of Europe: A Survey of Political and Social Values and Attitudes.* Washington: 1991.

United States. Congress. *Minority Rights: Problems, Parameters, and Patterns in the CSCE Context.* Washington: n.d.

United States. Congress. Commission on Security and Cooperation in Europe. *Presidential Elections and Independence Referendums in the Baltic States, the Soviet Union, and Successor States.* Washington: GPO, 1992.

United States. Department of State. *Country Reports on Human Rights Practices for 1992.* (Report submitted to United States Congress, 103d, 1st Session, Senate, Committee on Foreign Relations, and House of Representatives, Committee on Foreign Affairs.) Washington: GPO, 1993.

United States. National Technical Information Service. *Lithuania: An Economic Profile.* Washington: September 1992.

Van Arkadie, Brian, and Mats Karlsson. *Economic Survey of the Baltic States.* New York: New York University Press, 1992.

Vardys, V. Stanley. *The Catholic Church, Dissent, and Nationality in Soviet Lithuania.* New York: Columbia University Press, 1978.

Vardys, V. Stanley. "Lithuanian National Politics," *Problems of Communism,* July–August 1989, 53–76.

Vardys, V. Stanley. "The Role of the Baltic Republics in Soviet Society." In Roman Szporluk, ed., *The Influence of East Europe and the Soviet West on the USSR.* New York: Praeger, 1976.

Vardys, V. Stanley, ed. *Lithuania under the Soviets.* New York: Praeger, 1965.

Vilnius universiteto istorija (History of the University of Vilnius). 3 vols. Vilnius: Mokslas, 1976–79.

World Bank. *Lithuania: The Transition to a Market Economy.* Washington: 1993.

(Various issues of the following periodicals were also used in the preparation of this chapter: *Atgimimas* [Vilnius]; *Kataliku pasaulis* [Vilnius]; *Lietuvos aidas* [Vilnius]; *Literatura ir menas* [Vilnius]; *Mazoji Lietuva* [Vilnius]; *Metai* [Vilnius]; and *Tiesa* [Vilnius].)

Glossary

Cheka (Vserossiyskaya chrezvychaynaya komissiya po bor'be s kontrrevolyutsiyey i sabotazhem—VChK)—All-Russian Extraordinary Commission for Combating Counterrevolution and Sabotage. The political police created by the Bolsheviks in 1917, the Cheka (also known as the Vecheka) was supposed to be dissolved when the new regime, under Vladimir I. Lenin, had defeated its enemies and secured power. But the Cheka continued until 1922, becoming the leading instrument of terror and oppression in the Soviet Union, as well as the predecessor of other secret police organizations. Members of successor security organizations continued to be referred to as "Chekisty" in the late 1980s.

Commonwealth of Independent States (CIS)—A loosely structured alliance of most of the former republics of the Soviet Union that facilitates consultation and cooperation in economic and security matters of common concern. Members in 1995 were Armenia, Azerbaijan, Belarus, Georgia, Kazakhstan, Kyrgyzstan, Moldova, Russia, Tajikistan, Turkmenistan, Ukraine, and Uzbekistan.

Communist International (Comintern)—An international organization of communist parties founded by Russian Communist Party (Bolshevik) leader Vladimir I. Lenin in 1919. Initially, it attempted to control the international socialist movement and to foment world revolution; later, it also became an instrument of Soviet foreign policy. The Comintern was dissolved by Soviet leader Joseph V. Stalin in 1943 as a conciliatory measure toward his Western allies.

Conference on Security and Cooperation in Europe (CSCE)—Established in 1972, the group in 1995 consisted of fifty-three nations—including all the European countries—and sponsored joint sessions and consultations on political issues vital to European security. The Charter of Paris (1990) changed the CSCE from an ad hoc forum to an organization having permanent institutions. In 1992 new CSCE roles in conflict prevention and management were defined, potentially making the CSCE the center of a Europe-based collective security system. In the early 1990s, however, applications of these instruments to conflicts in Yugoslavia and the Caucasus were largely ineffective. In January 1995, the organization was renamed the Organization for Security and Cooperation in Europe (OSCE).

Congress of People's Deputies—Established in December 1988 in the Soviet Union by constitutional amendment, the Congress of People's Deputies was the highest organ (upper tier) of legislative and executive authority in the Soviet Union. As such, it elected the Supreme Soviet of the Soviet Union. The Congress of People's Deputies that was elected in March through May 1989 consisted of 2,250 deputies. The Congress of People's Deputies ceased to exist at the demise of the Soviet Union.

Council of Europe—Founded in 1949, the Council of Europe is an organization overseeing intergovernmental cooperation in designated areas such as environmental planning, finance, sports, crime, migration, and legal matters. In 1995 the council had thirty-five members.

European Community (EC)—A grouping of primarily economic organizations of West European countries, including the European Economic Community (EEC), the European Atomic Energy Community (Euratom or EAEC), and the European Coal and Steel Community (ECSC). The name changed to European Union (*q.v.*) in November 1993. Members in 1993 were Belgium, Britain, Denmark, France, Germany, Greece, Ireland, Italy, Luxembourg, the Netherlands, Portugal, and Spain.

European currency unit (ECU)—Established in 1979 as a composite of the monetary systems of European Community (*q.v.*) member nations, the ECU functions in the European Monetary System and serves as the unit for exchange-rate establishment, credit and intervention operations, and settlements between monetary authorities of member nations.

European Union (EU)—Successor organization to the European Community (*q.v.*). The EU was officially established by ratification of the Maastricht Treaty of November 1993. The aim of the EU is to promote the economic integration of Europe, leading to a single monetary system and closer cooperation in matters of justice and foreign and security policies. In 1995 members consisted of Austria, Belgium, Britain, Denmark, Finland, France, Germany, Greece, Ireland, Italy, Luxembourg, the Netherlands, Portugal, Spain, and Sweden.

glasnost—Russian term for public discussion of issues; accessibility of information so that the public can become familiar with it and discuss it. *Glasnost* is the name given to Soviet leader Mikhail S. Gorbachev's policy in the Soviet Union in the mid- to late 1980s of using the media to make information available on certain controversial issues to provoke public discussion, challenge government and party bureaucrats, and mobilize greater support for the policy of *perestroika* (*q.v.*).

gross domestic product (GDP)—A measure of the total value of goods and services produced by the domestic economy during a given period, usually one year. GDP is obtained by adding the value contributed by each sector of the economy in the form of profits, compensation to employees, and depreciation (consumption of capital). Only domestic production is included, not income arising from investments and possessions owned abroad, hence the use of the word "domestic" to distinguish GDP from the gross national product (*q.v.*). Real GDP is the value of GDP when inflation has been taken into account.

gross national product (GNP)—The gross domestic product (*q.v.*) plus the net income or loss stemming from transactions with foreign countries. GNP is the broadest measurement of the output of goods and services by an economy. It can be calculated at market prices, which include direct taxes and subsidies. Because indirect taxes and subsidies are only transfer payments, GNP is often calculated at factor cost, removing indirect taxes and subsidies.

International Monetary Fund (IMF)—Established along with the World Bank (*q.v.*) in 1945, the IMF has regulatory surveillance and financial functions that apply to its more than 150 member countries and is responsible for stabilizing international exchange rates and payments. Its main function is to provide loans to its members (including industrialized and developing countries) when they experience balance of payments difficulties. These loans often have conditions that require substantial internal economic adjustments by the recipients, most of which are developing countries. Estonia, Latvia, and Lithuania joined the IMF and the World Bank in 1992.

Karaites—Members of a religious group practicing Karaism, a Jewish doctrine originating in Baghdad in the eighth century A.D. that rejects rabbinism and talmudism and bases its tenets on Scripture alone.

kroon (EKR)—Estonia's prewar currency (1928–40), reintroduced in June 1992 after Estonia became the first former Soviet republic to leave the Russian ruble zone. The kroon was officially pegged to the deutsche mark (DM) within 3 percent of EKR8 = DM1. In March 1996, the exchange rate was EKR11.83 = US$1.

lats (LVL)—Latvia's unit of currency prior to the Soviet annexation in 1940. Reintroduced in March 1993, the lats became the sole legal tender in Latvia in October 1993. In March 1996, the exchange rate was LVL0.55 = US$1.

Latvian ruble—Interim unit of currency introduced in Latvia in May 1992 and circulated in parallel to and valued at par with the Russian ruble, a vestige of Soviet rule, until July 1992. Sole legal tender until March 1993. Replaced by the lats (*q.v.*).

litas (pl., litai)—Lithuania's unit of currency prior to the Soviet annexation in 1940. Reintroduced in June 1993, the litas became the sole legal tender in Lithuania in August 1993. In March 1996, the exchange rate was 4.0 litai = US$1.

nomenklatura—The communist party's system of appointing key personnel in the government and other important organizations, based on lists of critical positions and people in political favor. The term also refers to the individuals included on these lists.

Nordic Council—Founded in 1952, the Nordic Council promotes political, economic, cultural, and environmental cooperation in the Nordic region. Members in 1995 were Denmark, Finland, Iceland, Norway, and Sweden.

Old Believers—A sect of the Russian Orthodox Church that rejects the reforms of liturgical books and practices carried out by the head of the church, Patriarch Nikon, in the mid-seventeenth century.

perestroika—Literally, restructuring. The term refers to Mikhail S. Gorbachev's campaign in the Soviet Union in the mid- to late 1980s to revitalize the economy, communist party, and society by adjusting political, social, and economic mechanisms.

value-added tax (VAT)—A tax levied on the value-added income of a business. The VAT is defined as the difference between the total sales revenue and the costs of intermediate inputs, such as raw materials, used in the production process.

World Bank—Name used to designate a group of four affiliated international institutions that provide advice on long-term finance and policy issues to developing countries: the International Bank for Reconstruction and Development (IBRD), the International Development Association (IDA), the International Finance Corporation (IFC), and the Multilateral Investment Guarantee Agency (MIGA). The IBRD, established in 1945, has the primary purpose of providing loans to developing countries for productive projects. The IDA, a legally separate loan fund administered by the staff of the IBRD, was set up in 1960 to furnish credits to the poorest developing countries on much easier terms than those of conventional IBRD loans. The IFC, founded in 1956, supplements the activities of the IBRD through loans and assistance designed specifically to encourage the growth of productive private enterprises in less developed countries. The president and certain senior officers of the IBRD hold the same positions in the IFC. The MIGA, which began operating in June 1988, insures private foreign investment in developing countries against such noncommercial risks as expropriation, civil strife, and inconvertibility. The four institutions are owned by the governments of the countries that subscribe their capital. To participate in the World Bank group, member states must first belong to the International Monetary Fund (*q.v.*).

Index

Abisala, Aleksandras, 231
abortion: in Estonia, 31
Abrene (Latvia): annexation by Russia, 104, 158
Academy of Sciences (Lithuania), 206
acquired immune deficiency syndrome (AIDS): in Estonia, 32; in Latvia, 120; in Lithuania, 195
Agricultural Bank (Lithuania), 212
agriculture in Estonia: collectivization, 20, 56, 58; cooperatives, 60; private farming, 16, 58, 60
agriculture in Latvia, 133–35; collectivization, 134–35; cooperatives, 130; drainage projects, 108; erosion problems, 104; livestock farming, 135; private farming, 105, 115, 135, 146
agriculture in Lithuania, 213–15; collectivization, 182, 208, 213–14; private farming, 208, 210, 215; production, 213, 215, 223
AIDS. *See* acquired immune deficiency syndrome
air force. *See* armed forces
airline industry: in Estonia, 63; in Latvia, 137; in Lithuania, 217
air pollution. *See* environmental pollution
alcoholism: in Latvia, 120–21; in Lithuania, 195
Aleksiy (patriarch), xxv, 36
All-Estonian Congress, 15
All-Russian Constitutional Assembly (Latvia), 95
Alver, Betti, 37
Alviekste River (Latvia), 107
amber: from Latvia, 110; from Lithuania, 204
Andrejevs, Georgs, 156
architecture: in Estonia, 37
area: of Estonia, 28; of Latvia, 93, 104; of Lithuania, 186
armed forces: of Estonia, xxv, 76–77; of Latvia, 159–62; of Lithuania, 238–39
arts: in Estonia, 38; in Latvia, 129; in Lithuania, 202, 204
Atdzimsana un Atjaunosana. *See* Rebirth and Renewal
Ayala Lasso, José, 240

Baker, James A.: visit to Baltic states, 74
Baltic Agreement on Economic Cooperation, 155
Baltic Battalion, xxviii, 159
Baltic Council, 73
Baltic Independent (newspaper), 71, 159
Baltic Treaty on Unity and Cooperation, 155
Baltija Bank (Latvia): collapse of, xxi–xxiii
Bank of Estonia, 40, 41, 42
Bank of Latvia, 140, 145–46
Bank of Lithuania, 211–12, 230
bank reforms: in Estonia, 40–42; in Latvia, xxi; in Lithuania, xxii, xxv, 211–12
baptisms: in Latvia, 124–26
Baptists: in Estonia, 36; in Latvia, 122, 128; in Lithuania, 200
Barons, Krisjanis, 129
Belarus: relations with Latvia, 159; relations with Lithuania, 236; trade with Lithuania, 236
Belarusian/Belorussian population: in Estonia, 30; in Latvia, 111; in Lithuania, 191
Beriozovas, Vladimiras, 185
Berklavs, Eduards, 101, 107, 131
Bildt, Carl, 73
Birkavs, Valdis, 152
birth control: abortions in Estonia, 31
birth rate: in Estonia, 30; in Latvia, 113; in Lithuania, 189
births outside of marriage: Latvia, 115
Black Berets. *See* Soviet Ministry of Internal Affairs, Special Forces Detachment
black market: in Estonia, 78
blockade. *See* economic blockade

Contributors

Juris Dreifelds is Associate Professor, Department of Politics, Brock University, St. Catharines, Ontario, Canada.

Walter R. Iwaskiw is a Senior Research Specialist in East European Affairs, Federal Research Division, Library of Congress, Washington, DC.

Vello A. Pettai is Visiting Lecturer, University of Tartu, and a Ph.D. Candidate, Department of Political Science, Columbia University, New York, New York.

William A. Slaven is a Foreign Service Officer and Political/Economic Analyst for the Baltic States and Moldova, Department of State, Washington, DC.

V. Stanley Vardys (deceased) was Professor Emeritus, Department of Political Science, University of Oklahoma, Norman, Oklahoma.

Published Country Studies

(Area Handbook Series)

550–65	Afghanistan	550–36	Dominican Republic
550–98	Albania		and Haiti
550–44	Algeria	550–52	Ecuador
550–59	Angola	550–43	Egypt
550–73	Argentina	550–150	El Salvador
550–111	Armenia, Azerbaijan,	550–113	Estonia, Latvia, and
	and Georgia		Lithuania
550–169	Australia	550–28	Ethiopia
550–176	Austria	550–167	Finland
550–175	Bangladesh	550–173	Germany, East
550–112	Belarus and Moldova	550–155	Germany, Fed. Rep. of
550–170	Belgium	550–153	Ghana
550–66	Bolivia	550–87	Greece
550–20	Brazil	550–78	Guatemala
550–168	Bulgaria	550–174	Guinea
550–61	Burma	550–82	Guyana and Belize
550–50	Cambodia	550–151	Honduras
550–166	Cameroon	550–165	Hungary
550–159	Chad	550–21	India
550–77	Chile	550–154	Indian Ocean
550–60	China	550–39	Indonesia
550–26	Colombia	550–68	Iran
550–33	Commonwealth Carib-	550–31	Iraq
	bean, Islands of the	550–25	Israel
550–91	Congo	550–182	Italy
550–90	Costa Rica	550–30	Japan
550–69	Côte d'Ivoire (Ivory	550–34	Jordan
	Coast)	550–56	Kenya
550–152	Cuba	550–81	Korea, North
550–22	Cyprus	550–41	Korea, South
550–158	Czechoslovakia	550–58	Laos

550–24	Lebanon	550–70	Senegal
550–38	Liberia	550–180	Sierra Leone
550–85	Libya	550–184	Singapore
550–172	Malawi	550–86	Somalia
550–45	Malaysia	550–93	South Africa
550–161	Mauritania	550–95	Soviet Union
550–79	Mexico	550–179	Spain
550–76	Mongolia	550–96	Sri Lanka
550–49	Morocco	550–27	Sudan
550–64	Mozambique	550–47	Syria
550–35	Nepal and Bhutan	550–62	Tanzania
550–88	Nicaragua	550–53	Thailand
550–157	Nigeria	550–89	Tunisia
550–94	Oceania	550–80	Turkey
550–48	Pakistan	550–74	Uganda
550–46	Panama	550–97	Uruguay
550–156	Paraguay	550–71	Venezuela
550–185	Persian Gulf States	550–32	Vietnam
550–42	Peru	550–183	Yemens, The
550–72	Philippines	550–99	Yugoslavia
550–162	Poland	550–67	Zaire
550–181	Portugal	550–75	Zambia
550–160	Romania	550–171	Zimbabwe
550–37	Rwanda and Burundi		
550–51	Saudi Arabia